NFL 1965

ALSO BY DAVID KAISER

Baseball Greatness: Top Players and Teams According to Wins Above Average, 1901–2017 (McFarland, 2018)

NFL 1965
The Most Exciting Season

DAVID KAISER

McFarland & Company, Inc., Publishers
Jefferson, North Carolina

ISBN (print) 978-1-4766-8645-5
ISBN (ebook) 978-1-4766-4436-3

LIBRARY OF CONGRESS AND BRITISH LIBRARY
CATALOGUING DATA ARE AVAILABLE

Library of Congress Control Number 2021051742

© 2022 David Kaiser. All rights reserved

No part of this book may be reproduced or transmitted in any form or by any means, electronic or mechanical, including photocopying or recording, or by any information storage and retrieval system, without permission in writing from the publisher.

Green Bay Packers kicker Don Chandler (34) boots the game-winning field goal in overtime of the Western Conference playoff game against the Baltimore Colts on December 26, 1965 (Vernon J. Biever)

Printed in the United States of America

*McFarland & Company, Inc., Publishers
Box 611, Jefferson, North Carolina 28640
www.mcfarlandpub.com*

To George Plimpton, with thanks.

To Tom Matte (1939-2021),
the man of the hour.

"Ours was the great era of professional football, because it was the players' game then."—Sonny Jurgensen, quarterback, Philadelphia Eagles (1957–63) and Washington Redskins (1964–74)

"There has never been a year like 1965. All the years I was in pro football, I always looked back and said, 'That's the greatest season I ever lived through.'"—Upton Bell, executive, Baltimore Colts (1960–71) and New England Patriots (1971–72)

Table of Contents

Preface 1

1. Preseason 5
2. The First Month 34
3. Sheep and Goats 50
4. The Baltimore Boom 66
5. The Climax 101
6. The Playoff (December 26, 1965) 123
7. The Championship 132

Epilogue 143
Chapter Notes 151
Bibliography 153
Index 155

Preface

No decade was more significant to the development of the NFL than the 1960s. The decade began with expansion on two fronts: the inauguration of the first of two new NFL teams in Dallas, with Minnesota to follow a year later, and the beginnings of the rival American Football League (AFL). Jim Brown of the Cleveland Browns and Johnny Unitas of the Baltimore Colts were the first two NFL players to achieve the stature of baseball stars like Mickey Mantle and Willie Mays. The 1960 season also saw the emergence of the Green Bay Packer dynasty under Vince Lombardi, as the Packers lost a close championship game to the Philadelphia Eagles. The NFL grew rapidly in popularity during the next three years, led by the success of the New York Giants, who played fortuitously in the nation's largest city and media capital. With baseball in a declining period, the NFL now began to rival it as the nation's most popular sport. Starting in 1965, and especially after 1967, a new generation fed the league with a great deal more talent. The 1966 merger of the AFL and NFL put the league on a sound financial footing, and at the end of that season, the Packers and Kansas City Chiefs played the first Super Bowl. Two years later, interest in that game, and the league in general, reached new heights after the AFL's New York Jets upset the favored Baltimore Colts behind brash young quarterback Joe Namath. In 1969, the teams of the two leagues decided to merge their schedule.

During this decade, the 14 teams of the NFL played out the most exciting season in the league's history. Although the Cleveland Browns of the Eastern Conference were the defending NFL champions and made their way to the title game again in 1965, the season's drama took place in the Western Conference, fueled by an extraordinary constellation of strong teams. On the one hand, the three teams that had won the last seven conference championships—the Colts (1958–59, 1964), the Packers (1960–62), and the Bears (1963)—fought an incredibly exciting race for the conference title. All three had a chance to win going into the last weekend, and two of them met in a conference playoff game. One contender, the Baltimore Colts, caught the nation's imagination when it lost its two leading

Preface

quarterbacks to injury late in the season and had to finish up with halfback Tom Matte, who had not played quarterback since college, at that position.

Meanwhile, the rest of the league included the Detroit Lions, who had contended annually from 1960 through 1962, and three teams destined to take over the league later in the decade: the Los Angeles Rams, the Minnesota Vikings, and the San Francisco 49ers. Three of the greatest coaches in NFL history—Vince Lombardi of the Packers, Don Shula of the Colts, and George Halas of the Bears—led the leading teams. The Bears also boasted the most extraordinary pair of rookies ever on an NFL team in running back Gale Sayers and middle linebacker Dick Butkus.

Having lived through this amazing season in my first year in college, I have dreamed for decades about writing a history of it. My career as a professional historian and other projects continually intervened, but several years ago, I decided that the time had come. I only regret that I did not get to it at least ten years earlier when so many more of the participants in that season would have been available for interviews. Fortunately, the 1960s also generated several extraordinary books about NFL football, including three by George Plimpton and several books about Vince Lombardi and the Packers. I hope I have added a worthy companion to those that came before.

Unless otherwise noted, all quotes from participants in the 1965 season come from my telephone or Zoom interviews. Bill Curry and Dave Robinson of the Packers; Tom Matte, Dan Sullivan, Dennis Gaubatz, and Upton Bell of the Colts; Andy Livingston and Johnny Morris of the Bears; Fran Tarkenton of the Vikings; Dick LeBeau of the Lions; Ken Willard of the 49ers; Roman Gabriel of the Rams; Charley Johnson of the Cardinals; Sonny Jurgensen of the Redskins; and Ernie Green, Gary Collins, and John Wooten of the Browns were very generous with their time and their many insights about games, coaches, and players. I look forward to presenting each of them with a copy of the book. Like the great George Plimpton, I discovered that talk among football players was a lot more interesting than talk in some places where it's supposed to be good and that football, paradoxically, is both the most violent and most intellectually demanding of all our major sports. Sadly, several surviving key players were not well enough to be interviewed. Several very famous players never responded to my attempts to contact them, and one made clear through his manager that he would expect to be paid. I declined that offer.

The accounts of most games are based on specific local newspapers: the *Baltimore Sun*, the *Green Bay Press-Gazette*, the *Chicago Tribune*, *The Washington Post*, the *Cleveland Plain Dealer*, the *Dallas Morning News*, *The*

Preface

New York Times, the *Detroit Free Press,* the *Minneapolis Star-Tribune,* and the *Los Angeles Times*. I did not routinely note the news accounts that I relied on for the details of games. All the statistics came from the website www.pro-football-reference.com, except for some mid-season totals that came from newspapers.

A great many excellent highlight films of games from the 1965 season are now available on YouTube, including both Packers-Bears games, the remarkable Colts-Vikings game in Minnesota, games between the Browns, Eagles, and Cowboys, the Bears and Gale Sayers's great game against the 49ers, the season finale between the Packers and 49ers, the Colts-Packers playoff, and the championship game. More wonderful footage can be seen in season highlight films of the Colts, Packers, Cowboys, Bears, Vikings, 49ers, and Rams. Many of my detailed descriptions of plays are based on those films. I have no idea whether CBS kinescopes or tapes of any televised broadcasts have survived.

My other source was my memory. In 1965, I was a college freshman. I had started watching the NFL obsessively in 1957, when I was ten, but had spent 1961–64 in Africa, where there was no television of any kind, and then at boarding school, where access to television was severely restricted. Nineteen sixty-five was the first year that I could watch as much as I wanted. Since I was living in New England, the bulk of the available games involved the New York Giants, but thanks to national broadcasts and the advent of doubleheaders, I also saw the first game between the Colts and the Vikings, the game in the fog between Baltimore and Green Bay, the Thanksgiving game between the Colts and the Lions, and the Dallas-Washington thriller the following Sunday. Key plays from all of those games have stayed with me for 55 years. Unfortunately, I missed the climactic last weekend, the playoff, and the championship because I spent the Christmas holiday overseas with my family. I am delighted that I finally carried out my long-delayed dream to recreate the whole season for myself, for other fans, for the surviving participants, and for posterity.

1

Preseason

The United States appeared to have reached a new equilibrium early in 1965. Lyndon Johnson and the Democratic Party had just won a massive victory over Barry Goldwater, a foe of peaceful coexistence and Civil Rights legislation who struck most Americans as an extremist, and President Johnson was making the most of it. He had already signed the Civil Rights Act of 1964, opening access to public accommodations. He then introduced the Voting Rights Act while Medicare, federal aid to education, and poverty programs moved through Congress. The economy was booming, and inflation was low. The country did not know that Johnson had already given the "go" signal for a long process of escalation that would put a total of half a million American soldiers in South Vietnam. The new Baby Boom generation was filling up college campuses, and the threat of nuclear war had faded steadily in the more than two years since the Cuban missile crisis.

Pro football, meanwhile, had been taking over from baseball as the nation's leading sport. It had turned out to be ideally suited to television, which had passed the movies as the nation's preferred form of entertainment. In the last six years, the new American Football League, centered in the Sun Belt, where the population was already beginning to move, had put itself on the map bidding up salaries for players fresh out of college and attracting a television audience with a wide-open style of play. But the NFL remained supreme, and some of its owners still expected the AFL to go away. The NFL had also adjusted to the growth of the country, expanding into Minnesota and Dallas in 1960–61, but it essentially maintained the same simple structure that it had used for several decades. More than half a century later, we can only marvel at its classic simplicity.

The league had featured an Eastern and a Western conference since 1933. In the 1950s, the league had 12 teams, and each team played every conference rival twice and played two games against teams from the other conference. There were no playoffs as we know them today. In a typical year, the winners of the Eastern and Western conferences played the NFL Championship two weeks after the end of the regular season in the second week of December. Once, in 1958, the championship game had ended in a tie, and the Colts had beaten the Giants in the first sudden-death overtime game in football history. Occasionally, of course, two teams would tie for a conference title, in which case they would play a one-game playoff in the next week. In 1957, the Detroit Lions had staged a remarkable second-half comeback to beat the San Francisco 49ers 31–27 in such a playoff. In 1958, a very exciting season, the Cleveland Browns had gone to New York for the last game of their season, leading the New York Giants by one game, only to lose 13–10 to the Giants from a last-second field goal in the snow by Pat Summerall. They lost 10–0 in the playoff the following week. In general, the league's structure and the need to win one's conference to reach the playoffs gave every week's game an importance that today's contests do not have. Without wild cards, a contending team had to play every game as if it were its last—and they did.

As the 1965 training camps opened, the Baltimore Colts were coming off a tremendous season with only one major blemish—their disastrous 27–0 defeat at the hands of the Cleveland Browns in Municipal Stadium in the NFL Championship. The 1964 season had been just the second season for the Colts under their new head coach, Don Shula, who had replaced Weeb Ewbank in 1963 after three consecutive disappointing seasons.

The team had gone 9–5 in 1963, finishing third behind the Chicago Bears and the Green Bay Packers, whom they had been unable to beat. But in 1964, they had gone 12–2, scoring 428 points while allowing only 225, both league-leading figures. Their team leader and quarterback was Johnny Unitas, who had come almost literally out of nowhere in 1957, established himself as a national figure in 1958, and remained, with Jim Brown, one of the two biggest stars in the league.

Descended from Lithuanian immigrants, Unitas, whose father had died when he was five, was raised by his mother in the Pittsburgh suburb of Mt. Washington, high above the Monongahela River. He became a star quarterback for a small Catholic school, and Notre Dame gave him a tryout but turned down the lanky kid who weighed less than 140 pounds. An indifferent student, he failed the entrance exam at the University of Pittsburgh. An alumnus of his high school had fortuitously become an assistant coach at the University of Louisville, and Unitas went there on scholarship in 1951. It was very much a second-tier football school, and Unitas became the starting quarterback as a freshman. Although he played in only one winning season, his hometown team, the Pittsburgh Steelers, drafted him in the ninth round of the 1955 draft. They then cut him in training camp. He returned to Pittsburgh, got an outdoor construction job, and played a

1. Preseason

season of semi-pro football. The following year, he wrangled an invitation to the Colts' training camp and made the team. When starting quarterback George Shaw—in only his second year—was injured midway through 1956, Unitas became the starter.[1]

With the help of Unitas, running back and wide receiver Lenny Moore, fullback Alan Ameche, wide receiver Raymond Berry, offensive tackle Jim Parker, guard Alex Sandusky, and a defensive line featuring Gino Marchetti, Art Donovan, and Big Daddy Lipscomb, the Colts became contenders in 1957 and champions in 1958. Unitas caught the nation's imagination in the 1958 NFL Championship against the New York Giants when he took the team down the field in the last two minutes with the help of three passes to Berry to tie the game and then led them into the end zone in the Colts' first possession in the first sudden-death overtime in the history of the NFL. The team repeated in 1959, beating the Giants again. In 1960, as some key players aged, they dropped to 6-6 after losing their last four games and followed that up with seasons of 8-6 and 7-7 as the Packers took over the Western Conference. The 1962 season cost veteran coach Weeb Ewbank his job, and he moved, fatefully, to the New York franchise in the new AFL. Don Shula had improved the Colts to 9-5 in 1963, losing all five games against the strongest teams in the league—the Bears, Packers, and Giants—and then to 12-2 in 1964.

The offense had prospered because of a balanced attack. Johnny Unitas, who had taken over as the team's quarterback during the 1956 season and led it to championships in 1958 and 1959, had thrown just 305 passes during the 1964 season and completed 158, after throwing between 367 and 420 passes in each of the previous five seasons. But he had thrown only six interceptions all year while passing for 19 touchdowns, earning himself the designation of the NFL's Player of the Year for the second time. Meanwhile, the Colts had rushed for 2,007 yards during the season, fifth in the league and only 269 yards behind the league-leading Packers. Lenny Moore, one of the great pass receivers in the league, had moved to running back in 1964 and had rushed for 584 yards while catching 21 passes, good for 472 more yards, making 1,056 yards of total offense and scoring a league record 20 touchdowns. Tony Lorick, Jerry Hill, and Tom Matte were the other running backs. The stars of the offensive line were left tackle Jim Parker, one of the greatest in NFL history, and right guard Alex Sandusky, whom Detroit's Alex Karras rated as his most formidable opponent. Veteran split end Raymond Berry and flanker Jimmy Orr caught 43 and 40 passes, respectively. Going into his third year in 1965, John Mackey was a brilliant tight end, one of the biggest in the league, and had averaged 18.5 yards for his 22 receptions.

NFL 1965

Nineteen sixty-four was the final year for two of Baltimore's defensive stars, end Gino Marchetti—long regarded as the NFL's best—and linebacker Bill Pellington. In previous years, the 1958–59 team had also lost defensive tackles Art Donovan, who retired, and Big Daddy Lipscomb, who had been traded to Pittsburgh before dying of a heroin overdose.[2] Thirty-year-old Lou Michaels, a veteran and one of the league's better field goal kickers, took over for Marchetti in 1965, joining tackles Billy Ray Smith and Fred Miller and right end Ordell Braase. The secondary featured cornerbacks Bobby Boyd and the speedy Lenny Lyles and safety Jerry Logan.

Don Shula had had a meteoric rise as a coach. After seven years as a defensive back for the Browns (1951–52), the Colts (1953–56), and the Redskins (1957), he had retired at the tender age of 27 and spent two years as a college assistant. He then became the defensive secondary coach for the Detroit Lions in 1960 and the coordinator of their great defense in 1961 and 1962. When the Colts hired him as head coach in 1963, he was only 33 years old—just three years older than Johnny Unitas and Lenny Moore and years younger than defensive stars Gino Marchetti and Bill Pellington. Yet, he quickly established his authority.

Dan Sullivan

I had grown up in Dorchester and graduated from Boston College in 1962. The Colts drafted me. There weren't many New Englanders in the NFL in those days, but Art Donovan, who also went to BC, was very good to me in my rookie year. I was a backup for three years. In my first year, I played one quarter at center and one at defensive tackle. Then I backed up all over the offensive line until I eventually became the starting left guard.

Shula came in my second year, and he was very different from Weeb Ewbank. Ewbank was very structured—every practice had 15 minutes for one part of the team. Shula used the same structure, but if 15 minutes weren't enough to get something right, he would extend it. Shula also had a young college kid standing next to him with a notebook. If he saw you make a wrong move, he would tell the kid to write it down, and the next day he would review all the mistakes from the day before. He would chew you out, telling you something you needed to hear. He was a master at finding the right guys to pick on—like me.

Things between Unitas and Shula were quite tense—professional, but tense. Shula would not coddle Unitas. Sometimes Shula would send in a play, and Unitas wouldn't execute it, and that caused problems. Unitas would complain after a few beers. Also, John would have liked to pass 60–70 percent of the time—he didn't like to hand the ball off. You had to be able to pass block on that team!

1. Preseason

I think the real Shula emerged when he went to Miami to coach. He turned Bob Griese into his idea of a quarterback, and he built the offense around the run.

Upton Bell was the second son of the NFL's long-time commissioner Bert Bell, who had died at an Eagles game early in 1959, when Upton had just graduated from college. Upton had gone to work for the Colts in the summer of 1960. He initially worked in the ticket office, and then, in 1962, he became a scout. He saw himself as a future general manager, and Shula gave him a chance to learn, giving him his own role in practice and afterward.

Upton Bell

In training camp, the team filmed every practice. I would go into the huddle, listen to the play call, and write it down, and we would know what the play was when we watched the film that night. I learned attention to detail from Shula. Be on time, be prepared, do the extra work. He would see me talking with someone from across the field and yell, "Upton, stop fucking around and get with it." I was there for the four-hour film sessions when they graded all the players, and I came to understand how they evaluated talent. He trained Chuck Noll, his assistant and future Hall of Fame coach of the Steelers, that way too.

Shula and Unitas were two young guys with their own way of doing things. On the field, they managed it; off the field, it didn't work.

When the Colts lost Big Daddy Lipscomb, Allen Ameche, and Gino Marchetti, they lost their most physically dominating players, with the exceptions of offensive tackle and guard Jim Parker and tight end John Mackey. When center Bill Curry joined them in 1967 after two years with the Packers, he was immediately struck by how physically unimpressive they looked in their locker room.[3] They compensated by becoming the thinking man's team. "We had a variety of personalities and backgrounds," Raymond Berry said later, "but we were all alike in one way. We were serious about football." The great Jim Parker honed his blocking skills by spending hours studying films of Giant tackle Roosevelt Brown.[4] Tom Matte had joined the team in 1961 as a halfback and by 1963 carved out a role as a pass receiver coming out of the backfield. In 1963, he had caught 48 passes for 466 yards that way, although his role was scaled back in 1964–65 after Lenny Moore was shifted into the backfield from flanker.

Tom Matte

> Unitas had a lot of confidence in me to read the defenses. He would call my pass play, and I would look at the linebackers and figure out where I could get open. When the ball snapped, I would go there, turn around—and there it was. He read the defense the same way. We would go to [assistant coach] Don McCafferty's house in the evening and watch movies. I could find the dead spots.

The Colts made up for the retirement of middle linebacker Bill Pellington in the off-season with a clever trade. Before the 1964 season started, they acquired the New York Giants' top draft pick, a very fast 230-pound running back from Texas named Joe Don Looney, who would not put up with the treatment the Giants doled out to rookies. Talented and rich—his father was a Texas oilman—Looney had already attended three different colleges and was as uncontrollable off the field, where he frequently got into fights with strangers, as he was talented on the field. Looney averaged 5.5 yards a carry in just 27 rushes for the Colts during 1964, but in November, a judge put him on probation for assaulting a neighbor in his apartment building. In the offseason, the Colts traded him to the Lions for Dennis Gaubatz, who had been learning his middle linebacker trade backing up all-pro Joe Schmidt. Looney wound up playing for four different teams in five seasons before his career ended in 1969, while Gaubatz became a key to the Colt defense.

The Green Bay Packers had established themselves as a dynasty under coach Vince Lombardi in 1960–62, winning three consecutive conference titles and two consecutive championships. The second championship was won in 1962, with a record of 13–1. A shadow fell across the team in early 1963, however, when Commissioner Pete Rozelle suspended star halfback and Lombardi favorite Paul Hornung for betting on games. The Chicago Bears had stunned the Packers 10–3 in the first game of the 1963 season and had beaten them decisively in their second encounter later that year. Hornung returned for 1964 but became one of the goats of the season when his place kicking failed him at several crucial moments. The Packers got their revenge on the Bears, beating them twice, but lost to the Colts twice, 21–20 and 24–21. They also lost once each to the up-and-coming Minnesota Vikings, the Los Angeles Rams, and the San Francisco 49ers and finished the season 8–5–1, a full 3.5 games behind the Colts.

Lombardi's coaching has been immortalized in a number of books. They include his own *Run to Daylight* (New York, 1963), ghosted by the great sportswriter W.C. Heinz, about a single week's preparation and game in 1962; Jerry Kramer and Dick Schapp's *Instant Replay* (New York, 1968), a

1. Preseason

diary of the 1967 season; *One More July* (New York, 1977), by George Plimpton and Bill Curry; *Coach: A Season with Lombardi* (New York, 1970), by Tom Dowling, about Lombardi's one year at the helm of the Washington Redskins before he died; and David Maranniss' superb biography, *When Pride Still Mattered* (New York, 1999). His leadership had many features. Like Paul Brown, the first modern NFL coach, Lombardi wore business clothes on the sideline and insisted that his players act professionally at all times. He had a relatively simple offensive system and counted on superior personnel (of which he had inherited quite a bit in 1959), careful study of his opponents, and well-prepared practices to win. Lombardi had broken into pro football as the offensive coordinator of the New York Giants from 1954 through 1958, while another future coaching great Tom Landry ran their defense. The rivalry between their units gave the Giants one championship in 1956 and another title game appearance two years later.

The Giants had become Paul Brown and the Cleveland Browns' nemesis in the late 1950s, and Brown apparently helped convince Lombardi to leave his native New York—where he had hoped to become head coach—and take over the hapless Green Bay Packers in 1959. That put him in the Western Conference, where Brown wouldn't have to compete with him.

Ernie Green

> I graduated from Louisville in 1962, and I got a call from the Packers—they had drafted me. I reported for camp. We played the Cowboys in the first exhibition game and beat them, and I was called in to see Coach Lombardi. *Oh no*, I thought, *they're sending me home*. "Don't worry," Lombardi said, "we're not sending you home. Paul Brown and I are pretty good friends. He convinced me to take the job here at Green Bay, and he told me that he would do what he could to help me." And he had! He sent Lombardi [defensive ends] Willie Davis and Bill Quinlan, and [defensive tackle] Henry Jordan! "Paul Brown needs running backs," he said, "and if you can demonstrate to him what you've demonstrated to me, I have no doubt you can play in this league." So, I reported to the Browns training camp the next day.

Davis and Jordan became keys to Lombardi's defense for the whole of his Green Bay career. He also inherited the makings of a great offensive line, including center Jim Ringo, guard Jerry Kramer, and tackle Forrest Gregg, as well as backs Paul Hornung and Jim Taylor and quarterback Bart Starr. It took him just one year to turn Green Bay into a winner, a second year to get them into the championship game, and a third year to win it. He spent essentially all of his time coaching the offense, leaving the defense to an excellent assistant, Phil Bengtson. All of Lombardi's players appreciated his encyclopedic knowledge of football, his ability to dissect game films, and his remarkable communication skills. But more than anything else, they remembered his managerial style, which was, in turn, a function of his demon-driven personality and his rather dark view of human nature.

The son of Italian immigrants, Lombardi had grown up in New York and attended then-football power Fordham in the Bronx. He was a deeply religious Catholic who took communion every day, was extremely sensitive to slights of all kinds, and felt that he would have become a head coach much earlier but for his Italian ancestry. (It is something of a shock to realize that he was only 45 when the Packers hired him.) Only a man driven by shame, in my opinion, could have been so terrified of losing. As a coach, he continually passed that terror on to his players, screaming at them over every mistake and trying to make them utterly dependent emotionally upon himself. In reality, no athlete or coach can function at any level of competition without somehow coming to terms with the inescapable fact that everyone, at times, must lose. But Lombardi, like so many of them, insisted that every loss was a preventable aberration and told his players that if they simply did as they were told, they would always win. Film played a key role in game preparation, of course, and Lombardi's Tuesday film sessions with his offense became legendary. So scathing were his comments on his players' mistakes that many of them felt their heart sink on the field whenever they missed an assignment, anticipating their humiliation less than 48 hours away.

Lombardi believed that fear and hatred drove men more than anything else, suggesting that ultimately those emotions drove him. He told his players to hate their opponents, whom he accused of trying to take away their livelihoods by beating them, and he clearly kept their hatred honed by turning it against himself. A master of what some psychologists call intermittent reinforcement, Lombardi manipulated players in many ways. He humiliated them in front of their teammates, and they melted in gratitude whenever he favored them with a compliment. He did have a great deal of respect for the talents of both his players and those of the opposition, but he rarely showed it to the Packers themselves.

As the 1965 season approached, both Lombardi and his players were beginning to show some strain because they had had to face losing for two years. Lombardi and the team had suffered an awful shock early in 1963 when Commissioner Pete Rozelle suspended golden boy Paul Hornung—Lombardi's personal favorite on the team—for betting on games, along with Alex Karras of the Lions. The Packers lost only two games in

1. Preseason

1963—only one more than in 1962—but the Bears lost only one, beating the Packers and taking the title. In 1964, even though Hornung returned, they had lost five, and another one in the Playoff Bowl for second-place teams, a game that Lombardi regarded with contempt. The breaks had gone against the Packers in both 1963 and 1964, but the Bears and Colts, meanwhile, had produced teams that were as good as, and in some respects superior to, the Packers. The league was beginning to catch up to Lombardi, and the core of his team was getting older. There was strain in his home life as well, and his wife had survived an apparent suicide attempt in February.[5] In one of the team's preseason games in Cleveland on September 4, the strain showed when a sellout crowd packed Municipal Stadium to watch the Packers play the newly crowned NFL Champion Browns. The Packers had gotten control of the game in the third quarter, leading 17–7, and Bart Starr led the team about 70 yards down the field to the Green Bay four-yard line for a first down. On the next play, Starr failed to get the play started in time, and the Packers were assessed a five-yard penalty for delay of game.

On the sidelines, rookie center Bill Curry watched as Lombardi screamed across the field at Starr and the Packers at the top of his lungs, asking what in the hell was going on, all in front of 80,000 fans—not in the NFL championship game, but a meaningless exhibition that the Packers were obviously on their way to winning. Starr never turned a hair but simply went into the huddle, called a new play, and threw a bullet pass to Boyd Dowler in the end zone. Curry got up and stepped onto the field to take his place on the kicking team for the extra point but was astonished to see Starr, to whom he would snap the ball, running toward the sideline. Starr, a quiet Southerner, was in many ways the opposite of Lombardi, an equally dedicated warrior but one who never complained and was rarely known to raise his voice. Starr ran right up to his coach in front of those same 80,000 fans and the Packer bench and unleashed a stream of abuse such as Curry had never seen aimed at an authority figure in his life. Lombardi, quite simply, had pushed his most important player too far. The coach maintained an unaccustomed silence for the rest of the game and eased up on his players for some days afterward. Then, of course, he returned to normal.[6]

The team had now changed significantly from the lineups that had dominated the early 1960s. Quarterback Bart Starr, Paul Hornung, and fullback Jim Taylor remained the backfield, and Taylor in 1964 remained the league's second-leading rusher, about 300 yards behind Jim Brown. But center Jim Ringo had been traded to Philadelphia after 1963, and young

Ken Bowman replaced him. Jerry Kramer returned from a year of injury and serious illness, along with Fuzzy Thurston, as the team's guards, and the tackles remained Forrest Gregg and Bob Skoronski. Neither Kramer nor Thurston were ready to play when the season opened, however, forcing Gregg to shift from right tackle to left guard while two young players, Dan Gregg and Steve Wright, filled in the right side of the line. Veteran tight end Ron Kramer had played out his option and signed with the Packers' bitter rivals, the Detroit Lions, and Marv Fleming initially replaced him. Boyd Dowler remained the flanker, but Lombardi made a key trade in the spring of 1964, acquiring a potential replacement for veteran receiver Max McGee.

Dave Robinson

I had played offensive and defensive end in college at Penn State. Lombardi drafted me after 1962. He thought rookies usually needed to sit on the bench for two years. On Thanksgiving Day, 1963, Ray Nitschke broke his arm, and I got to play the last few games of the season at left linebacker while Dan Currie moved into the middle. In 1964, Lombardi had acquired Leroy Caffey from Philadelphia for Jim Ringo, but he became the backup, and I became the right linebacker with Nitschke and Currie. But then I hurt my knee.

When we went to the Playoff Bowl, Lombardi told me not to tape my knee on the first day of practice. "If it's ok," he said, "you'll play. If it isn't, we'll send you back to Green Bay for surgery." In the very first drill, I heard a pop, and I couldn't straighten my knee. The cartilage had torn. I went back, had the surgery, and watched the game from a hospital bed. The doctors said I could play again in six weeks.

I went home to New Jersey after that and went to a surgeon whose son had played with me in high school, and he gave me a rehab program. I started riding a bike. When I could ride three miles out and three miles back, I started jogging. On May 3, they flew me to Green Bay, and Vince and the team doctor met me and took me to the training room that morning to evaluate me. I left for home that afternoon, and they brought in Curry to evaluate him. The next day, Vince traded Curry to Los Angeles for Carroll Dale.

Max McGee was getting older, and Carroll Dale could block. Max McGee couldn't spell "block"—it made it hard to run to the weak side. So now, I became the left linebacker, and Caffey took over on the right.

Dick LeBeau (Lions Cornerback)

McGee never blocked me! McGee, Dowler, and Dale were all tall and fast. That's what Lombardi liked. It made them hard to cover.

1. Preseason

There were other changes on defense. Defensive end Lionel Aldridge and tackle Ron Kostelnik now joined all-pros Willie Davis and Henry Jordan. In the secondary, right cornerback Jesse Whittenton retired, and his replacement, Doug Hart, and strong safety Tom Brown joined veterans Herb Adderley and Willie Wood. Hornung's place-kicking days were over after a disastrous 1964 kicking season, and Don Chandler had been acquired from the New York Giants to punt and place kick. The Packers' defense had nearly matched the Colts in 1964, but their once-legendary offense had lagged well behind, sixth in the league overall, even though they had outgained the Colts in both of their close losses to them.

In early 1965, in a portent of things to come, Paul Hornung attempted to reinforce and rehabilitate his reputation and make extra money by publishing an autobiography, *Football and the Single Man*, ghosted by sportswriter Al Silverman.[7] The title was an obvious play on *Cosmopolitan* editor Helen Gurley Brown's *Sex and the Single Girl*, which had appeared three years earlier. Hornung's book mixed the story of his football career with brief accounts of some of his countless romantic exploits. The vast majority of young football players were already married in the early 1960s—many of them before they graduated from college—and Hornung not only enjoyed his sexual freedom but reveled in talking about it. His final chapter bragged shamelessly about his "little black book" of phone numbers arranged by city and the many young women who were delighted to fly to Green Bay just to see him for a couple of days. He was evidently Joe Namath before Joe Namath, although since he played in Green Bay instead of New York, he never became quite the national figure that Namath did.[8]

Next to the Colts, the most fancied team in the Western Conference was the Minnesota Vikings, who had tied the Packers for second place in the conference in 1964—only their fourth year in existence—under their coach, former star quarterback Norm Van Brocklin.

Although the 1964 Vikings already included the defensive ends from their Purple Gang of the late 1960s, Carl Eller and Jim Marshall—and the 1965 version added tackle Gary Larsen—they were known mainly as an offensive team. Their small, agile quarterback, Fran Tarkenton, the league's most notorious scrambler, had captured the country's imagination with his twists and turns. In 1964, Tarkenton had thrown for 22 touchdowns while rushing for 330 yards and two additional touchdowns. Halfback Tommy Mason and fullback Bill Brown were also stars, and Brown had rushed for 866 yards and caught 48 passes worth 703 additional yards. Drafting wisely, Minnesota had emerged as a contender in only its fifth year in the league and had beaten the Colts and the Packers once each in 1964.

In *Sports Illustrated*'s Pro Football Preview edition in early September, lead NFL writer Tex Maule wrote his main feature on the Vikings, coach Norm Van Brocklin, and Tarkenton and speculated that they might dethrone the Colts in the Western Conference. Van Brocklin—a long-time star with the Los Angeles Rams who had won the NFL title with the Philadelphia Eagles in his last year, 1960—had gone directly from his playing career to the head coaching position of the expansion Vikings, a move without precedent. With Tarkenton's scrambling filling highlight films, the team had managed to win a remarkable three games, including their opener against the Chicago Bears (37–13) and a later game against Johnny Unitas and the Colts. Maule's article showed that Van Brocklin still had an aura of greatness that he could cast over writers and the public. While acknowledging that Van Brocklin "had a hot temper," "was not notably tactful," and he "still erupts occasionally during the course of a game," Maule boldly declared that "he has proved that he is as good a coach as he was a quarterback."[9] The Vikings' young players were much too respectful to share their feelings with the press, but they were experiencing something very different.

Fran Tarkenton

> Van Brocklin was a brilliant offensive mind and quarterback. He taught me offense. But he was probably the most dysfunctional coach in the history of the world. He was a cancer in the clubhouse.
>
> [Chicago quarterback] Bill Wade and I became friends when I was in college. He had played with Van Brocklin in Los Angeles. In early 1961, I was on a speaking tour with Bill Wade. He said, "I'm really sorry for you having to play for Van Brocklin. He's the worst human being I've ever known." He was a nutcase. He hated everybody—Christians, Jews, blacks, and whites. Once on a plane home from a loss, he got drunk and punched out our equipment manager, a little guy who had lost a leg in World War II.

Van Brocklin's personality would emerge at a critical moment during the coming season.

The Detroit Lions had been the Packers' principal conference rival in 1960–62, beating them once a year and winning the Playoff Bowl between second-place teams three times running. They had slumped very badly in 1963 after their best player, defensive tackle Alex Karras, had

1. Preseason

been suspended along with Hornung for betting on games, but they had rebounded smartly in 1964, finishing with a 7–5–2 record, including a decisive win over the Colts after Baltimore had clinched the conference. Their strong defense still featured their legendary front four of Karras and 300-pound Roger Brown at tackle and Darris McCord and Sam Williams at the ends, as well as linebackers Joe Schmidt and Wayne Walker and cornerback Dick LeBeau. Another legendary defender, however, cornerback Night Train Lane—who even today holds the NFL record with 14 interceptions in a single season—was cut during training camp in 1965, ending his career. Safety Yale Lary, for years the NFL's best punter, also retired.

The offense remained a problem. The fourth game of the 1962 season, when the Vikings faced the defending champion Packers in a battle of unbeatens, had left the team with a wound it could not heal. The brutal defensive battle—immortalized in *Run to Daylight*, the book Vince Lombardi wrote about the game with the help of W.C. Heinz—had come down to the last few minutes of the game, with the Lions leading 7–6. On a third down with less than three minutes remaining, their new quarterback, Milt Plum, had completed a down and out pass to end Gail Cogdill for the first down, forcing Green Bay to use up its timeouts during the next series. With 1:46 remaining, rather than play it safe and let Yale Lary punt, Plum tried another pass to the other side of the field. The intended receiver, Terry Barr, lost his footing on the wet field, and Packer Herb Adderley intercepted the pass and ran the ball back inside the Lion ten-yard line. A few plays later, Paul Hornung kicked the winning field goal. In the dressing room, Alex Karras threw his helmet across the room at Plum, just missing him. For weeks afterward, whenever middle linebacker Joe Schmidt passed Plum as the offense came on to the field, he would say, "Pass, Milt, three times, and then punt."[10] Although the Lions got some revenge on Thanksgiving Day in Detroit later that year, winning 26–14 after leading 26–0 at the half and sacking Bart Starr for a total loss of more than 100 yards, they lost two other games and could not overtake the Packers. The offense had never become the equal of the defense.

Dick LeBeau

> I did not hold that play against Milt. He was trying to win. But Milt Plum in 1962 had just come over from another team. Teams really were family in those days. That play in 1962 may have kept him from becoming part of the family.

NFL 1965

The also-rans of the conference in 1964 were the Los Angeles Rams (5-7-2), the Chicago Bears (5-9), and the 49ers (4-10). The Rams had given up well over 300 points despite the presence of the league's best front four, the Fearsome Foursome of Deacon Jones, Merlin Olsen, Rosey Grier, and Lamar Lundy. Their offense included some fine players, but their quarterback situation was confused, with Bill Munson and fourth-year man Roman Gabriel competing for time. The always-promising 49ers had quarterback John Brodie, already an eight-year veteran, and fine wide receivers in Bernie Casey and big Dave Parks, at 6'2" and 220 pounds. The team also added rookie Ken Willard, destined to establish himself as an outstanding fullback, and acquired long-time star back John David Crow from St. Louis. Their defense, however, was mediocre even though it featured two of the league's best cornerbacks, Kermit Alexander and Jim Johnson.

Ken Willard

I was from Richmond, Virginia. My father died when I was very young, and my mother raised me. She worked in a department store. I went to the University of North Carolina on a football scholarship. I thought about playing professional baseball, and I could have signed with the Red Sox out of high school, but I decided to go to North Carolina on scholarship for two years. I got married after my sophomore year, and I had had a miserable year in baseball that year, so I decided I wanted to play in the NFL.

The war between the AFL and NFL was reaching its peak my senior year, 1964. I wanted to play for the Detroit Lions. I had grown up watching them play on Thanksgiving Day. Bill Dudley, a Lions scout, actually signed me on Thanksgiving Day 1964, after our season was over and before the draft. There was a lot of that going on in those days. The Buffalo Bills said they wanted me, but they had Cookie Gilchrist at fullback, my position. Their coach, Lou Saban, came down to Richmond to talk to me and said they would get rid of Gilchrist. I didn't believe him. He asked, "For equal money, do we have equal chances?" I said, "No."

The leagues were babysitting top prospects, and the NFL sent Bill Fisher, a broadcaster, to look after me. I told him I wouldn't meet with him, but he showed up anyway. I told him I wanted to play with the Lions, and he said he would try to make that happen. But the 49ers had the second pick in the draft, and the Lions the 11th, and the 49ers wanted me. So, Fisher said I had to talk to Lou Spadia of the 49ers, and I said I would. I thought San Francisco was right next to Japan!

Spadia asked me what it would take to play in San Francisco.

I said, "Double what I got from Detroit!" He said, "It's yours." I said, "I'm yours!" He informed me, "Jack White will fly into Richmond tonight."

1. Preseason

> I signed for a $50,000 bonus and three years for a total of $80,000. He wrote me one $10,000 check for my mother and $40,000 for me, and she put her check in the bank.

The Chicago Bears had fallen a very long way in 1964 after their championship season the year before, in which they had lost just one game. Thirty-four-year-old Rudy Bukich had replaced Billy Wade at quarterback and had passed very often and effectively. Flanker Johnny Morris led the league with a record-setting 93 receptions, and tight end Mike Ditka was second with 75, but the running game was very weak. Star runner Willie Galimore had died in a car accident during training camp. The defense had let them down, partly because of its advanced age. Defensive tackle Stan Jones, end Doug Atkins, and linebackers Joe Fortunato and Bill George were all in their mid-thirties, and George retired after 1964. Their famous 1963 secondary of cornerbacks Bennie McRae and Dave Whitsell and safeties Rich Pettibon and Roosevelt Taylor had intercepted only six passes in 1964.

In November of that year, however, the Bears had hit one of the greatest jackpots in the history of the NFL draft. Their first two picks were a new middle linebacker to replace George, a University of Illinois graduate named Dick Butkus, and a slim, fast halfback from Kansas named Gale Sayers.

Butkus was a Chicago native, and like Johnny Unitas, the child of an Eastern European immigrant family. He had seven older siblings, including three brothers with whom he shared one of the three bedrooms in the family home on the south side of Chicago, and his father worked at the Pullman railroad car factory. Obsessed with sports from an early age, he became a football star at Chicago Vocational High School and was the city player of the year as a junior. A flirtation with Notre Dame did not pan out, and the local University of Illinois snapped him up instead. Butkus helped lead the team to the Rose Bowl in his junior year, and a coaches' poll named him College Player of the Year. A Chicago lawyer named Arthur Morse adopted Butkus as a client, dangled him before the Denver Broncos and the New York Jets of the AFL (where he might have become a teammate of Joe Namath), and eventually arranged his signing with the Bears. Halas got him for a $6,000 signing bonus and a five-year contract increasing from $18,000 to $60,000—much less, evidently, than many of his top contemporaries received. Years later, writing his autobiography, Butkus wondered exactly for whom Morse had really been working.[11]

Gale Sayers, a black Kansan, had had a more difficult childhood. Although his father came from a very high-achieving family, including two lawyers, he worked as a car mechanic, and both Sayers's parents had alcohol problems. By the time he entered high school, the family was living in Omaha, Nebraska, and he became a star halfback for Central High. A shorter, older brother, Win Sayers, was a track star who in college once defeated Bob Hayes in a 100-yard race and was on a U.S. team that competed against the USSR. Gale was also a star hurdler and broad jumper in high school. He received 100 college scholarship offers and settled on the University of Kansas, where he would set a three-year record for rushing. Sayers had already shown an extraordinary knack for open-field running, and the Bears drafted him fourth overall in early 1965 and outbid Lamar Hunt and the Kansas City Chiefs of the AFL. While quiet and shy, Sayers was also extremely ambitious, and he wanted to play in the stronger league.[12]

Earlier in 1964, the Bears had acquired an even more remarkable rookie, a 6'1", 230-pound fullback from Arizona named Andy Livingston, who had been signed at the age of 19. Livingston, whose older brother Warren had been a Dallas Cowboys cornerback since 1961, had been a three-sport star athlete in Mesa, Arizona, hitting over .400 in baseball and winning decathlons in track while starring in football. His life was derailed somewhat early in his senior year in high school when he had to marry a pregnant girlfriend. Many colleges wanted him, and he signed a letter of intent for Arizona State, which was already turning out a string of great running backs. In 1962–63, Arizona State encouraged Livingston to enroll in Phoenix Junior College because he was a few credits shy of high school graduation and could play more football there than as a freshman at Arizona State. During that year, another black Arizonan, Wilfrid White, who had played for two seasons with the Bears in the early 1950s, suggested to Livingston that he try to play in the NFL, even though rules normally barred anyone from the league whose college class had not graduated. "Let me make some calls," White said.

In the summer of 1963, Don Kellett, general manager of the Baltimore Colts, invited Livingston to Baltimore and signed him to a contract. The next day, he had to withdraw his offer because Commissioner Pete Rozelle had ruled Livingston ineligible. A year later, the phone rang again.

Andy Livingston

In the middle of 1964, I got a call from George Halas. "Do you know who I am?" he said. "Yes," I said, "you just won the World Championship." He invited me to Chicago, and I told him the commissioner had ruled me ineligible. "I don't give a damn what the commissioner said," he said. "I put him there." He told me

1. Preseason

to fly to O'Hare and come to his office. "Andy," he said, "this first-year money is not the most important thing. The most important thing is proving to me and everyone else that you can play on the professional level. I'm going to sign you for the minimum," which was $8,500 at the time.

In the midst of training camp, as other hopefuls disappeared right and left, Livingston was summoned to see Halas at 2:30 a.m. Instead of cutting him, Halas offered Livingston three contracts with small raises in the second and third years. He signed. The first time he got into a game, late in the season, he returned a kickoff 86 yards for a touchdown. Sayers, however, was already getting far more publicity during the 1965 training camp and figured to be the outstanding new face in the Bears' offense.

The Western Conference in 1964 had a combined record of 49–43–6 while the East had gone 43–49–6, with only two teams over .500. The Cleveland Browns, with an offense very nearly the equal of the Colts, had won the conference by a half-game over the St. Louis Cardinals, going 10–3–1. The Browns, who had dominated the NFL during their first six years in the league from 1950 through 1955, reaching the championship game six times and winning thrice, were in the midst of their second great run near the top of the league from 1963 through 1969, under their second coach, Blanton Collier.

Paul Brown, who had founded the team as part of the new All America Conference in 1946, had led the Browns to six consecutive conference titles and three NFL championships from 1950, when the team joined the NFL, through 1955. He had become too rigid in his thinking in the late 1950s, however, and had won the Eastern Conference title just one more time, in 1957. He had finally been let go after 1962. As fullback Jim Brown had explained in his 1964 autobiography, *Off My Chest*, Paul Brown's insistence on calling all the plays and sticking to the same stereotyped offense had stirred his players to contemplate actual rebellion late in a disappointing 1962 season. Meanwhile, coach Brown was also having trouble with the team's new owner, Art Modell, who, hearing about the players' plans to confront Brown, advised them to be patient and fired Brown when the season ended, replacing him with Collier.[13]

A quiet and intense man, Blanton Collier—largely forgotten today—had an extraordinary life and career as a coach. Born in 1906 in Kentucky, he had gone straight from college to a high school football coaching job in Paris, Kentucky, where he remained from 1928 through 1943. In 1944, he became an assistant to Paul Brown at the Great Lakes Naval Station training center, where Brown really got his start, and he served as Brown's backfield coach for the Browns from 1946 through 1953. Then he spent eight years as the head coach of the University of Kentucky. After 1955, when star quarterback Otto Graham retired, the Browns offense became predictable and conventional. Collier had returned to coach the backfield again in 1962 and taken over after yet another disappointing season. He had immediately brought a new spirit and philosophy to the Browns.

Gary Collins

I graduated from Maryland in 1962. The Browns and the Boston Patriots drafted me. The Patriots were talking about a lot more money, but I preferred to play with the Browns. I signed for two years at $25,000 a year. That was a lot of money in those days. My brother-in-law was working in a factory for $2,800 a year. I should have started in 1962. I was playing behind Ray Renfro at flanker, and his knees were shot, but when Paul Brown had an opinion, he stuck with it.

Blanton Collier immediately made some changes. I remember, in my first away game my first year, when we landed at the airport, there were two buses. The first bus had all the coaches, the rookies, and the black guys. The second bus had the white guys. Blanton changed that right away.

He was a great teacher and deeply knowledgeable about every phase of the game. I was the punter, and we talked about my steps. I remember him in deep conversations with the middle linebacker, the offensive linemen, the defensive linemen. He was stern, but he didn't chew you out. He would use reason. That was what I responded to, too.

John Wooten (Browns Guard)

The black guys did ride in the bus with the coaches, but that wasn't from segregation. Most of the players were smokers, but none of the black guys smoked. That's why we rode in that bus.

Collier, as fullback Jim Brown put it years later, "turned us loose," allowing new quarterback Frank Ryan to call the plays, which Paul Brown had always sent in via "messenger guards." He also gave new instructions to the offensive line.

Dick Schafrath

With Paul Brown, you normally blocked a guy and just stayed with him and tried to drive him in the ground. But that wasn't enough when you played under

1. Preseason

Blanton. Once Jimmy Brown would see you start with your hit on one side or the other of a guy, as soon as you hit him, you didn't stay with him another two seconds. You tried to go past him and get a second block because Jim Brown didn't mess around—he was going. It became an obsession with the offensive line to make more than one block.[14]

The Browns had led the NFL East for most of the 1963 season before fading suddenly at the end of the season and finishing second and had won the conference and the NFL title in 1964.

The key to the Browns, of course, was Jim Brown, now 29 years old and entering his ninth season in the league. For all that time, Brown had been and remains today the most dominant player in the history of the NFL. He had never missed a game from injury, and he had led the league in rushing in every year but one, 1962, when injury limited his effectiveness and allowed Jim Taylor of the Packers to surpass him. Nineteen sixty-two was also only the second year in which Brown failed to gain 1,000 yards rushing for the season. In the following year, 1963, he had rebounded from 996 yards gained to a new all-time record of 1,863—breaking his own record of 1,528 yards in twelve games in 1958—with an average of 6.4 yards per carry. At 6'2" and 235 pounds, Brown was one of the largest running backs in the league, with above-average speed and extraordinary balance that often allowed him to bounce off two or three tacklers at once and continue on his way to the end zone.

Brown's early 1964 autobiography—the first of two that he would eventually publish—made a very interesting contrast with Paul Hornung's. While Hornung stuck pretty much to his early life, the football field, and his love life, Brown talked at length about his contract negotiations, which he spiced up with threats to leave football and try either soccer or boxing. It also included a frank chapter about race, in which Brown claimed that "the black Muslims' basic attitude toward whites" was shared by 99 percent of black people. (Since the Muslims, then led by Elijah Muhammad, claimed that whites were alien devils, this was an intentionally inflammatory exaggeration.) He explicitly said that he did not want the love of white people. Having followed up the book with the first championship season he had ever had, Brown had started looking ahead to the next phase of his life. He had appeared in a film, *Rio Conchos*, which had been shot during the 1964 offseason, and was already signed to appear in a bigger picture, *The Dirty Dozen*, which would shoot early in 1966.

Like most great runners, Brown worked behind a terrific offensive line, featuring pulling guards Gene Hickerson and John Wooten and tackle Dick Schafrath. His running mate in the backfield, Ernie Green, had managed to gain 436 yards, averaging 3.9 yards per carry in 1964, while Brown piled up 1,544 yards with an average of 5.3 yards per carry. The Browns had ranked just behind the Packers as the leading rushing team in the league, albeit with a significantly higher average.

The Browns had also found their first effective passing quarterback since the retirement of Otto Graham after 1955. Dr. Frank Ryan, a Ph.D. in mathematics from Rice University, was not the equal of Unitas, Charley Johnson of the Cardinals, or Sonny Jurgensen of the Redskins, but the Browns had led the league with 28 touchdown passes in 1964. They had featured two outstanding receivers, the very fast rookie Paul Warfield at split end and Gary Collins at flanker. Collins, an imposing figure at 6'5" and 215 pounds, had outstanding moves and could, by virtue of his height, catch touchdown passes that his defenders simply could not reach. He had caught three of them against the Colts in the 1964 championship game, embarrassing Colt cornerback Bobby Boyd.

Gary Collins

> That was the biggest day of my career and Frank Ryan's career. It was a very windy day, not conducive to throwing. It was 0–0 at the half, and I think that was the first time all year our defense shut a team out in the first half! In the second half, everything worked.

Collins and Warfield were one of the best pairs of receivers in the league, but sadly, Warfield broke his collarbone in the annual College All-Star Game in late July 1965 and was lost for most of the season. Walter "The Flea" Roberts, one of the smallest players in the league at 5'9" and 163 pounds, replaced him as the season opened.

The Browns' defense lacked any really great players, and although they had ranked fifth in points allowed in 1964 behind the Colts, Packers, Lions, and Dallas Cowboys, they had given up the most yardage of any team in the league. Forty takeaways—just one behind the league-leading Colts and Packers—had evidently bailed them out of a lot of difficult situations. It seemed a very open question as 1965 began if they could maintain their microscopic edge over the Cardinals.

The Cardinals had suddenly emerged as an Eastern Conference power in 1963 with a 9–5 record, their third-place finish matching their third-best offense and defense, as measured by points. They had improved marginally in 1964 to 9–3–2, tying and beating the Browns in their two meetings but losing to the weak New York Giants and Dallas Cowboys. Charley Johnson,

1. Preseason

entering his prime at 26 and ranked among the league's better passers, had thrown 24 interceptions along with 21 touchdown passes. His leading receivers were flanker Bobby Joe Conrad, with 61 receptions, and tight end Jackie Smith with 47 receptions and a 14-yard average. The rushing game, led by fullback John David Crow, the league's eighth-leading rusher, was also among the league's best. The Cardinal defense, however, was not in the elite of the league. The team had shocked the Packers and the football world in the Playoff Bowl in Miami between the second-place teams, winning 24–17 behind two touchdown passes from Charley Johnson to reserve Billy Gambrell and two interceptions that stalled Packer drives. It was the first time that an Eastern Conference team had won the Playoff Bowl.

Charley Johnson

> We showed up to play. Billy Gambrell had a great day against [Packers defensive back] Jesse Whittenton.

The Eastern Conference's teams fell into three groups in 1964. After the contenders, the Browns and the Cardinals, came two teams that finished the season with 6–8 records, the Washington Redskins and the Philadelphia Eagles. They coincidentally had swapped quarterbacks before the 1964 season began, with the Eagles sending Sonny Jurgensen to Washington in exchange for Norm Snead. The Redskins were in the midst of an exciting but frustrating era of their long history, one which had begun in 1962 when the team belatedly became integrated under pressure from the federal government, acquiring the great Bobby Mitchell from the Browns. Mitchell had been Jim Brown's running mate for four years, rushing for as many as 743 yards in 1959 and catching about 35 passes a season. The Redskins immediately shifted their first black player to flanker, and although Mitchell—like his fellow Redskin Charley Taylor, who joined the team two years later—resented the switch, he and Taylor almost surely had much longer, injury-free and productive careers as receivers than they could have had in the backfield. Mitchell made a sensational debut at flanker in 1962, leading the league with 72 receptions and 1,384 receiving yards as the Redskins remained unbeaten for seven games before fading, and matched those figures the following year.

Mitchell fell off to 60 receptions in 1964, but rookie halfback Charley Taylor—who, like his fellow Arizonan Andy Livingston, dreamed of becoming the next Jim Brown—had an extraordinary season, rushing for 755 yards and catching 53 passes for 814 additional yards. Jurgensen ranked second in the league to Charley Johnson in passing yards but ranked fifth overall as a passer because of his 13 interceptions. Unfortunately, the defense had very few bright spots, although rookie free safety Paul Krause, who intercepted 12 passes, was one of them, and the defense gave up as many points as the offense scored. The team suffered a big blow during training camp in 1965 when Taylor chipped his ankle, but he managed to return for the second game of the season.

Norm Snead did much less well for the Eagles than Jurgensen for the Redskins in 1964. The team fielded an extraordinarily undistinguished lineup, save running back Tim Brown, in retrospect its most impressive performer on offense. The defense was even less memorable, and the team's prospects were anything but encouraging for 1965.

The Dallas Cowboys, who had begun life in 1960 under coach Tom Landry, had not progressed nearly as rapidly as their expansion counterpart Minnesota Vikings. After a disastrous first season that ended 0–11–1, they had improved slowly to 4–9–1 in 1961 and 5–8–1 in 1962, slipping back to 4–10 in 1963, and then 5–8–1 in 1964, despite playing in the weaker conference. Landry, himself a Texan and former defensive back, had coached the Giants defense in the late 1950s while Lombardi coached their offense, developing the innovative 4–3 defense that tried to funnel enemy runners toward middle linebacker Sam Huff. Devoutly religious, Landry was as reserved as Lombardi was volatile. Something of a control freak, he was now the only coach in the league to call all his offensive plays. In five years, he had not been able to settle on a quarterback, partly because fellow Texan Don Meredith was such a free spirit and refused to become an automaton. The team had managed to run the competing AFL team, the Dallas Texans, owned by oil magnate Lamar Hunt, out of town to Kansas City, but they had not won the heart of their city yet.[15]

Still, Landry and Dallas general manager Tex Schramm had laid the foundation of a very strong team. The 1964 starting roster included quarterback Don Meredith, fullback Don Perkins, and tight end Frank Clarke on offense, and defensive end and tackle George Andrie and Bob Lilly, linebacker Chuck Howley, and safety Mel Renfro on defense. But the offensive line was weak, and the team offense had been among the league's weakest. Help was on the way. In early 1965, the Cowboys signed tackle Ralph Neely, who had originally been chosen in the second round of the draft by the Colts and signed by the Oakland Raiders of the AFL only to change his mind and land with Dallas. NFL teams had decided to treat any draft picks who signed with the AFL as free agents. The Cowboys also landed another rookie, wide receiver Bob Hayes, the world's fastest human, who had won

1. Preseason

the Olympic gold medal in the 100 meters the previous fall in Tokyo. They did not, however, look likely to mount a serious challenge to the Browns and Cardinals.

In 1963, the Pittsburgh Steelers had come within one game—their final game of the season against the New York Giants—of making it into the NFL Championship for the first time in many years. They had lost that game and in 1964 slipped to a 5–9 record despite one of the more extraordinary performances in NFL history. Their 36-year-old quarterback, Ed Brown, had performed very poorly, but 35-year-old John Henry Johnson, their fullback, had rushed for an astonishing 1,048 yards, second in the league behind Jim Brown. The Steelers, however, provided the first really big news story of the NFL season in the first week of September.

Steelers coach Buddy Parker was one of the more respected leaders in the NFL. He had coached the Detroit Lions from 1951 through 1956, in the era of Bobby Lane, Leon Hart, Jim David, and Joe Schmidt. The Lions had won the NFL title game against the Browns in 1952–53, lost it in 1954, slumped badly in 1955, and just missed winning the Western Conference in 1956 with a 9–3 record. At the end of the Lions' training camp in 1957, at a boosters' banquet in Detroit, Parker stood up to give the closing speech and announced that he was quitting. The team had gotten too big for him. George Wilson replaced him a week before the opening game. The team won the Western Conference in a playoff with the 49ers and destroyed the Browns in the NFL title game.

On September 5, 1965, Parker did the same thing again, quitting the Steelers on the eve of the season opener after the team had lost four straight preseason games. He was replaced by coach Mike Nixon, and the ill omen proved out during most of the rest of the 1965 season.

One team remained: the New York Giants, who had dominated the NFL East from 1956 through 1963, winning the conference six times, but taking the league championship title only once, in 1956. The Giants owed their remarkable success to the two greatest assistant coaches in NFL history: Vince Lombardi and Tom Landry. Both, of course, had become head coaches at Green Bay and Dallas, respectively. The team was very strong defensively in the late 1950s thanks to Roosevelt Grier, Andy Robustelli, and Sam Huff and became more offensive beginning in 1961 when Y.A. Tittle took over at quarterback. The team became the toast of New York, the nation's largest media market, just as baseball's National League allowed two of its best teams to decamp for San Francisco and Los Angeles, leaving a vacuum that the NFL eagerly filled. The Giants ruled the television market all over New England as well as in New York itself. But the team was aging by 1963, and they had suddenly collapsed in 1964, finishing with a record of 3–11. Allie Sherman remained the head coach. The team used the first pick in the draft on Tucker Frederickson, a running back from Auburn, passing up Sayers and Butkus. It acquired veteran quarterback Earl Morrall from Detroit to replace Tittle, who had retired, along with star pass-catcher Frank Gifford, Robustelli, and a good many more. As the season dawned, many were wondering if the Giants would be able to improve at all in 1965.

The NFL of the mid–1960s played a simpler version of the game it plays today, fifty-plus years later. The game-day rosters numbered only 40 players, about 25 percent less than they do today. Every team relied on the same basic formations on offense and defense. The offensive formation featured two wide receivers, a split end (usually on the left side), and a flanker, who played outside the tight end and usually lined up on the right. Two running backs lined up behind the quarterback. On defense, teams usually played a 4–3–4 formation with four linemen, three linebackers, two cornerbacks, and two safeties. Middle linebacker had become the key defensive position, making stars out of players like Sam Huff of the Giants and Redskins, Joe Schmidt of the Lions, and Ray Nitschke of the Packers. Crucially, most pass defense was man-to-man, with the cornerbacks assigned to the opposing team's split end and flanker, a strong safety detailed to watch the tight end, and a free safety to go where he might be most needed. Almost no cornerback could consistently cope with the league's best receivers, making long touchdown passes to men like Paul Warfield, Bobby Mitchell, Jimmy Orr, Carroll Dale of the Packers, and Dave Parks of the 49ers a constant threat. Teams sometimes assigned an extra safety or linebacker to cover an enemy receiver with two men, but that inevitably opened up territory for someone else—the kind of opportunity Johnny Unitas or Bart Starr or Sonny Jurgensen relished.

Field goals were also an important part of the game, but kickers approached the ball from directly behind it and moved the toe of their shoe straight through the ball with little follow-through. Pete Gogolak, a Cornell graduate and Hungarian refugee, had just been drafted by the Buffalo Bills of the AFL, but no one had tried a field goal with his instep in the NFL. Still, kickers like Lou Groza of the Browns and Lou Michaels of the Colts could reach the goalposts—which were set on the goal line—from around the 50-yard line on occasion. Because kicking was weaker, most kickoffs were returned, and those returns frequently might give a team excellent field position or even a touchdown—another feature of the game that was far more exciting than it is now. There were no two-point conversions (although the NCAA had adopted them in 1959), no replays to overturn

1. Preseason

officials' calls (although CBS had begun using instant replay in its telecasts in 1964), and no overtime, except in postseason play. A tie was a tie, worth half a game in the standings.

While professional football was recognizably the same game in 1965 as in 2016, statistics show several key differences between gridiron contests then and now. Remarkably, an average team scored almost exactly the same number of points per game in 1965 and 2016, 23.1 and 22.8, respectively. Passing yardage accounted for over half of the league's offense in 1965, but it accounts for substantially more now. Yet the 1965 offenses were better at getting the ball into the end zone. They averaged 36 touchdowns per season compared to 33.6 per season in 2016. (All 2016 seasonal figures have been adjusted downward to represent a 14-game season, as in 1965, rather than the actual 16 games.) Because kicking distance and accuracy have improved so much, field goals now account for 22 percent of all points scored, compared to 13 percent in 1965. But the 1965 game was also more volatile because offenses were not as skilled at hanging on to the ball.

Fumbles lost were almost twice as high per game in 1965 than in 2016. Some long-time observers think that tackling was more punishing then, but another reason is surely the sticky substances that running backs and receivers now apply so liberally to their hands. Interceptions were nearly twice as frequent as well, and even the best quarterbacks seem to have taken many more chances. As a result, defenses in 1965 were much more of an *offensive* threat than they are today. Defenses scored a full 8 percent of their team's touchdowns in 1965 (and obviously set up a lot more), while they scored just 4 percent of their team's touchdowns in 2016. The dramatic changes of fortune turnovers create occurred far more frequently than now, keeping coaches, teams, and fans on their proverbial toes at all times. And because the rules against offensive holding on pass plays have been relaxed in recent decades, sacks were about 20 percent more common in 1965 than in 2016.

The NFL was rapidly eclipsing baseball as the national pastime. While baseball's minor leagues had fallen to a fraction of their prewar size during the 1950s, college football programs were expanding. The National League had given the NFL a big opening in 1958, when it abandoned the nation's media capital and allowed the Giants and Dodgers to move to the West Coast, and the New York Football Giants, who played in the NFL title game for five of the next six years, had taken full advantage of it. Under the leadership of its young commissioner Pete Rozelle, the league had adopted a critical new approach to its television contract. Rozelle sold the regular season rights for the entire league to CBS, and the teams evenly divided the money, regardless of the size of their market or their record on the field. The league's popularity was mushrooming. In 1962, CBS bought the rights to the entire season's NFL games for $4.65 million, with another $1.6 million for the NFL Championship. Two years later, a new contract gave the league more than $14 million per year for the regular-season games. Revenue sharing, along with restrictive player contracts, allowed the Green Bay Packers, with their tiny fan base, to compete effectively with the New York Giants, Chicago Bears, and Los Angeles Rams. The teams, however, still regarded their paying customers as their most important asset, and home games could not be televised by local stations. This was already creating some interesting new migratory patterns. In the early sixties, thousands of New York Giant fans jumped into their cars and drove to motels in central Connecticut to pick up broadcasts of Giants home games from the Hartford CBS affiliate. In November 1963, one small group of New York–based NFL fanatics drove far into the Midwest to catch the broadcast of the crucial second game between the Packers and the Bears.

Clearly, the system was not helping the NFL market the cream of its product to the nation. Vince Lombardi's Packers had been the talk of the league from 1961 through 1963, but most fans got to see them a maximum of two times a year, once on Thanksgiving when they always played the Lions and once in the NFL title game (until 1963). In 1962–63, the Giants, whose broadcasts had exclusive NFL rights north and northeast from New York to the Canadian border, contended for the title. But the Northeast suddenly had to make do with a second-rate product in 1964, when the Giants slumped to 3–11 while the Packers, Colts, Browns, and Cardinals fought out exciting races for the Eastern Conference and Western Conference titles. By the time the 1965 season began, that situation had set people thinking at CBS and in the headquarters of the NFL.

While television was booming, newspapers remained the main source of information for sports fans, and the NFL was peculiarly suited to newspaper coverage as well. Monday was traditionally a slow news day, and Sunday's games gave readers something to turn to. And with just seven games every Sunday—compared to ten Major League Baseball games on most days of the season—the papers could easily print a reasonably complete account of every single game, complete with a box score, and provided by the AP or UPI. *Sports Illustrated*, founded in 1954, was now the nation's leading sports periodical, and the NFL dominated it during the fall.

The NFL had not come into its own architecturally. While the Rams, 49ers, Eagles, Cowboys, and Steelers played in dedicated football stadiums—most of them built for the college game—the Giants, Redskins,

1. Preseason

Browns, Bears, Cardinals, Lions, Vikings, and Colts shared their stadiums with major league baseball teams. (The Packers split their home schedule between Lambeau Field in Green Bay and Milwaukee County Stadium.) Parts of early-season games, in particular, took place on top of baseball infields. Sellout crowds filled the home games of the Packers, Colts, and Giants week after week, and attendance all over the league was quite healthy.

Nineteen sixty-five also marked the peak of the modern Civil Rights Movement. The integration of the NFL was very visible but not very extensive. This was not altogether the league's fault: the major college programs were integrating very slowly in the Midwest and Far West and not at all in the Deep South. The league had only occasionally drawn on the deep pools of talent at historically black colleges such as Grambling. A survey of integration among the leading teams tells a straightforward story: black players were mostly restricted to certain very visible positions and performed on the average at a very superior level.

Thus, the Colts' offensive lineup included halfback Lenny Moore, tight end John Mackey, and offensive tackle Jim Parker—all of whom had long careers and earned places in the Pro Football Hall of Fame. Their defense in 1965 had just one black starter, the fast, hard-hitting cornerback Leonard Lyles. The Packers' offensive starting lineup had been all white during their championship years and began 1965 with only one black starter, new tight end Marv Fleming. On the other hand, Willie Davis, Lionel Aldridge, Dave Robinson, Herb Adderley, and Willie Wood made their defense nearly 50 percent black. The Browns, the pioneers of integration under Paul Brown, had Jimmy Brown and Ernie Green in the backfield, Paul Warfield or Walter Roberts at flanker, and John Wooten at guard on offense, but their starting defensive lineup had only one black player, cornerback Walter Beach. The Cardinals had three black starters on offense—Willis Crenshaw and Bill Triplett in the backfield and tackle Ernie McMillan—and Sam Silas and Luke Owens on their defensive line. The young Dallas Cowboys, interestingly enough, appear to have ranked just behind Green Bay with six black starters: fullback Don Perkins, tight end Frank Clarke, and split end Bob Hayes on offense, with Cornell Green, Warren Livingston, and Mel Renfro in the defensive backfield. The Rams had three black players in their defensive front four—Deacon Jones, Rosey Grier, and Lamar Lundy—and rookie cornerback Clancy Williams in the secondary, but no black starters on offense. Five out of 22, in short, seemed to be the customary limit for black starters, who seemed to be clustered on either the offense or defense. When the Pro Bowl squads were selected at the end of the season, however, the percentage was somewhat higher: 19 out of 70 were black. Quite a few teams evidently wanted to avoid having too many black players in visible positions, and that would have at least one major impact on the 1965 title race.

Nineteen sixty-five marked a turning point generationally as well. In one of his articles in the *Sports Illustrated* Football Preview edition, Tex Maule listed the stars who had just retired, including Y.A. Tittle, Frank Gifford, Andy Robustelli, and Alex Webster of the Giants; Gino Marchetti and Bill Pellington of the Colts; Dave Hanner of the Packers; the Lions safety and punter, Yale Lary, and runner Hugh McElhenny.[16]

Although demographers have always defined the Baby Boom as having begun in 1946, students of generations now date it from 1943, largely because the boys and girls born in that year were the first to grow up with no memory at all of the Second World War. That cohort reached the NFL for the first time via the 1965 draft, and it was one of the more distinguished in NFL history. Draft selections that year included halfback Tucker Frederickson and cornerback Spider Lockhart of the Giants, fullback Ken Willard of the 49ers, receiver Roy Jefferson of the Steelers, the all-time greats Dick Butkus and Gale Sayers of the Bears, quarterback Craig Morton and defensive tackle Jethro Pugh of the Cowboys, tight end Jerry Smith and linebacker Chris Hanburger (a very low pick) for the Redskins, receivers Jack Snow and Lance Rentzel for the Vikings, and linebacker Mike Curtis and tackle Ralph Neely for the Colts.[17] Two picks who got away from the NFL and signed with the rival AFL were receiver Fred Biletnikoff, drafted by the Lions, and quarterback Joe Namath, who signed a big contract with the New York Jets. All of these players played in Pro Bowls, and many of them are in the Hall of Fame.

The NFL's coaches, as a group, were far less distinguished than the players. Vince Lombardi had set a new standard for coaching at Green Bay. Young Don Shula of the Colts was not far behind, and in Dallas, Tom Landry was using innovative ideas on both offense and defense while showing how the draft could build a championship team. Blanton Collier had done brilliantly with the Browns in his first season as head coach and continued to have success for the rest of the decade. George Halas of the Bears was a link to the earliest days of the NFL but was never known for creativity—but his defensive coach, George Allen, had a great career ahead of him with the Los Angeles Rams and Washington Redskins. None of the other coaches in the league left a lasting mark upon the game. All of them, however, played their part in the drama that became the most exciting and most intensely watched season that the NFL had ever had.

The battle between the NFL and the upstart AFL was escalating on

1. Preseason

several fronts. The younger league had opened with eight teams in 1960. Texas oil money lay behind both the new AFL and the NFL's decision to expand into Dallas, perhaps because the extraordinarily generous treatment of oil profits in that era allowed oilmen to accumulate fortunes that other businessmen could only dream of. When one prominent oilman, Clint Murchison, got the Dallas Cowboys franchise in the NFL, another, young Lamar Hunt, decided to go ahead with the AFL instead. The AFL initially decided not to raid the NFL, but competition for top college prospects began even before the AFL had ever played a game, with several of them signing contracts with teams from either league. Lamar Hunt's team, the Dallas Texans, eventually had to leave for Kansas City after the Cowboys outbid him for both coach Tom Landry and quarterback Don Meredith, a local hero. It turned out, in any case, that the NFL wasn't big enough to absorb all the quality football talent in the United States, and players like quarterbacks Len Dawson and Jack Kemp and wide receiver Don Maynard, who had gone nowhere in the older league, became stars. The Buffalo franchise also picked up Hungarian refugee Pete Gogolak, who had introduced soccer-style place-kicking to college football at Cornell.

The interleague war entered a new phase early in 1964, when the AFL signed a new TV contract with NBC. Its existing ABC contract would earn it just $2.35 million in 1964, but the new contract would earn the league about $7 million a year for five years starting in 1965.[18] The new money enabled the Kansas City Chiefs to outbid Dallas for wide receiver Otis Taylor and allowed Sonny Werblin, the owner of the New York Jets, to sign Alabama quarterback Joe Namath after the 1965 draft to a reputed $400,000 contract. The war was now costing both sides a great deal of money. It had raised the price of good rookies, who were often better paid than seasoned veterans. The NFL owners were divided on their future, with some still hoping to put the new league out of business, while others talked openly of the need for a merger. Larry Wilson, a trucking magnate who owned the league champion Buffalo Bills, knew Carroll Rosenbloom, the owner of the Colts, well, and had opened informal talks about a merger with him. In the fall of 1965, Rosenbloom got Tex Schramm of the Cowboys and Commissioner Pete Rozelle into a merger meeting as well. Rozelle expressed interest in a merger that would temporarily maintain separate schedules but create a common draft, but there was one catch. He demanded $50 million, a huge sum in 1965, as an initiation fee from the AFL owners—about $6 million per team, more than ten times what each owner had paid to join their own league. The AFL owners said no, but talk of a possible merger continued. It became the biggest story of the offseason in 1966.[19]

2

The First Month

The Green Bay Packers traveled to Pittsburgh for the first of their two interconference games on Sunday, September 19, and got their season off to a rousing start in the midst of a late summer heatwave. Pittsburgh stopped the Packer offense cold in the first half, and their new young quarterback, Bill Nelsen, who had replaced veteran Ed Brown, led the Steelers to two field goals. Shortly before halftime, however, Herb Adderley got in front of rookie Roy Jefferson, intercepted a pass, and ran it 29 yards for a touchdown. The Steelers replied with yet another field goal and left the field leading 9–7. Vince Lombardi and his staff apparently gave some effective instructions in the locker room. The Packer defense made two more interceptions and recovered a fumble in the second half, and the offense scored the first six times that they had the ball on the way to a 41–9 victory. Injuries forced Green Bay to shuffle its offensive line, and Jim Taylor and Paul Hornung gained less than 100 yards between them, but Bart Starr gave a typically impeccable performance at quarterback, completing 17 of 23 passes for two touchdowns with no interceptions. The Steelers, only four weeks into the tenure of their new coach, Mike Nixon, also lost their star running back, John Henry Johnson, in the first quarter. Lombardi returned home well pleased, looking forward to the first crucial contest of the season the following week against the Colts in Milwaukee.

The first week's marquee attraction matched the Western Conference champion Colts with the highly touted Minnesota Vikings in Baltimore, where the temperature was also well over 90 degrees and 56,562 fans jammed Memorial Stadium. The Vikings got off to a truly spectacular start, returning the kickoff to the Colt 38-yard line and scoring on a 60-yard pass from Fran Tarkenton to receiver Hal Bledsoe on their second play from scrimmage. Minnesota had beaten the Colts in their opener a year before and looked as if they might do it again. Their defense promptly stopped Unitas and the Colts cold, and a poor punt gave the Vikings possession around midfield. This time, however, Tarkenton threw an interception only to have

2. The First Month

Unitas return the favor. The Vikings moved the ball close enough for a Fred Cox field goal and led 10–0. Unitas moved the Colts down the field and into the end zone with passes to four different receivers. On the next series, Jerry Logan intercepted another Tarkenton pass and ran it in for a touchdown and a 14–10 halftime lead. The Vikings continued to move the ball and made the score 14–13 with another field goal early in the third quarter.

The Colt defense, however, was proving more aggressive and tougher than its Viking counterpart, and during the second half, the Vikings could manage only three field goals while the Colts scored three touchdowns en route to a 35–16 victory. Backup Gary Cuozzo replaced Unitas late in the game and was driving for a touchdown when the gun sounded. "Credit the defense for giving us the chance to come back," coach Don Shula told the press. Fran Tarkenton completed only 11 of 27 passes.

Fifty miles south in D.C. Stadium, the Redskins took on the champion Browns and came up short. Jim Snowden, their massive young offensive tackle, lost 22 pounds during the game, and Sonny Jurgensen was red-faced and exhausted in the locker room. Both teams fielded very effective pass defenses, and Jurgensen had such a dreadful day that coach Bill McPeak replaced him late in the first half with young Dick Shiner, who had performed well in the preseason. Shiner eventually threw a touchdown pass to split end Angelo Coia for the Redskins' only score, but by then two big plays—an 80-yard bomb to Walter "The Flea" Roberts, who juggled and caught the ball on the dead run, and a 35-yarder to Frank Ryan's favorite target, Gary Collins—had already given the Browns a 17–0 lead. The Redskins rushed for just 24 yards. Thanks largely to his long-time antagonist Sam Huff, Jim Brown gained just 65 yards, but his running mate Ernie Green picked up some slack with 89 yards. For the second consecutive official game—the first being the 1964 title game—the Cleveland defense had almost completely shut down one of the league's best passers.

Meanwhile, in San Francisco, the Chicago Bears defense completely collapsed, suggesting that 1965 was going to be an even worse nightmare than 1964. "The last vestige of the defensive greatness that carried the Chicago Bears to a championship two years ago was shot away here today," wrote George Strickler of the *Chicago Tribune*, after George Halas's team had gone down to its worst opening day defeat ever, 55–24. 49er quarterback John Brodie, now hitting his peak in his ninth season, threw four touchdown passes, and his superb wide receivers Dave Parks and Bernie Casey scored three touchdowns between them. As if that were not enough, John David Crow, rookie Ken Willard, and fullback Gary Lewis rushed for 197 yards. The 49ers scored six consecutive times in the second and third periods, while Billy

Wade and Rudy Bukich, sharing the quarterback spot, were ineffective. The Bears tried a new formation to try to spring their rookie halfback Gale Sayers on some long runs, but he repeatedly slipped in the mud of Kezar Stadium. Although Sayers, Strickler wrote, "gave some evidence of one day becoming a star," he suffered in his debut from slips and fumbles. The Chicago press gave coaches George Halas and George Allen a very hard time after the game, asking whether rookie Dick Butkus had performed effectively (Halas said he had) and questioning other personnel decisions as well.

Back on the Great Lakes, the Detroit Lions did much better against the league's other California entry, humiliating the Los Angeles Rams 20–0. As they had so often in the past, Detroit's great defensive tackles Alex Karras and Roger Brown repeatedly reached the opposing quarterback, Bill Munson, and the Rams could go nowhere on the ground, either. The Rams gained just 119 yards and never penetrated beyond the 43-yard line of the Lions. The score was only 3–0 at the half, but Milt Plum threw 34- and 47-yard touchdown passes to flanker Terry Barr and halfback Joe Don Looney (one of the league's freest spirits), respectively, in the fourth quarter to put the game away. Coming off a winning season, the Lions re-inserted themselves as a possible winner in the Western Conference.

Back east, the real shock result of the week occurred in Philadelphia, when the supposedly mediocre Eagles edged the highly touted St. Louis Cardinals 34–27 in a seesaw thriller. Cardinal quarterback Charley Johnson passed for 383 yards, the third-best performance of his career, but the Eagles, using an unusual double-wing formation with a single setback, stuck with them in the first half, which finished 20–20, and had the last word in the fourth quarter on a 38-yard pass from Snead to wide receiver Ray Poage. The lone setback was star Eagle runner Tim Brown, who rushed for 50 yards and caught seven passes for 129 additional yards.

Meanwhile, the fall of the once-mighty New York Giants continued in Dallas, where the Cowboys annihilated the Giants revamped, youthful aggregation by a humiliating margin of 31–2. The Giant offense, led by new acquisition Earl Morrall, was completely inept in the first half, gaining 24 yards rushing but losing 27 passing, and gained only 150 yards without scoring in the second half. Two Dallas rookies, Olympian Bob Hayes at wide receiver and halfback Dan Reeves, made very impressive debuts, while the Giants lost two fumbles and threw two interceptions. New Yorkers must have wondered if the team would be able to match its 3–11 record of 1964. The Cowboys, meanwhile, found themselves tied with the Browns and the Eagles for first place in the Eastern Conference.

2. The First Month

Week 2

The St. Louis Cardinals, whose defense had let them down so badly in their opener against the Eagles, found themselves face to face with the champion Browns in Cleveland on September 26. The result met their fondest hopes—but left the Dallas Cowboys in first place in the Eastern Conference.

The game started promisingly enough for the 80,000-plus fans in Municipal Stadium. Although the Cardinals jumped off to a 7–0 lead on a 78-yard pass from Charley Johnson to back Willis Crenshaw, Lou Groza answered with a field goal, and Frank Ryan threw a 33-yard touchdown pass to Gary Collins, who outjumped the much shorter Pat Fisher in the end zone. Unfortunately, Ryan also incurred a severely bruised foot and had to leave the game after the first half. Rather than try to rely on his running game, Ryan threw interceptions on three consecutive series of downs, and the Cardinals followed each one up with a touchdown. Ryan's replacement, Jim Ninowski, was little better, throwing two interceptions of his own.

Meanwhile, Cardinal spotters noted that Browns cornerback Walter Beach was playing too tightly on split end Sonny Randle, and Johnson went straight to work on him. Randle finished the day with seven receptions good for 198 yards and three touchdowns, and Erich Barnes, recently acquired from the Giants, replaced Beach. Overall, Johnson completed only 11 passes, but they included six touchdowns, one shy of the league record shared by Sid Luckman, Adrian Burk, and Y.A. Tittle. Jim Brown rebounded from his slow start in Washington and gained 110 yards, but the Browns finished on the short end of a 49–13 score, with Ryan doubtful for the next week's game. They had now failed to beat the Cardinals in three consecutive games.

In Dallas, meanwhile, rookie Bob Hayes put himself squarely on the NFL map with three touchdowns as the Cowboys humiliated a hapless Washington Redskins team 27–7. Hayes opened the scoring by leaving veteran cornerback Johnny Sample in the dust on a 45-yard reception and scored his second touchdown on an end-around. Meanwhile, the Redskins offense outperformed the Cowboys' offense with 25 first downs to 16—although the Cowboys outgained them by a few yards—but threw the game away with four fumbles and numerous penalties, which allowed the Cowboys to prolong two drives. Charley Taylor missed the game with a re-injured ankle, and until the very last few minutes, the Cowboys successfully contained Bobby Mitchell by double-teaming him. The Cowboys found themselves in undisputed first place in the Eastern Conference, and as luck would have it, they were scheduled to face the Cardinals the following week.

The struggling New York Giants trailed the Eagles 7–0 in Philadelphia in the second quarter when quarterback Earl Morrall put together a 45-yard drive on the ground and pitched out to Joe Morrison, who went 11 yards for the score. "The Giants," screamed the CBS commentator, "score their first touchdown of the 1965 season!" His tone strongly suggested that he had wondered if they would ever manage that feat. The team had traded its long-time placekicker and punter, Don Chandler, to the Packers, and defensive end Andy Stynchula provided three field goals to edge out the Eagles 16–14.

In San Francisco, the 49ers won the week's interconference game against the Pittsburgh Steelers 27–17. John Brodie had another excellent day, completing 16 of 20 passes for 236 yards and a touchdown, and the 49ers rushed for 191 yards as well, led by rookie Ken Willard with 88 yards. Three fumbles held down the San Francisco score. Meanwhile, the other six Western Conference teams played three thrillers, each decided in the last minute of play. The Rams opened the scoring against the Bears with an interception runback for a touchdown, although Bruce Gossett missed the extra point. On their next possession, the Bears blocked a field goal attempt, and defensive back Rosey Taylor picked the ball up and ran it back 60 yards to go ahead 7–6. Just three plays later, the Bears' great defensive end Doug Atkins hit Ram quarterback Bill Munson hard enough to force a fumble, and rookie Dick Butkus picked it up and returned it 22 yards to the Bears' 18-yard line. Gale Sayers took the ball on a halfback option, faked a pass, and picked his way through several Rams on his way to the end zone to make the score 14–6, scoring his first NFL touchdown. In the third quarter, Munson's passes, including two to flanker Tommy McDonald, took the Rams to the Bears' four-yard line, but the defense stiffened, and the Rams had to be content with a field goal, making the score 14–9. Quarterback Rudy Bukich replaced Bill Wade on the next play from scrimmage and delivered an 80-yard pass to Johnny Morris. The Bears defense promptly forced a fumble, and on third down, a scrambling Bukich found rookie Jimmy Jones in the end zone, making the score 28–9.

The Rams, remarkably, had lost to the Bears 11 times in a row in the last six years, and George Halas's team initially seemed determined to make it 12 and reach the .500 mark. But Munson suddenly caught fire, repeatedly connecting with halfback Terry Baker, a Heisman Trophy winner as a quarterback at Oregon. Munson took the ball in himself after a pass interference

2. The First Month

call on Bennie McRae gave the Bears a first down on the one-yard line. The Chicago offense promptly failed to go anywhere, and Munson took the Rams in again from 42 yards out with two key passes to McDonald. Once again, Bukich failed to move the ball, and Munson finished off yet another drive with another touchdown pass to Baker in the 21-point fourth quarter, giving the Rams a 30–28 victory. Without a first-string quarterback, the Bears were outgained once again and fell two games back of the league leaders.

The Lions, who had decisively beaten the Rams a week earlier, traveled to Minnesota, where the Vikings sought to right themselves after losing to the Colts. Neither team moved the ball very well in the first half, but late in the second period, trailing 10–7, Detroit quarterback Milt Plum threw a 16-yard touchdown pass to Amos Marsh, a big, fast running back whom the Lions had recently acquired from Dallas. Then Alex Karras caught Tarkenton at the end of a scramble, forced a fumble, and his fellow tackle Roger Brown recovered it on the Viking one-yard line. Plum snuck it in for a 21–10 halftime lead.

Coach Norm Van Brocklin apparently did a good job rallying the Vikings at halftime. Tarkenton drove down the field for a score after the second-half kickoff, and a Fred Cox field goal closed the gap to 21–20 just a few minutes later. Then, with the Lions pinned to their own goal line, defensive end Carl Eller tackled Plum in the end zone for a safety and a one-point lead. Although Tarkenton had another poor day passing, completing just nine of 22 passes, he increased the lead to eight points with another score midway through the fourth quarter. Wayne Walker kicked a Detroit field goal to make it 29–24, but by the time the Lions got the ball back on their own 25, there were only 69 seconds on the clock. The Lions managed to hold off the Vikings rush, and Plum completed three passes to three different receivers to get the ball to the Lion 48-yard line. Then the Lion wide receivers spread out the Viking defense, and Amos Marsh beat two defenders to score the winning touchdown and give Detroit an amazing 31–29 victory, a 2–0 record, and a share of first place.

The Colts and the Packers, meanwhile, fought out the renewal of their rivalry in Green Bay. The Colts had won the 1964 conference title thanks to two razor-thin victories over Lombardi's men, 21–20 and 24–21, and this game fit right into the same pattern. The defenses dominated the first half, with Willie Davis and Henry Jordan repeatedly chasing Unitas around the pocket and Ordell Braase and Billy Ray Smith sacking Bart Starr, eventually knocking him out of the game in the third quarter. (The Colts finished the game with six sacks.) The harried Unitas tried to hit Jimmy Orr on a turn-out at the 50-yard line, but Herb Adderley, who had played Orr loosely, cut in front of him at top speed, got his hands on the ball and juggled it for at least five yards without slowing down, allowing him to beat the whole Colt team into the end zone for the first Packer touchdown. He also intercepted a second pass later in the half. The Pack played the entire game without Jim Taylor, who, like his Redskin cousin Charley, had a bruised ankle, and the Colts defense also put Paul Hornung out of the game in the third quarter. Unitas managed to direct a long drive made up almost entirely of running plays, and with each team kicking a field goal, the half finished at 10–10. The Colts had already surrendered the ball twice on fumbles and twice on Adderley's interceptions.

The third quarter was scoreless. Veteran Zeke Bratkowski had now replaced Starr at quarterback. Starting a drive on his own 26-yard line, Bratkowski moved to the Colts 34 with the help of a 27-yard pass to halfback Elijah Pitts, and Don Chandler kicked a go-ahead field goal. Colt Tony Lorick made an ill-advised attempt to return the ensuing kickoff and was dropped on the three-yard line. Unitas got the team out of the hole with a 27-yard pass to John Mackey, but the team soon had to punt. The Packers promptly fumbled, however, and four plays later, Unitas hit Raymond Berry on a corner pattern in the left of the end zone to lead 17–13 with 8:30 remaining in the game.

The defensive battle continued. On the next Colts possession, two holding penalties forced the Colts to punt from their own goal line, and the Pack took over on the 32-yard line. Forsaking a field goal that would have left them a point behind, the Packers lost the ball on downs with three minutes left. The game was in the Colts' hands, but Lenny Moore—who lost his 18-consecutive game touchdown streak—promptly fumbled, and Willie Wood recovered. Veteran receiver Max McGee had now replaced an injured Boyd Dowler—another casualty of the Colts' defense—and after consulting with Bratkowski, caught a zig-out pattern behind Lenny Lyles to put the Packers ahead 20–17 with 2:38 left.

No one moved the ball better in the last two minutes than Unitas. He passed to back Tony Lorick for six yards, to John Mackey for 20 yards, and to Berry again for 13 yards, reaching the Packer 37-yard line. His next pass, to Tom Matte on the 24-yard line, put the Colts close enough for a tying field goal, but Matte fumbled the ball, and Herb Adderley recovered with just seconds left. The Colts had outgained the Packers' 309 yards to 184 yards but had committed six turnovers to the Packers' three. For the first time in over a year and only the second time in three years, the Packers were tied for the lead in their conference. Lombardi paid tribute to the team's fortitude despite its worst offensive day in years, while Shula blamed

2. The First Month

the team's mistakes for the defeat, and Unitas blamed himself for Adderley's two interceptions. Only the television audience in parts of Wisconsin and around Baltimore had the opportunity to watch this amazing game. The 1965 season was well and truly launched.

Week 3

The NFL in 1965 was six years away from expansion, and both Minnesota and Dallas were establishing themselves as more than respectable teams. The league's weak sisters—the Steelers, Eagles, Giants, and Redskins—all played in the Eastern Conference and played 10 games in 14 weeks against each other. While even the best teams, such as the Browns and Cardinals, were subject to occasional blowouts, most games were close. On October 3–4, the seven league games were decided by an average margin of a shade over one touchdown, and the largest margin was only 18 points.

Playing away, the Browns started their game against the Eagles with Jim Ninowski at quarterback in place of the injured Frank Ryan, and Norm Snead joined Ryan on the sidelines in the first quarter with an injured knee. Ninowski called a far more conservative game than Ryan, completing only nine of 20 passes while Jim Brown and Ernie Green led a rushing attack good for 239 yards. The Eagles, playing behind quarterback King Hill—a teammate of Frank Ryan's at Rice University in the late 1950s—led 10–7 at halftime, but Ninowski managed a drive after the break that culminated in a typical Gary Collins touchdown to make it 14–10. The Eagles regained the lead with a long drive, 17–14, and forced the Browns to punt. But Tim Brown fumbled the ball, and the Browns recovered on the Eagle two-yard line. Jim Brown promptly scored. Two plays after the kickoff, Cleveland safety Ross Fichtner intercepted Hill's pass and ran it 32 yards for a touchdown. Then on the next series, Larry Benz intercepted, and Jim Brown scored again, finishing the scoring at 35–17—a far more comfortable-looking victory than the game had really been. Meanwhile, in Pittsburgh, new Giants quarterback Earl Morrall recovered his passing form, and a good defensive effort ran the Giants record to 2–1 with a 23–13 victory.

In Detroit, the Lions ran their record to 3–0 with a 14–10 victory over the Redskins in what was surely the most inept, ludicrous game of the whole season. "The Detroit Lions defeated the Redskins today," wrote the great *Washington Post* columnist Shirley Povich, "at some kind of a game that faintly resembled pro football." In a defensive battle, the Lions gained only 118 yards and the Redskins 196—while each team lost two fumbles and the Lions intercepted six passes to the Redskins' four. The Redskins scored their only touchdown on a 54-yard runback of a fumble recovery, while the Lions scored one of theirs on an interception and the other after recovering a fumble on the Redskins four-yard line. Dick Shiner replaced Sonny Jurgensen at quarterback after Jurgensen's fourth interception. Although two future Redskin stars, linebacker Chris Hanburger and tight end Jerry Smith, had found their way into the lineup, the team threw away late chances to win the game. The Lions most fortunately remained tied for the Western Conference lead with a 3–0 record while the Redskins, having lost to the Browns, Cowboys, and Lions, now faced the Cardinals twice as well as the Colts over the next three weeks. The next day, Redskin coach Bill McPeak announced that Dick Shiner would replace Jurgensen, who had completed just 28 of 62 passes, at quarterback in next Sunday's game with the St. Louis Cardinals.

In Baltimore, the Colts faced off against the undefeated 49ers in a wild duel between Johnny Unitas and John Brodie. Ahead 3–0 in the first quarter, Unitas found himself with a fourth down and inches at the 49er 45-yard line. Taking a leaf from the Green Bay playbook, he faked a run and hit Lenny Moore at the 49er seven-yard line. Moore scored a few plays later. Then cornerback Bobby Boyd picked off his second pass of the day and ran it 18 yards for a 17–0 lead. Brodie promptly retaliated with a 53-yard touchdown pass to big Dave Parks, who beat the smaller Lenny Lyles, but Unitas managed to run the score up to 24–7 at the half with a long drive that finished with a touchdown pass to Moore.

Parks, however, scored again on an option pass from John David Crowe in the third quarter from 45 yards out, making the score 24–14. The teams traded field goals early in the fourth quarter, and then Parks scored on another 45-yard pass from Brodie to close within three points, 27–24. That, however, ended the scoring. Brodie outgained Unitas in the air 268 yards to 236 but threw three interceptions to Unitas's one. Although the 49ers lost the game, their offense was emerging as one of the league's most dangerous thanks in large part to their new offensive coordinator—their one-time quarterback Y.A. Tittle, who had retired from the Giants as a player the preceding winter.

Ken Willard

> Jack Christiansen, our head coach, was a great guy, very low-key, your best friend. He would have been a great drinking buddy. He was a laissez-faire guy

2. The First Month

who let everybody do their job. Y.A. and John Brodie were our brain trust, and everything came together thanks to Y.A.

Out in Los Angeles, the Minnesota Vikings gave up more than 30 points for the third week in a row yet managed to escape with their first victory of the season against the Rams. The Rams roared out to a 14–0 lead behind a fine performance by Bill Munson, but the floodgates opened when Munson went to the locker room with an injured leg and Roman Gabriel took over. The Vikings promptly scored four touchdowns before halftime thanks to a 92-yard kickoff return, a blocked punt, a fumble recovery, and one long drive. The Rams pulled back to 28–21 in the third quarter when a Tarkenton pass was blocked, grabbed, and run back 59 yards by a substitute tackle. Tarkenton passed to Bill Brown for 31 yards on third and nine and then handed off to him for a touchdown to make it 35–21 in the third quarter. The Rams returned the ensuing kickoff 56 yards, and Munson returned to the field and threw a 28-yard touchdown pass to halfback Dick Bass. Munson directed a brilliant drive in the fourth quarter, completing nine passes in a row and finishing with a touchdown heave to rookie Jack Snow, who had a fine day as a receiver and blocker. But the Vikings had the last word and won 38–35 with a short field goal after Tarkenton drove them down the field. Tarkenton had his first really good day of the season, 17 for 25 for 249 yards and two touchdowns, scrambling and rolling out almost every time. Much of the Los Angeles front four missed the game with injuries, making life easier for the Vikings.

In Green Bay, the Chicago Bears unveiled their new star, Gale Sayers, but managed to do just about everything a team could do on a football field but win. George Halas started Sayers for the first time as Billy Wade remained the starting quarterback. Wade took the team practically to the Packer goal line on the Bears' first possession, then called a trap play to Gale Sayers, but Packer tackle Ron Kostelnik broke through the line and forced Wade to fumble as he tried to get Sayers the ball, ending the drive. An unnecessary roughness penalty promptly helped the Packers move to midfield, and Bart Starr, recovered from his injury against the Colts, took the team the rest of the way for a score. On the first play after the kickoff, Packer linebacker Leroy Caffey intercepted Wade's pass and ran it in for a second touchdown. The Bears made a couple of first downs, and a great punt put the Packers in a hole on their own two, but Starr got them out of it with a 41-yard pass down the middle to fullback Jim Taylor. Shortly thereafter, a pass interference penalty kept the Packer drive alive, and Starr finished the drive with a 48-yard touchdown pass to substitute wide receiver

Bob Long. Don Chandler's extra point missed, but the Bears had, in effect, spotted the Packers a 20–0 halftime lead.

Rudy Bukich took over as the Bears' quarterback, as it turned out, for good. His first drive miscarried when a touchdown pass was called back for a penalty, and the Bears surrendered the ball on a fourth down near the goal line rather than try for three points. The Packers managed to keep their momentum going when a 61-yard pass play from Starr to Hornung set up a field goal and a 23–0 lead. Starr extended his record for most passes without a single interception, running it to 277. Then, however, the Bears turned their season around. The Bear defense—like the Colts defense a week earlier—had stopped the famous Packer running game cold, holding them to just 78 yards. Gale Sayers and Andy Livingston accounted for 67 yards of an 80-yard drive to get the Bears on the board. Sayers began showing the league what he was made of on the last two plays of the drive. On the first, a sweep to the left, he simply ran right between his two leading blockers without giving them a chance to throw a block and was stopped only on the six-yard line after a 10-yard gain. On the second, going from left to right, he appeared to run directly at two all-time greats, linebacker Dave Robinson and cornerback Herb Adderley, only to step around them both and reach the end zone untouched. The Bears came up empty and surrendered the ball on downs after another long drive. Later in the half, Sayers once again devastated the Packers on both sides of the field, this time on pass receptions from Bukich. Sayers caught the second pass in full stride near the left sideline and simply outran the entire Packer secondary to make the final score 23–14. The Bears had outgained the Packers' 413 yards to 299, and their defense had sacked Starr five times, but turnovers and penalties cost them the game. "I think the fans will see an improved Bear team next Sunday," said George Halas, who had called the team's plays from the bench in the second half. "The kind of team we have been promising them." Unfortunately, they had already lost three games.

On Monday, October 5, the NFL staged a Monday night football game for the second year in a row when the St. Louis Cardinals hosted the undefeated Dallas Cowboys. Pete Rozelle was already scheming to get the NFL on primetime television, but this contest, like the one a year earlier between the Packers and Lions, was not televised nationally. The Cardinals dominated the game, moving the ball very easily in the air in the first half and on the ground in the second, but won only 20–13 thanks mainly to one play. Twenty seconds before the end of the first half, leading 14–0 on the Dallas 10-yard line, Charley Johnson threw an interception to Dallas safety Mel

2. The First Month

Renfro, one of the fastest men in the league, and Renfro ran it back 90 yards for a touchdown. Chastened by this play and another interception in the second half, Johnson kept the ball on the ground, and neither team could manage a touchdown after the break. Don Meredith completed only nine of 25 passes and threw two interceptions, and rookie Bob Hayes caught just two passes for 21 yards. Three weeks into the season, the Cardinals, Cowboys, Browns, and, remarkably, the Giants found themselves tied for the Eastern Conference lead with 2–1 records. Those old rivals, the Packers and the Lions, were tied for the Western Conference lead with 3–0 records, with the Colts one game behind.

Week Four

Week four began on Saturday evening, October 3, when the Browns entertained the lowly Steelers before 80,187 fans in Cleveland. With Frank Ryan still limping, the Browns gave Jimmy Brown the ball 29 times, and he responded with 168 yards, averaging more than five yards a carry. Ernie Green was injured, but second-year man Leroy Kelly replaced him, rushing for 67 yards and catching passes for 60 more. Kelly's patience as a backup paid off years later when he turned out to be one of the leading rushers in the NFL. Still, the Browns found themselves behind 19–17 with three minutes left after a 67-yard punt return by Steeler rookie Roy Jefferson had set up a Pittsburgh touchdown. Ryan managed to move the ball down the field and reached the Steeler 14-yard line with 44 seconds left. A field goal would have won the game, but Ryan completed his favorite pass, the post pattern, to Gary Collins for the winning touchdown, and the fans breathed a sigh of relief.

In Washington, an angry Redskin crowd brought banners demanding the replacement of coach Bill McPeak and booed the team off the field as the Cardinals crushed the Redskins 37–16. Flanker Bobby Joe Conrad beat cornerback Johnny Sample for a 36-yard touchdown in the first quarter, and the Cardinals led 10–7 at the half. They ran the score out to 13–7 in the third quarter and were driving for another score when Charley Johnson called a down-and-in to Conrad in the end zone. CBS's isolated camera watched Sample and Conrad on the play, and Sample—who later entitled his autobiography *Confessions of a Dirty Football Player*—slugged Conrad three times as he ran his pattern, then stepped in front of him and intercepted the pass, downing the ball for a touchback.

NFL 1965

Charley Johnson

That was Johnny Sample. He was dangerous.

On the next play, Dick Shiner faded back and threw the ball about 50 yards down the right sideline. Bobby Mitchell, who had dropped a bomb in the clear in the first half, caught the ball at top speed behind Pat Fisher and took it the whole 80 yards for a touchdown. But the Cardinals took advantage of sacks and fumbles to run up a 37-10 lead before the Redskins scored a consolation touchdown. Charley Taylor was still playing hurt, and Shiner gained most of the Redskins 65 yards worth of rushing yardage. So far, the Redskins had the most inept offense in the league.

In Dallas, Tom Landry also benched his starting quarterback, Don Meredith, and shuttled two rookies, Craig Morton and Jerry Rhome, in and out on alternate plays against the Eagles, whom he had expected to beat comfortably. Landry had tried the two-quarterback strategy early in the Cowboys' history with Meredith and Eddie LeBaron, and Rhome and Morton went a combined 15-25 for 234 yards and no interceptions. Bob Hayes had his most remarkable day yet, scoring on a 49-yard pass from Morton and an 82-yard pass from Rhome, but the Cowboy running game was inept. Eagle quarterback King Hill, still filling in for the injured Norm Snead, did even better than his Dallas counterparts, and 14 fourth-quarter points gave the Eagles a 35-17 lead and an eventual 35-24 victory.

The New York Giants had scheduled their first four games away, including this week's match with the Vikings, on the assumption that the Yankees, as usual, would be using Yankee Stadium through early October. Instead, the Minnesota Twins found themselves in the midst of a close World Series with the Los Angeles Dodgers, and the Vikings played their game with the Giants on Saturday night so as not to conflict with the afternoon baseball game. Meanwhile, a long newspaper strike finally came to an end in New York—not in time to report the result on Sunday, but early enough for postmortems on Monday. The Vikings controlled the game on the ground, rushing for 173 yards and three touchdowns to the Giants' 61 rushing yards, and ran up a 17-7 halftime lead. Then a Minnesota score and two fumbles in four plays by the Giants led to three quick Viking touchdowns, and Minnesota finished with a 40-14 victory, running their record to 2-2 and lifting hopes that the team might justify its preseason hype. The Western Conference was now 4-0 against the Eastern Conference.

In Baltimore, Johnny Unitas showed for the first time all year that he was still the most devastating quarterback in the NFL. Although the Lions

2. The First Month

sacked Unitas four times, he picked apart the Lions' secondary by focusing on its weak spots. While his favorite target, Raymond Berry, did not catch a single pass against left cornerback Dick LeBeau, Lions' right cornerback Bobby Thompson was simply no match for fleet Jimmy Orr, who caught nine passes for 167 yards and two touchdowns. The Lions could not move the ball against the Colt defense at all, and Unitas ran the score up to 28–0 before halftime after John Mackey pulled in a pass that linebacker Wayne Walker had tipped and carried it in from 35 yards out. The final score was 31–7 after a quiet second half, and the Lions dropped into a tie for second place with the Colts with a 3–1 record and returned home to regroup.

On the shores of Lake Michigan, the Packers hosted the 49ers while the Bears played the first rematch of the young season against the Rams. Like the Colts in Baltimore, the Packers made everything work for the first time all year. After the 49ers missed a short field goal, Starr directed a 67-yard drive that finished with a touchdown pass to Bob Long, alternating with Carroll Dale. The drive had appeared to be stalled with fourth and four on the Packer 45-yard line, but Don Chandler decided to fake a punt and ran for the first down. John Brodie, passing to his great wide receivers, Dave Parks and Bernie Casey, managed to tie the score, but that was his last hurrah. The Packers lost a chance to extend the lead when Starr finally threw his first interception in over a year on the goal line to Jim Johnson, but two field goals gave the Pack a 13–7 lead at the half. Fine running by Jim Taylor and Paul Hornung, who had their first impressive day of the year together, ran the lead to 27–7. The 49ers threatened twice, but a fine goal-line stand by the Packers and an interception by Willie Wood stopped them. Chandler enlivened the proceedings once again late in the game when he let fly a punt from three yards inside his own end zone that landed on the 49er 25-yard line and bounced into the end zone—a 90-yard punt, the longest in league history. A restrained Vince Lombardi allowed that the Packers had played their best game of the year. While unspectacular on offense, they had combined passing, running, and tough defense to win a solid victory against a coming team.

After three road losses in a row, the Chicago Bears finally showed what they could do in their home opener against the Rams. George Halas had finished retooling his elderly 1963 championship team, and the entire backfield, half the defensive line, and one of the linebackers were new. Sayers knew all week that he would start this game, with the result that the young man threw up in the locker room before the game, something that became a ritual for him for several years.[1] The Bear lines dominated the Rams on both sides of the ball—as well as in the secondary, a weakness since

1963—and the team suddenly recovered its championship form, intercepting two passes and forcing and recovering two fumbles. The Bears led 10–3 at the half and outscored the Rams 21–3 in the second half. Rudy Bukich had a day that Starr or Unitas might have been proud of, 16 for 22, good for two touchdowns.

Young Gale Sayers once again provided the biggest highlights. In the third quarter, he took a screen pass from Bukich on the left sideline, a perfect call against a Ram blitz. Sayers cut back into the middle of the field, broke two tackles, and outran the whole secondary. Tight end Mike Ditka wiped out the last defender with a great block, but Sayers was clearly going to outrun him for the 80-yard touchdown anyway. Ditka, who had missed the whole preseason with a foot injury, caught five passes. After the secondary forced the last turnover in the third quarter, Bukich pitched out to Sayers going to his left from the Bear 26-yard line. The young back slowed, cocked the ball in his left hand, and passed somewhat tentatively to Dick Gordon, who had to slow down to catch the ball but still carried it in for the Bears' last touchdown and a 31–6 victory. Meanwhile, the tough Bear pass rush, always a threat to quarterbacks, put Bill Munson out of the game, and Roman Gabriel replaced him. "It was a great victory," said Bukich, "but I wasn't completely satisfied. I think we can do even better."

Livingston had led the team with 47 yards rushing on nine carries and caught three passes for 64 more yards against the Rams. At 230 pounds, he was about the size of Jim Brown, and *Chicago Tribune* reporter Cooper Hollow speculated that he might be the next Jim Brown in a feature later that week. "Ever watch the way [Brown] carries the ball, I mean really watch?" Livingston asked Hollow in his hotel room. "He goes into the line in a semi-crouch and not at full speed. He hits the hole at three-quarter speed so he can adjust if the hole isn't there." He amazed Hollow with his football insights. "It helps when you get to know the moves of the other running back in the backfield," Livingston said. "I'm learning how fast Gale Sayers hits off-tackle when I'm blocking. It's important because I have to get the linebacker out of the way before Gale climbs up my back." Sayers never used three-quarter speed in holes. Livingston thanked older Bears for the help they had given him, especially Billy Wade and fellow running back Jon Arnett. He wanted, Cooper reported, to be the best ball carrier of all time.[2]

A month into the season, individual standouts were emerging around the league. With Frank Ryan fighting an injury, the Browns had given Jim Brown the ball 94 times, and his 476 rushing yards were more than twice as many as his nearest rivals, Tommy Mason of the Vikings (228) and Timmy

2. The First Month

Brown of the Eagles (217). Brown also led all pass catchers with 23 receptions, followed by Ram veteran Tommy McDonald with 22, Johnny Morris of the Bears and Dave Parks of the 49ers with 19 each, and Bobby Mitchell of the Redskins and the Cardinals' Sonny Randle with 18. Gary Collins had caught only 15 passes, but his four touchdowns tied him with Parks and Bob Hayes for the lead. Rudy Bukich was rated as the NFL's top passer over Starr, Charley Johnson, John Brodie, and Unitas largely because he had not thrown a single interception, but Johnson and Brodie led in touchdown passes with 11 and eight, respectively.

The Packers were now the only undefeated team in the league but still led the Colts and the Lions—their next opponent—by just one game. The red-hot Cardinals, who owned by far the league's best point differential, looked a better club than the Browns, with whom they were tied at 3–1. The following week, the Packers had to play their old rivals, the Lions, while the Bears and the Vikings would try to get into the title race in Minnesota. In the Eastern Conference, Dallas had a chance to move into a tie with the Browns. So far, the league's stars had suffered no crippling injuries, while rookies like Tucker Frederickson in New York, Roy Jefferson in Pittsburgh, and Butkus and Sayers in Chicago were making an impact. The year was well and truly launched.

Standings

Eastern Conference	W	L	T	Pct	Pf	Pa
St. Louis	3	L	0	.750	133	76
Cleveland	3	1	0	.750	89	92
Dallas	2	2	0	.500	95	64
Philadelphia	2	2	0	.500	100	102
New York	2	2	0	.500	55	98
Washington	0	4	0	.000	40	95
Pittsburgh	0	4	0	.000	58	115

Western Conference	W	L	T	Pct	Pf	Pa
Green Bay	4	0	0	1.000	111	50
Baltimore	3	1	0	.750	110	87
Detroit	3	1	0	.750	72	70
San Francisco	2	2	0	.500	113	95
Minnesota	2	2	0	.500	123	115
Chicago	1	3	0	.250	97	111
Los Angeles	1	3	0	.250	71	117

3

Sheep and Goats

In Cleveland, on October 17, the Browns prevailed over their young rivals, the Cowboys, 23–17. Touchdowns by Jim Brown and Walter Roberts and a field goal got them off to a 17–0 first-half lead, but they managed just two more field goals in the second half. Tom Landry still could not settle on a quarterback, and rookies Jerry Rhome and Craig Morton split the first quarter before giving way to the veteran Don Meredith in the second. Meredith got the score to 17–10 at halftime. The Browns moved the ball well in the second half but had a touchdown called back for clipping, and Meredith managed to get Dallas one touchdown on a pass to Pete Gent. Asked to compare the Browns and Cardinals, Landry replied judiciously, "The Cardinals rely on overall team execution," he said. "The Browns rely on Jimmy Brown." St. Louis seemed to prove Landry right in Pittsburgh, where a new Steeler defensive setup stopped their running game cold, limiting it to 69 yards, compared to nearly 400 total in the previous two weeks. Charley Johnson responded with 18 completions in 30 attempts for 287 yards and two touchdowns, while a ferocious St. Louis pass rush held the Steelers to negative passing yardage. Unfortunately for the Cardinals, they lost Johnson and defensive backs Pat Fisher and Jim Burson, who ran into each other, to injuries. Steeler coach, Bill McPeak, pronounced the Cardinals the best team he had encountered, including the Packers, who had trounced the Steelers on opening day. Earlier in the week, Tex Maule of *Sports Illustrated* had picked the Cardinals to win the Eastern Conference.

The New York Giants finally returned to Yankee Stadium for a wild game that illustrated the random elements of NFL football in the mid-1960s. King Hill, continuing at quarterback for the Philadelphia Eagles in place of the injured Norm Snead, completed 23 passes for 311 yards but also threw four interceptions. The Giants' Earl Morrall, on the other hand, completed only 10 passes, but they included four touchdowns, three of them long bombs. The longest, 80 yards, went to fleet-footed second-year man Homer Jones, who replaced the injured veteran Del Shofner, long Y.A. Tittle's favorite target. The packed Yankee Stadium crowd went home very

3. Sheep and Goats

happy with the 35–27 win. The Giants had already matched their three wins in 1964, and a victory over the Browns in the following week could put them in a tie for first place.

In Los Angeles, the 49ers firmly established themselves as the rulers of the West Coast and sent the 1–4 Rams deep into the conference cellar, blitzing the home team with a 28–7 first half and running the final score up to 45–21. The Coliseum was more than half-empty, and with a tough Ram schedule ahead—including both the Cardinals and the Browns from the Eastern Conference—their season looked as catastrophic as the Redskins'. John Brodie had his most efficient passing day yet, with 18 of 26 passes completed and three touchdowns, and the unheralded 49er pass rush was far more effective than Los Angeles's famed Fearsome Foursome. Had the 49ers not lost three fumbles, the rout might have been much worse. Harland Svare of the Rams now ranked with Bill McPeak of the Redskins as the coach "Least Likely to Return," but as it turned out, the Rams had too many fine players to do so badly for the whole year.

The Bears, 1–3, traveled to Minnesota to face the 2–2 Vikings, who were fighting to remain within two games of the lead. The wild game firmly established Gale Sayers as the most exciting player to reach the NFL since Jim Brown.

The Bears opened the game with the veteran Ronnie Bull in the backfield next to Sayers, in place of Andy Livingston. The Bears scored their first touchdown from 33 yards out when Bukich faked a pitch to Sayers to the left, pivoted, and handed the ball to Bull, going up the middle. The whole Viking defense was already heading to its right after Sayers and Bull streaked straight into the end zone. The Vikings proceeded to fumble the ensuing kickoff, and Bukich immediately passed to Johnny Morris for a touchdown and a 14–0 lead. Tarkenton's scrambling and Bill Brown's running allowed the Vikings to climb back into the game, cutting the lead to 17–13 at the half and 17–16 early in the third quarter. Then came the most extraordinary sequence of the season so far—six consecutive touchdowns without a single punt.

First, Bill Brown took a simple hand-off off tackle, bounced off a couple of tacklers, and ran 43 yards for a touchdown to give Minnesota a 23–17 lead. Then Bukich scrambled and passed the ball to the 18-yard line, hit Sayers on a comeback pass around the six-yard line, and watched the Kansas rookie go through two tackles to score. Sayers was having little trouble getting open because the Vikings were double-teaming the Bears' tight end, Mike Ditka. Watching the game films 50 years later, it is still hard to see why the slim Sayers was so extraordinarily hard to bring down. Early in the fourth quarter, Tarkenton, who frequently took off on scrambles well before he was directly threatened by linemen, ran the ball much of the way to the end zone and scored on a rollout to regain the lead 30–24. Sayers was also receiving punts and kickoffs, and he took the next kickoff at the 15-yard line and ran smoothly to the Viking 49. After two fine runs by Ronnie Bull, Bukich found Sayers in the end zone again, and the Bears took the lead 31–30. But with two and a half minutes left, a terrible pass interference call against the Bears on their own four-yard line allowed the Vikings to score again and make it 37–31.

The Viking defense didn't even get back on the field. Sayers took this kickoff on the four-yard line, swept up the field through a big hole, made one spectacular cut to his left at top speed, and pulled away from the entire Viking kickoff team, scoring his third touchdown without a hand being laid on him. The thoughtful Sayers even slowed, turned, and called to his teammates not to throw any more blocks at around the Viking 20-yard line because he feared a clipping penalty. Tarkenton started the ball back up the field, but when he faded back and the Bears put on a big rush, he passed hurriedly rather than scrambling. The throw was short, and Dick Butkus grabbed it and stumbled to the Viking nine-yard line. A fine trap play opened a big hole for Sayers, and he scored his fourth touchdown, good for a 45–37 lead that sewed the wild game up.

Sayers finished with 297 yards total offense but did not receive the game ball because he had already gotten it the previous week against the Rams, and 70-year-old coach George Halas had a rule against any one player getting more than one per season. That rule would be sorely tested as the fall went on. In the dressing room, Halas said that as a back, Sayers could be compared to Red Grange and Ken McAfee, two players from earlier eras, and that he might be better than both. He also pronounced Butkus "a great linebacker for a rookie." Asked if anyone could stop Green Bay, Halas replied that the Packers "still have to play a lot of good teams" and said the Vikings could beat them if they played as they had today. The Bears suddenly had the most spectacular player and the most spectacular offense in the league, but they were only 2–3, three games off the lead with nine to go.

Sadly, the previous week's Packers game also marked the high point of Andy Livingston's season. After racking up 107 yards total offense (rushing and receiving) against the Packers in the Bears' first game against them and 111 yards against the Rams, he had just 40 yards rushing and none receiving this week. And in the second half of the season, he played only occasionally, for the simple reason that George Halas refused to start him at fullback

3. Sheep and Goats

and Sayers at halfback at the same time. There was no informal league rule against playing two black running backs at once, as there was against black quarterbacks. Both the Browns, with Jim Brown and Ernie Green, and the Cardinals, with Willis Crenshaw and Bill Triplett, were doing just that. But one black star was all Halas wanted in his backfield, and the second position was generally filled by veterans Jon Arnett or Ronnie Bull.

Andy Livingston

The sportswriters used to ask Halas, "Why don't you play Sayers and Livingston together?" What he said was, "If we did, Sayers would carry the ball 90 percent of the time, which would be bad for Andy. We'd rather play him with another back and get it 80 percent of the time." But that turned out to be 80 percent of about 20 percent because Gale was in 80 percent of the time.

Livingston finished 1965 with 363 yards rushing in just 63 attempts, a 5.8 yards per carry average—slightly higher than Sayers's 5.2 yards per carry average. In 1966, Livingston tore knee ligaments in an exhibition game against the Packers and missed the whole season, and he never became a regular for the Bears. He quit Chicago in disgust after just seven carries in four games in 1968 and declined to return when Sayers was lost for the season late in the year. In 1969, when he was still only 25, he rushed for 671 yards for the newly minted New Orleans Saints, averaging 4.2 yards per carry. Another injury in 1970 ended his career.

In Detroit, the Lions aimed to prove that they belonged at the top of the Western Conference by beating the Packers and regaining a share of the top spot. Their great defense and their dangerous pass receivers had always posed problems for the Packers, and they had beaten the Lions once each year during Green Bay's title years of 1960, 1961, and 1962. Their most dramatic victory had occurred on Thanksgiving Day 1962, in Detroit, when their front four, led by Alex Karras and Roger Brown, had repeatedly sacked Bart Starr on the way to a 26–14 victory that was not nearly as close as the score indicated. With the Packers missing middle linebacker Ray Nitschke and all-pro tackle Forrest Gregg from injuries, this game opened up almost the same way.

After Don Chandler opened the scoring with a 48-yard field goal, the Lions moved the ball down the field through the air and scored on a 15-yard pass from Milt Plum to tight end Ron Kramer, who had played out his option and left the Packers in the off-season. Then Roger Brown got his hands on a Starr pass, and rookie Lion defender Wayne Rasmussen intercepted it and ran it back 36 yards for a touchdown. Only five minutes later, the Lions had the ball back again, and Plum hit flanker Terry Barr for 55 yards and a third touchdown. So far, Alex Karras, the quick, eccentric, verbal Lions tackle, was having the time of his life. "What do you think of that, you big fat Jap?" he yelled to Lombardi as the teams left the field at the half.[1]

Bill Curry

I thought the gods would strike Karras dead.

Dick LeBeau

(Chuckles) That isn't exactly what Karras said. We did have a nickname for Vince. Yes, "Jap" was part of it, but I don't see any reason to give you all of it now.

Dave Robinson

Wayne Walker and the Lions also called Vince "the Jap." When we went into the locker room at halftime, Lombardi didn't say anything, didn't holler and scream. "You guys are playing so poorly," he said. "Everybody has a bad day. We may not win, but we can play with pride. You are my team—go out and play like the Green Bay Packers." [Defensive coach] Phil Bengtson also talked to us. "I never saw the coach so despondent," he said. "He never thought he would see something so bad." He got us fired up by not saying anything.

The Packers were having a terrible day on the ground—they wound up with just 83 yards rushing—and Lombardi changed personnel and strategy. Jerry Kramer had established himself as one of the best guards in the NFL by 1962 at the latest, but he had missed all of 1964 with a near-fatal injury and illness. Kramer, who eventually immortalized his Packer experiences in two books, the bestselling *Instant Replay* about the 1967 season and the sequel, *Farewell to Football*, was a remarkably accident-prone young man who had survived brushes with death going back to childhood. In one of them, a piece of wood had struck him in the abdomen, leaving several splinters in his intestines and around his liver. During 1964, they caused a series of nearly fatal infections and required him to have a colostomy. Eventually, in early 1965, his doctor realized some foreign body was lurking in his abdomen, operated again, and found the splinters. Kramer managed to

3. Sheep and Goats

return to training camp, but it took months to regain his strength, and he had not played very much in the first few games of the season. Dan Grimm, who had replaced Kramer in 1964 when he was ill, was having a very difficult time with Karras in this game, and Lombardi sent Kramer back in for the second half. He also told Starr to do more passing against the depleted Lions secondary.

The Packers were continually alternating wide receivers, using Dale, Dowler, and Bob Long, and the Lions were missing Bobby Thompson, their regular left cornerback. Two passes from Starr to Long gave the Packers a quick touchdown on their first possession in the third quarter when Long took a pass in full stride, slanting from right to left, and a Carroll Dale block took out the last Lion defender. The defense promptly forced a Lion punt, and Starr successively hit Dale, Paul Hornung, and Tom Moore, who scampered 31 yards, cutting across the middle of the field for the touchdown that made the score 21–17. After another quick Lion punt, three running plays gave the Packers a third and two on their own 23-yard line. With the whole Lion defense bunched at the line of scrimmage, Starr made his favorite move. He faked to Taylor and threw a quick pass to Carroll Dale cutting over the middle, who caught the ball behind the whole Detroit defense and went 77 yards into the end zone to take the lead. Starr ran for another touchdown in the fourth quarter while the Packers intercepted two passes to stop Lion drives. The frustrated Detroit fans booed so long and loudly that they brought the game to a halt for several minutes. In the dressing room, Lombardi said he had appealed to the Packers' pride, and Starr said the third quarter was the best of his career. "Green Bay will always have a good team as long as Vince remains coaching there," ex–Packer Ron Kramer said after the game. Despite the lack of a running game, the team was on top and looking better and better.

The weekly interconference games in the NFL included two traditional matchups played every year. One, between the Bears and the Cardinals, which dated from the days when the Cardinals had also played in Chicago, was booked for later in the year, while the other matched the Colts and the nearby Redskins, who could hardly have faced the 3–1 Colts at a worse time. Coach Bill McPeak of the Redskins announced that Sonny Jurgensen would be back at quarterback in D.C. Stadium against the Colts because his experience made it easier for him to cope with their complex defense. It didn't help. The Redskins ran 66 plays compared to 54 for the Colts but emerged with just one touchdown. Jurgensen completed 21 of 40 passes, but his receivers dropped several, and Bobby Mitchell had two touchdown catches called back due to penalties. Meanwhile, Unitas had a superb day, completing 12 of 18 passes for 221 yards, including two passes to tight end John Mackey for 92 yards. Unitas also made a remarkable play after completing a pass to reserve end Butch Wilson, sprinting into the secondary after the catch and taking out Sam Huff, of all people, with a cross-body block.

Upton Bell

> The players said the difference between Unitas and every quarterback is that Unitas is a football player first and a quarterback second. That's why they would do anything for him.

Backup Gary Cuozzo replaced Unitas in the fourth quarter. Jurgensen, remarkably, scored the only Redskin touchdown on a 24-yard run, and the Colts won 38–7. Washington was now a seemingly hopeless 0–5, tied with the Steelers, while the Colts, at 4–1, passed the Lions for second place in the Western Conference, which still had yet to lose a game against the Eastern Conference.

Week 6

In a battle of also-rans, the Pittsburgh Steelers managed their first victory at the expense of the Eagles, 20–14, dropping the Eagles to 2–4. With Norm Snead still injured and King Hill coming off a four-interception game, the Eagles alternated him with young Jack Concannon at quarterback, but they combined for four more interceptions. The Steeler offense scored only seven of the team's 20 points and gained only 232 yards to the Eagles' 388 yards. Meanwhile, in New York, the surprising Giants got a rude awakening from the Browns.

"I have a lot of friends here," Jim Brown, who had grown up on Long Island, said after the game. "They come to see me play, and I don't want to disappoint them." In their glory years from 1958 through 1963, the Giants had consistently been very tough opponents for Brown, but those days were over. Brown carried the ball 24 times for 177 yards, caught three passes for 17 more, and threw a 39-yard touchdown pass to Gary Collins on a halfback option play. Frank Ryan, meanwhile, had his most accurate day of the year, completing 10 of 15 passes, including two first-half touchdowns to Flea Roberts, who was proving a more than adequate

3. Sheep and Goats

replacement for Paul Warfield. The Giants gained a very respectable 312 yards but turned the ball over three times to the Browns' one, while Cleveland piled up 526 total yards. The score was 31–7 after three quarters, and second-string lineups traded touchdowns in the fourth quarter. The Browns looked more like the team that had won the 1964 title than they had all year, while the Giants showed that they were not yet ready to face the first tier of NFL competition.

Having destroyed the winless Redskins two weeks earlier in Washington, the Cardinals undoubtedly expected to keep pace with ease in a rematch. But they had to play without Charley Johnson, who had been seriously injured in the previous week, and they played against a fired-up Redskin team. Unfortunately, the injury was going to put an end to the Cardinals' title hopes.

Charley Johnson

> I got hurt in Pittsburgh. I separated my shoulder. I tried to play with that because I didn't want to miss games. It wasn't the coaches' fault—they were depending on my judgment.

On the previous Tuesday, October 20, Redskins' president, Edward Bennett Williams—the famed trial lawyer and power in the Democratic Party—had met with the team for two hours before their regular practice began. No one would talk about the unprecedented meeting, but the team's morale evidently improved. The game featured excellent performances by the men who continued to define the Redskins for the next decade or so: Jurgensen, who completed 12 of 14 passes with no interceptions; rookie linebacker Chris Hanburger, who blitzed effectively; flanker Bobby Mitchell, who evened the score at 10–10 in the second quarter with a 53-yard touchdown catch; halfback Charley Taylor, who at last began to recover his 1964 NFL Rookie of the Year form; and rookie tight end Jerry Smith. Although Cardinal reserve quarterback Buddy Humphrey performed well, with 17 completions in 28 attempts, the Redskins defense made a number of big plays to keep one of the league's top offenses in check. Two passes to halfback Taylor for 43 and 14 yards gave the team a 17–10 lead in the third quarter. St. Louis pulled back to 17–13 in the fourth quarter, but a pass interference call on a pass to Bobby Mitchell put the ball on the Cardinal one-yard line. Young Jerry Smith came off the bench with a play and caught Jurgensen's pass deep in the end zone. Then Johnny Sample, the controversial cornerback, saved the game with two interceptions off of Humphrey, and the Redskins had their first victory while the Cardinals fell two games behind the Browns with their third defeat.

As if that were not enough, on the next day, Monday, the Cardinals fell victim to the *Sports Illustrated* jinx when the cover featured them, and a story by Edwin Shrake touted them as the probable Eastern Conference champions, if not the victors in the NFL title game. Team coach Wally Lemm, Shrake explained, was a free spirit who held relatively short practices. The offensive line, led by right tackle Ernie McMillan and right guard Ken Gray, was rated the best in the Eastern Conference, if not in the whole league, given the injuries that were troubling Green Bay.[2]

In 1960, in their first year of operation, Tom Landry had entertained the Green Bay Packers in Dallas. The game had a special meaning for Landry and Vince Lombardi, who had broken in as professional coaches with the Giants in 1955 and worked together for four years. Not surprisingly, the Packers had annihilated the Cowboys 41–7. In 1964, the Cowboys had traveled to Green Bay and done only marginally better, losing 45–21. Their third meeting in Milwaukee turned out to be the toughest defensive battle of the season. The two teams punted 15 times in the first half, in which the Cowboys penetrated once to the Green Bay 34-yard line before a penalty stalled them, and the Packers got close enough for Don Chandler to kick a 44-yard field goal. The Cowboys took the second-half kickoff and put together a 66-yard drive featuring a 43-yard run by fullback Don Perkins and came away with a tying field goal.

Late in the third quarter came the sequence that decided the game. First, Cowboy Mel Renfro fumbled a long punt, and although the Packers once again failed to move the ball, Chandler kicked another field goal from 22 yards out. Then, Willie Davis sacked Craig Morton, again replacing Meredith, on the Green Bay 10-yard line, and Don Perkins fumbled the ball away on the next play. Jim Taylor promptly scored from seven yards out to make it 13–3, the final score. The Cowboys had five sacks of Bart Starr, and the Packers sacked Morton nine times. Both had dreadful days, and the two teams both wound up with negative passing yardage, the first time in NFL history that had occurred. Dallas actually outgained Green Bay 192–63, but they turned the ball over five times to the Packers' none. Their passing game suffered from the absence of rookie sensation Bob Hayes, who had hurt his ankle against the Browns. A crusty and defensive Vince Lombardi insisted that a win was a win and praised the defense and special teams, undoubtedly saving his actual opinion of the pathetic Green Bay offensive performance—surely one of the worst of his career—for the Tuesday movies. Landry credited his defense with its best performance ever and seemed

3. Sheep and Goats

to agree with Steeler coach Mike Nixon that the Cardinals and the Browns might be superior, overall, to the Pack. But Green Bay remained the only undefeated team in the league at 6–0. The next time the two teams met—more than a year later—they scored 61 points.

Having averaged 32 points scored and 32 points allowed in their first five games, the astonishing Minnesota Vikings outdid themselves in San Francisco, beating those averages by about a touchdown. The game was two different contests. The 49ers, with Brodie reaching new heights against the wretched Viking pass defense, raced to a 21–0 lead early in the second period thanks to two touchdown passes to Bernie Casey and a run by rookie Ken Willard. The Vikings answered with one touchdown thanks to running backs Brown and Mason, but when they next got the ball, the 49er defense forced them back to their own seven-yard line, where Mason fumbled, and San Francisco converted. Tarkenton, whose favorite target, Paul Flatley, finally had a good game, managed to make it 28–14 late in the first half, but Brodie orchestrated another brilliant drive with just two minutes left and finished it up with Casey's third touchdown catch and a seemingly safe 35–14 lead. But Van Brocklin managed to rally the Vikings for the second half.

A 72-yard drive and a pass to Hal Bledsoe from Tarkenton made the score 35–21. San Francisco answered with a Tommy Davis field goal, but a pass interference call led to a 21-yard touchdown run by Tommy Mason, making it 38–28. And two passes from Tarkenton to Flatley got Minnesota within three points just as the third period ended in a game many must have thought belonged in the American Football League.

Incredibly, Minnesota took the lead just 2:24 into the fourth quarter when Flatley wrestled a pass away from a 49er defender and ran the rest of the 58 yards to the end zone, making the score 42–38. Davis kept San Francisco in the game by faking a punt and making a first down, allowing him to kick the field goal that made the score 42–41. The 49ers got the ball back on the Minnesota 41-yard line with 4:42 remaining, but their last drive was halted when Brodie's attempt at Casey's fourth touchdown catch was intercepted, the only pick of the game. In a remarkable display, Brodie completed 19 of 29 passes for 264 yards, while Tarkenton had the best day of his career to date with 21 for 35, good for 407 yards and three touchdowns. Neither team rushed the passer effectively, and both Brodie and Tarkenton were sacked just once.

The 3–2 Lions met the 2–3 Bears in Chicago, trying to end their two-game losing streak. A rough, alert Bear defense took over in the first quarter as defensive end Doug Atkins forced two fumbles. Rudy Bukich immediately hit Johnny Morris for 27 yards and a touchdown after the first, and Gale Sayers scored on an eight-yard swing pass after the second when Bukich lofted the ball over blitzing linebacker Wayne Walker. Walker kicked a field goal to get Detroit on the board, but Jon Arnett hit Johnny Morris on a 59-yard halfback option pass for a 21–3 lead. The Detroit secondary, devastated by injuries, had called Night Train Lane out of retirement, but Mike Ditka hit him so hard on this play that Lane's helmet came off. In the third quarter, Ditka caught a touchdown pass on the next Bear drive after yet another Lion fumble, making it 31–3. The game finished at 38–10 after Bennie McRae ran an interception back 89 yards. This week, Chicago's defense won the game, and rookie Dick Butkus won the game ball. Sayers took a big hit early in the second period, and Halas held him out of the game for most of the second half. The Packers, he reminded the writers, would be coming into town the following week.

Over the last two weeks, Johnny Unitas had led the Colts to overwhelming victories over the Lions and the Redskins. This week was different. The 1–4 Rams came to Baltimore with something to prove, and their famed front four finally woke up, sacking Unitas five times. The Rams began briskly when Bill Munson hit rookie Jack Snow for 44 yards on the first play from scrimmage, leading to a Bruce Gossett field goal and a 3–0 lead. Unitas and the Colts retaliated with two long drives, culminating in a short touchdown pass to Raymond Berry and an unusual 18-yard scoring run by Johnny Unitas. But the Rams came back strong in the third quarter, scoring ten more points for a 20–14 lead. Then came the key play of the game.

The Colts had moved the ball near the Ram goal line but had to retreat to the 21-yard line when Raymond Berry was called for offensive pass interference. Unitas faded back to pass, and the great Deacon Jones, the Rams' left end, rushed him and leaped to block the pass. When he came down, as he admitted after the game, he accidentally, briefly grabbed Unitas' face mask—a tactic that had been outlawed only about six years earlier. The officials called the penalty, and Unitas promptly hit Jimmy Orr for a 15-yard touchdown and a 21–20 lead. Unitas took the Colts in for two more fourth-quarter touchdowns, the last with just 24 seconds left, to make it 35–20. Afterward, Shula praised Bill Munson and acknowledged that Deacon Jones and Merlin Olsen—two future Hall of Famers—would give anyone trouble. The Colts remained just one game behind the Packers, running their record to 6–1, and prepared for their second meeting with the 49ers in San Francisco the following week.

3. Sheep and Goats

Week 7

"On any given Sunday," the legendary NFL Commissioner Bert Bell had loved to remark, "any team can beat any other team." The October 31 games that closed out the first half of the season made Bell look good: four of the seven contests ended in major upsets. The trouble started in the Eastern Conference, where the top three teams all managed to lose.

In New York, an injured Charley Johnson returned to quarterback the Cardinals and did everything except get the ball into the end zone. The Cardinals outgained the Giants 438 yards to 259 but emerged with only 10 points. St. Louis took a 10–0 lead, thanks to a 59-yard touchdown run by Bill Triplett, who gained 176 yards on the day, but could not score a single point in the second half as the Giant defense repeatedly stopped them inside the Giant 30-yard line. Using a ground game based on rookie Tucker Frederickson, the Giants scored two touchdowns for a 14–10 victory that tied them with the Cardinals with 4–3 records. Their first touchdown occurred after wide-open tight end Aaron Thomas dropped a pass from Earl Morrall in the end zone from 21 yards out. Morrall brought the team into the huddle and called the exact same play again, and the Cardinals, who had not changed their coverage, watched helplessly as Thomas caught the pass on his second try.

The Dallas Cowboys, who had begun the season on such a bright note, lost their fifth straight game, this week to the Pittsburgh Steelers, who won their second game at home in Pittsburgh. Once again, the Cowboy offense was inconsistent, with Meredith completing just 12 of 34 passes while the team rushed for just 90 yards, and their pass defense was weak. Meredith wasted two promising second-quarter opportunities, one by overthrowing a long pass in a fourth-and-one gamble and one by fumbling within sight of the Steeler goal line. Steeler quarterback Bill Nelsen, who became a star three years later after being acquired by the Cleveland Browns, performed significantly better, although he threw for three interceptions. The Steelers took a 19–6 lead at halftime thanks to two touchdown passes from Nelsen to Gary Ballman (the teams missed three extra points between them) and held on for a 22–13 win. Both teams found themselves in a four-way tie for last place in the division with 2–5 records.

The Washington Redskins won their second straight game against the Eagles, giving both of those teams the same 2–5 record as well. An outstanding Redskins defense kept the Eagles in their own end for the whole first half of the game as Eagle's quarterback King Hill finally gave way to Norm Snead, who had been sitting on the bench since an early-season injury. Neither team could move the ball on the ground, but Jurgensen had a tremendous day, completing 23 of 36 passes for 293 yards. Nineteen of those completions went to tight ends Preston Carpenter and Pat Richter and running backs Charley Taylor and Dan Lewis, who had been acquired from Detroit. Washington led 16–7 early in the fourth quarter, but the Eagles came storming back and closed the gap to 23–21 with just a few minutes left. Taking the ball on his own 20-yard line, Jurgensen completed five successive passes to get the ball well into Eagle territory and ran 20 yards backward to eat up the last few seconds on the clock. The Eagles couldn't run another play.

In Cleveland, the Browns played their first game against a team from the Western Conference and received a rude awakening from the Minnesota Vikings. Having given up between 31 and 45 points in five of their first six games, the Viking defense righted itself and held the powerful Browns to just 167 yards total offense—including just 39 yards rushing by Jim Brown. Frank Ryan, playing with a sore elbow, completed just four passes and gave way to backup Jim Ninowski in the fourth quarter. Tarkenton, meanwhile, had another brilliant day, completing 17 of 27 passes for 234 yards and two touchdowns, while Bill Brown left his more famous namesake and rival in the dust with 138 rushing yards and two touchdowns. Cleveland remained a game ahead of St. Louis and the Giants at 5–2, losing by a solid margin of 27–17. The Vikings improved their record to 4–3—tied with the Bears for third place and close enough to dream that a hot second half might put them into title contention after all.

The Bears and the Packers played one of the pivotal games of the season. Bart Starr, who ran for more than 30 yards on an improvised quarterback draw, handed the ball off to Jim Taylor, who ran into the Bears' end zone on the opening drive for a 7–0 lead. The Packers couldn't move the ball much after that, however, and a poor punt gave the Bears the ball at midfield, whereupon Gale Sayers ran the ball into range for an easy field goal. After a second-quarter interception at the line of scrimmage gave the Bears the ball around midfield, runs by Andy Livingston, who repeatedly broke tackles, and Sayers advanced the ball to the Green Bay 13-yard line. Livingston, the youngest player in the league, was celebrating his 21st birthday. Bukich threw a touchdown pass to rookie Dick Jones for a 10–7 lead. Trying to come back, Starr threw one of his worst passes of the season, overthrowing Boyd Dowler by about 10 yards and finding the arms of cornerback Bennie McRae, who ran the interception back to the Packer 30-yard line. Bukich pitched out to Andy Livingston, going left. He appeared to be boxed in by Willie Davis, Willie Wood, and Leroy Caffey but simply slowed,

3. Sheep and Goats

accelerated again as they continued their pursuit, and ran around all three for a ten-yard gain. "Just call it instinct, I guess," said Livingston after the game. "Or maybe the will to survive."[3] Sayers then took the ball around the right end and outran Herb Adderley in similar fashion to make it 17–7. The athleticism of the Bears was simply too much for the great Packer defense.

In the third quarter, Sayers took a punt deep in Chicago territory and returned it 62 yards, cutting by five different Packers at top speed before Bob Jeter finally hauled him down. Backup halfback Jon Arnett now came into the game and gave the Bears a 24–7 lead with two fine runs. The Bears' offensive line was dominating the Packer defense, and Ronnie Bull scored the last touchdown in a 31–10 rout, the Pack's first loss of the season. Only twice, once in 1959 and once against the Colts in 1961, had Lombardi's Packers lost by a larger margin. Starr, who had been hit very hard by Rosey Taylor at the end of his long first-quarter run, threw three interceptions, and the Packers gained only 121 yards on the ground. In the dressing room, the Packers shook their heads in amazement after their first defeat and expressed hope that Baltimore would fare no better against the Bears the following week.

"Sayers just outran us," Lombardi said after the game. "He's got great speed—and we just misjudged him. He's a helluva football player—which I think is a high compliment. I think the whole Bear club has a big lift because of him and Livingston. Some of the veterans have caught fire as a result." The Packers' first loss of the season was bound to have consequences. Lombardi always feared that too many victories made his team overconfident and tried to keep them angry at himself. "Don't think you're responsible for this success," he would tell them. "Don't let it go to your heads and become impressed with yourselves because I want you to know that *I* did this. *I* made you guys what you are." The crushing defeat by the Bears gave him an opportunity. "Now I've got something to sink my teeth into," he told the team. "You!"[4]

Fresh from three devastating losses against the Colts, Packers, and Bears, the Detroit Lions rebounded with a 31–7 rout of the Rams in Los Angeles. The game was lost by the pathetic Rams—who played before a Los Angeles Coliseum that was almost 2/3 empty—rather than won by the Lions, as the Rams lost the ball five times on fumbles and three times on pass interceptions. The debacle began when the Rams fumbled the opening kickoff, the Lions recovered on the Ram 16-yard line, and big, powerful, flakey fullback Joe Don Looney—showing some of his outstanding speed and strength—scored on the first play. Coach Harry Gilmer had replaced Milt Plum with young George Izo at quarterback, and when the Lions next got the ball, he threw a 61-yard touchdown pass to Terry Barr. The Lions were only slightly superior in total offense, but the Rams continued to surrender the ball at crucial moments and managed only one touchdown. Like the Bears, the Lions would need a lot of help to turn their 4–3 record into a contending season, but with games against the Packers, Bears, and Colts in the next month, they had ample opportunity to affect the remarkable Western Conference race.

Two hours later, in San Francisco, Johnny Unitas and the Colts faced the surging 49ers. For the second week in a row, the 49ers roared out to a big lead. John Brodie passed for touchdowns to flanker Bernie Casey and fullback Ken Willard, who rushed for another, and San Francisco led 21–10 late in the second quarter. The Colts were double-covering Casey and league-leading receiver Dave Parks quite effectively, but Brodie compensated by passing to his running backs. Unitas, however, put on one of his signature drives with the clock running out in the first half, hitting Raymond Berry twice on the sidelines and finishing with a 31-yard screen pass to Tony Lorick to bring the Colts within four points, 21–17. They made it 21–20 in the third quarter, and the 49er momentum stalled when John David Crow threw an interception on a halfback option pass. Two big third-down passes by Unitas allowed the Colts to go 79 yards in 11 plays and take a 27–21 lead. John Brodie tried to respond but fumbled at the Colt 19-yard line, and another Colt drive finished with Jimmy Orr's second touchdown catch. Brodie did take the team almost all the way on the 49ers next series but was hit by linebackers Steve Stonebreaker and Dennis Gaubatz and separated his shoulder at the Colt three-yard line. His backup, George Mira, closed the gap to 34–28 with three minutes left. Mira got the ball again at the 49er 19-yard line with just 1:24 left and did a passable imitation of Unitas himself, moving the ball to the Colt 16-yard line thanks to two passes to Dave Parks with just 16 seconds left. On the next play, tackle Billy Ray Smith hit him hard and forced a fumble, and Lou Michaels recovered to save the game. The 49ers outgained the Colts 443 yards to 418, and while Unitas completed 21 of 34 passes, Brodie and Mira did even better with 25 out of 35. The wild win left the Colts tied with the Packers for the first time since the first week of the season. Unitas was having a better year even than in 1964, but the Colt defense clearly was not. Now the team had to fly back to Baltimore, practice for a week, and travel to Chicago to meet the hottest, scariest team in the NFL on November 7.

The Packers and Colts now sported identical 6–1 midseason records, with the Bears, Lions, and Vikings two games behind at 4–3. Chicago had both its games with the Colts remaining, but they would need help from

3. Sheep and Goats

elsewhere to catch up to Green Bay. Yet the Bears had established themselves as one of the league's top teams, and they, not the Packers, Colts, or Browns, had the finest young stars in the league in Gale Sayers, Andy Livingston, and Dick Butkus. They looked like the team of the future.

With the season half over, Jim Brown once again towered over every other rusher in the league with 777 yards gained and a 4.9 yards per carry average. Tommy Mason of the Vikings, Don Perkins of the Cowboys, Mason's teammate Bill Brown, rookie Tucker Frederickson of the Giants, Bill Triplett of St. Louis, and 49er rookie Ken Willard all trailed Brown with between 358 and 420 yards gained. John Brodie and Johnny Unitas stood alone among all the passers in the league with 14 touchdown passes each and almost 1800 yards gained. Brodie's main target, Dave Parks, led all receivers comfortably with 35 receptions, and his teammate Bernie Casey had 27 receptions. For the Colts, Raymond Berry had 31 receptions and Jimmy Orr 29—including a league-leading seven touchdowns. Gale Sayers ranked 12th in the league in rushing, but first in kickoff returns and first in touchdowns with 10. Jim Brown, with eight touchdowns, was the only other non-kicker in the top ten in scoring. Never had the NFL played a more exciting brand of football. More was to come.

4

The Baltimore Boom

Week 8

Back among the more comfortable confines of their own conference after their disastrous trip to Minnesota, the Cleveland Browns managed to maintain their one-game lead over St. Louis in a wild home game against the Philadelphia Eagles on November 7. Norm Snead, finally restored to starting quarterback, completed 18 of 36 passes for 362 yards. The Eagles finished the day with 582 yards of total offense to the Browns' 369 yards, but brilliant special team play kept the Browns in the game. Philadelphia opened the scoring when fleet halfback Tim Brown found room around left end, accelerated, and went 54 yards into the end zone without a hand laid on him. Flea Roberts immediately retaliated with a great 88-yard kickoff return to the Eagle 10-yard line, and Ryan promptly tied the game on Collins's favorite post pattern. The rest of the first half featured another great kickoff return by substitute halfback Leroy Kelly and two touchdowns by Jim Brown, one rushing and one on a 32-yard pass from Ryan.

The second half opened with the Browns leading 21–17, but the Eagles promptly went ahead on a long pass from Snead to his favorite target, Pete Retzlaff. The teams traded field goals, and the Browns moved quickly down the field for another score on a long post pattern from Ryan to Collins and a fine end sweep by Jim Brown, making the score 31–27. The teams traded touchdowns again, and the Browns finished on top 38–34 in a typically wild struggle featuring big plays on both sides. In one of the greatest days of his career, Tim Brown outgained Jim Brown 186 yards to 131 yards on the ground, and Norm Snead outpassed Frank Ryan 362 yards to 220 yards, but the Browns managed to come up with the big play just a little more often.

The Cardinals remained one game behind at 5–3 with an even closer victory in St. Louis. Charley Johnson, still hampered by his injured left shoulder, had a mediocre first half, but a Larry Wilson interception of a Bill Nelsen pass eventually gave the Cardinals the ball on the Steeler three-yard line, and they took a 7–3 lead. A long third-quarter drive led to a 15-yard

4. The Baltimore Boom

touchdown pass to Sonny Randle, but Nelson answered quickly with a 50-yard pass to rookie speedster Roy Jefferson to make the score 14–10. After a long defensive battle, Nelsen managed to pass the Steelers down the field again for a 17–14 lead with just 1:12 left. Johnson came out throwing. He missed three of his first four passes, but on the fifth, a third down and 10, he hit Bobby Joe Conrad with a very soft pass that Conrad ran out of bounds at the Cardinal 41-yard line with 46 seconds remaining. The Cardinals were using a double-wing formation, with Billy Gambrell flanked on the left inside Sonny Randle. Randle went wide, Gambrell cut toward the post, beat the Steeler safety, caught Johnson's rifled pass around the Steeler 20-yard line, and ran it in for the winning touchdown with just seconds left in perhaps the most thrilling finish of the entire season.

The Giants, meanwhile, fell out of their tie for second place with St. Louis with a 23–7 loss to the resurgent Redskins, who won their third straight. A 31-yard fumble recovery return by safetyman Paul Krause opened the scoring for the Redskins, and another end-zone interception by Johnny Sample stalled a Giant drive. Jurgensen then took the Redskins down the field, and they scored on an option pass from halfback Dan Lewis to rookie tight end Jerry Smith. Washington led 17–7 at the half. They knocked Giant quarterback Earl Morrall out of the game early in the second half and eventually managed to add two field goals, running their record to 3–5, one game behind the Giants.

The Cowboys had lost five consecutive games as they entertained the 49ers in the Cotton Bowl, and less than 40,000 fans turned out. They saw one of the wildest contests of the season. Safety Mel Renfro got the afternoon off to a rousing start with a 99-yard kickoff return for a touchdown, but even with John Brodie missing due to injury, the 49ers showed off their remarkable offense, which was emerging as perhaps the league's best. Both 49er sub George Mira—whose NFL career never really took off—and Meredith passed well, exchanging touchdown passes to Bernie Casey and Bob Hayes in the first quarter. With the score 14–10 for Dallas late in the second period, the Doomsday Defense—as it was already known—took over the game. First, cornerback Warren Livingston forced 49er Ken Willard to fumble, and linebacker Chuck Howley recovered and returned the ball 58 yards to the 49er 28-yard line. Meredith's try for a touchdown was promptly intercepted on the San Francisco five-yard line, but a few plays later, defensive end George Andrie recovered a 49er fumble in the end zone to make the score 20–10 after the extra point was missed. On the next series, George Mira hit tackle Bob Lilly in the stomach with a pass, and Lilly controlled the ball and ran it into the end zone for another score and a 27–10 lead. The

49ers got their act together in the second half, marching 78 yards in eight plays for a touchdown. Bob Hayes nearly took the ensuing kickoff in for another touchdown, but Meredith's passes failed repeatedly, and Dallas settled for a field goal and a 30–17 lead.

Mira came back quickly with passes to three different receivers—including league-leading Dave Parks—and another touchdown, making the score 30–24. The 49ers got the ball back again on a blocked field goal, and Mira finished off yet another drive with a 22-yard pass to Parks and a 31–30 lead. Meredith promptly threw another interception and was booed off the field, but the Dallas defense stopped San Francisco on the next drive and blocked a field goal themselves, running it back to the Dallas 47-yard line. Two fine passes from Meredith to Pete Gent—later the author of *North Dallas Forty*—and Bob Hayes made the score 36–31 after Meredith botched the hold for the extra point for the second time. A Mira fumble led to a Dallas field goal, and the defense held the 49ers one last time for a 39–31 win. The 49ers gained 411 yards to the Cowboys' 242 yards but lost. It was the first—and as it later turned out, the only—time in the 1965 season that an Eastern Conference club had beaten a team from the Western Conference.

Having overcome the Lions' first-half edge in Detroit three weeks earlier, the Packers faced the rematch at home with confidence. During the week, Vince Lombardi signed his fourth contract as Green Bay coach and general manager, this one taking him through 1974. A new tight end, Bill Anderson—who had sat out 1964 while coaching college football—took over for Marv Fleming. The Lions, meanwhile, had lost their outstanding flanker Terry Barr for several weeks with a knee injury, but Pat Studstill was a very capable replacement. The teams had almost identical offensive statistics, except that the Packers had surrendered 11 turnovers and the Lions 30. In another omen, while Packer quarterbacks had been sacked 21 times, the Lion signal callers had gone down only 11.

No team, not even the Colts, had consistently given Lombardi's Packers more trouble than the Lions, beating them once each in 1960, 1961, and 1962, and tying them in the last annual Thanksgiving game between the two clubs in 1963. Although Detroit's offense never equaled Green Bay's, their defense, based on their outstanding front four of Darris McCord, Alex Karras, Roger Brown, and Sam Williams—and linebackers Joe Schmidt and Wayne Walker—gave Lombardi nightmares, as he had explained at length in his 1962 classic book about the team's first game against the Lions that year, *Run to Daylight*. Green Bay had won that game 9–7 on a last-minute field goal after a fortunate interception, but the Lions had gotten some dramatic revenge on Thanksgiving that year, sacking Bart Starr repeatedly

4. The Baltimore Boom

while running out to a 26–0 halftime lead. This year's Lions offense was much weaker, but on November 6, 1965, they proved that their defense was still just as good.

Bill Curry

> The Lions were the only team that was not intimidated by the Packers.

The first quarter was scoreless, and the Packers took the lead in the second quarter when Jim Taylor scored to finish an 80-yard drive. The Lions' Tom Watkins proceeded to return the kickoff 62 yards to the Packer 35-yard line, however, and six plays later, Joe Don Looney, who was hitting his stride with Detroit, tied the game on the last play of the first half. Never again did the Packers take the ball into Lion territory.

In a debacle worse than Thanksgiving 1962, Bart Starr was sacked 11 times for a total loss of 109 yards and finished the game with -2 yards passing despite nine completions in 14 attempts. Meanwhile, the Pack rushed for a pathetic 70 yards. The Lion offense wasn't much more effective, gaining just 180 yards, and not until the last five minutes of the game did they manage to break the 7–7 deadlock after Paul Hornung's option pass was intercepted on the Packer 21-yard line and Wayne Walker kicked a field goal. Elijah Pitts decided to return a deep kickoff and was tackled on the Packer six-yard line, and on the first play from scrimmage after the kickoff, 300-pound tackle Roger Brown tackled Starr in the end zone for a safety. Detroit ran out the clock to preserve the 12–7 win. Joe Schmidt pronounced the game the best his defense had played since he joined the team in 1953. Alex Karras said specifically that the Lions had outdone their performance on Thanksgiving Day in 1962. He explained that the revamped Lion secondary had played the Green Bay receivers very tight to prevent Starr from getting off quick passes. He and his linemates had done the rest.

Both the Packers' regular guards, Jerry Kramer and Fuzzy Thurston, missed the game with injuries. This marked the third game in a row that the Packers had scored just one touchdown, moving Lombardi to remark, "We haven't generated any offense all year, really." The situation was all the more painful for Lombardi because he was, in essence, the offensive coach of the Packers, while Phil Bengston, his long-time assistant, handled the defense entirely on his own. The Packer defensive players joked that the offense made more money but that they had to earn it by enduring Lombardi's endless screaming over their mistakes.[1] As usual, Lombardi put a brave face on before the press and saved his wrath for the Tuesday film session with the offense. He was in the midst of the most frustrating series of games in his career as a head coach, and it seemed impossible that the Packers could prevail against the Colts, Bears, Vikings, and Lions—who still hoped to challenge for the title—without more of an offense.

Dave Robinson

> A lot of things Lombardi said and did, we ignored them. We knew Phil didn't second the motion.

In Chicago, the Colts faced the Bears in what turned out to be one of the pivotal games of the season. A win would give the Colts a game lead over the Packers, while a loss would leave the Bears just a single game behind Baltimore and Green Bay. In the second period, with the score 0–0, Unitas took the Colts from their own seven-yard line to the Bear 37 with the help of a controversial penalty. After Larry Morris knocked a screen pass away, nearly intercepting it, Unitas kicked the ball back into the end zone, and defensive lineman Dick Evey ran right into Unitas. Then young Dick Butkus accidentally piled into Evey, who had to leave the game, to the fury of the Chicago fans, who thought Unitas had injured him. Then Unitas noticed the Bears preparing to send their right linebacker to help out Dave Whitsell against split end Raymond Berry, still his favorite target. That left massive tight end John Mackey momentarily unguarded, and Unitas called an audible and hit him with a pass. No sooner had Mackey caught the ball than three different Bear defenders hit him, but he shook them all off and rumbled into the end zone, surviving one more attempted tackle on the five-yard line. Another long drive culminated in a field goal, and the Colts led 10–0 at the half as Ordell Braase wreaked havoc in the Bears' backfield. Unitas managed to make it 17–0 early in the third quarter on a brilliant 49-yard pass to fullback Tony Lorick, but he had been hit hard two plays earlier on a quarterback sneak and had to leave the game for good with back spasms. So far, the Colt defense had stopped the red-hot Chicago offense cold in their own park.

The Bears promptly came to life, going 86 yards for a touchdown in just six plays, but Unitas's backup, Gary Cuozzo—hitherto restricted to late-game stints in blowouts—replied with four completed passes on a six-play drive that ended with Raymond Berry juggling a touchdown pass that the officials ruled good. Trailing 24–7, the Bears finally got the ball back in the fourth quarter, and although the Colts had successfully devised

4. The Baltimore Boom

a strategy to do what no other team had—to contain Gale Sayers—Rudy Bukich began to connect on passes. Two long drives ended in touchdowns, and the score closed to 24–21 with five minutes left. A John Mackey fumble gave the Bears their chance, but they could not move the ball in four downs. They got the ball again on their own five-yard line with seconds left, but Sayers barely failed to catch a 60-yard pass, and on the next play, Bukich was tackled in the end zone for a safety, and the Colts won 26–21. In the dressing room, Halas bitterly attacked the officiating, claiming that Richie Pettibon had been denied an interception after wrestling the ball from Mackey and that Raymond Berry had never had possession of his touchdown catch.

Johnny Morris

That bad call cost us the title.

The Colt defense gave its best performance of the season—holding the Bears to just 17 yards rushing—and they suddenly, indisputably, looked like the best team in the NFL again. The Bears slipped to 4–4, two games behind the Packers and three behind the Colts, and their title chance suddenly appeared remote. With both the Lions and the Vikings picking up steam and the 49ers scoring at will, anything could still happen in the NFL West.

The Colt defenders could not match the raw physical power of the Packers' Willie Davis, Henry Jordan, Dave Robinson, and Herb Adderley, or the Bears' Dick Butkus and Doug Atkins, but they were making up for it with planning and smarts.

Dennis Gaubatz

I called the defensive signals. Sometimes the coaches sent the defense in, but if I didn't agree with it, I ignored it. Then, you had to look at the other team when they came up to the line. Not just the formation—lots of times, players give away what's coming—and I would call an audible.

The Vikings passed the Bears and pulled to 5–3, one game behind Green Bay and two behind the Colts, with a solid 23–13 victory over the hapless Rams in Bloomington, Minnesota. Both front fours were in top form, with the Vikings sacking Munson seven times while the elusive Tarkenton went down four times. Munson was slightly more effective in the air, but the Vikings more than made up for it on the ground. Star halfback

Tommy Mason went out early in the third quarter with an injured knee, but Dave Osborne filled in ably. The Vikings had rebounded from their disastrous start and were starting to look like the contenders pundits had expected them to be. Their fate was now squarely in their own hands, with home games against the Colts and Packers coming up in the next two weeks. Two victories would, at a minimum, leave them a game behind the Colts and tied with Green Bay.

The week's seven games had been decided by an average of 7.5 points, and four of them had gone down to the last minute. One game separated the first- and second-place teams in both the Eastern and Western conferences, and other teams remained in striking distance. And now, at last, CBS and the NFL had discovered the means of turning their league into a national obsession. On November 15, the fans of the Northeast would not be limited to either the Eagles or the Giants and would get a look at the class of the league for the first time.

Standings

Eastern Conference	W	L	T	Pct	PF	PA
Cleveland	6	2	0	.750	205	184
St. Louis	5	3	0	.625	204	138
New York	4	4	0	.500	125	196
Dallas	3	5	0	.375	167	153
Washington	3	5	0	.375	117	181
Philadelphia	2	6	0	.250	196	218
Pittsburgh	2	6	0	.250	124	183

Western Conference	W	L	T	Pct	PF	PA
Baltimore	7	1	0	.875	243	143
Green Bay	6	2	0	.750	172	111
Minnesota	5	3	0	.625	253	231
Detroit	5	3	0	.625	146	153
Chicago	4	4	0	.500	232	194
San Francisco	3	5	0	.375	259	231
Los Angeles	1	7	0	.125	132	252

Week 9

In a battle of Eastern Conference also-rans, Norm Snead and the Philadelphia Eagles got some revenge over the Washington Redskins, winning 21–14. Like the 49ers, the Redskins had an Achilles heel, their pass defense, and Norm Snead tormented his old club with 21 completions in 28 passes for 204 yards. Dropped passes by Bobby Mitchell and Charley Taylor spoiled a fine effort by Jurgensen.

4. The Baltimore Boom

In Dallas, a much larger crowd of 57,000 was rewarded by the Cowboys' second straight victory against the hapless Steelers. The game was close all the way, but Bill Nelsen threw five interceptions, stopping several Steeler drives. The last of those, by Chuck Howley at the Pittsburgh 31-yard line, allowed Meredith to throw the winning touchdown pass to Bob Hayes. The final score was 24–17.

The division-leading Browns entertained the Giants for their rematch in Municipal Stadium at 1:00 p.m., and Jim Brown put on another show for his fans on Long Island and all over New York and New England. The Browns took a 14–7 lead on two swing passes to halfback Ernie Green, who scored once and was only stopped the second time by the fantastic acceleration of Giants' safety Henry Carr, the Olympic gold medalist and world record holder at 200 meters. Jim Brown promptly ran the ball over for a 14–7 lead. He finished the day with 156 yards rushing and three touchdowns while Ernie Green caught seven passes for 160 yards and rushed for 62 more. Despite some fine passing by Earl Morrall, the Browns won a comfortable 34–21 victory and finished the day with a two-game lead over the Cardinals.

At about 4:00 p.m. on the afternoon of November 14, 1965, when the Browns-Giants game came to an end, the NFL fans of New York, New England, and the rest of the East got a wonderful surprise. Rather than revert to local programming, as usual, CBS cut to Bloomington, Minnesota, where the game between the Baltimore Colts and the Minnesota Vikings was now in progress. The NFL and CBS had announced this change in the national lifestyle in a full-page ad in the *New York Times* that morning, warning the nation's wives not to expect any yard work from their husbands this afternoon. The East Coast's introduction to the major leagues could hardly have been more exciting.

Winners of their last three games, the 5-3 Vikings got a very pleasant surprise when the Colts went out for their first series of downs. Johnny Unitas, who had hurt his back against the Bears the previous week but had practiced during the week and had been reported ready to play, was not on the field, and young Gary Cuozzo started his first game for the Colts.

The game began well for the Vikings, who moved the ball pretty easily until they lost the ball to a Bill Brown fumble. Phil King, replacing the injured Tommy Mason, also ran well in the Vikings' next possession, and Tarkenton began to connect with his wide receivers. The Colt pass rush came to life, however, and Tarkenton was soon faced with a fourth and more than 40 yards after two sacks and an intentional grounding penalty. Cuozzo failed to move the ball again as the first quarter ended without a score. Another Minnesota drive ended with a touchdown pass to Hal Bledsoe in the corner of the end zone, and they went ahead 7–0 early in the second quarter. Not until 22 minutes into the first half did Cuozzo and the Colts secure a first down. A beautiful pass to Raymond Berry on a slant, caught in full stride, got the ball to the Viking 17-yard line, and the drive led to a field goal. With just moments to go in the half, speedy Alvin Haymond returned a punt from his own 10-yard line to the Viking 34, and on third and 18, with just seconds remaining, Cuozzo hit Jimmy Orr on a straight fly pattern to the end zone to take the team into the locker room with a rather lucky 10–7 lead.

A different Colt team came out of the locker room to receive the second-half kickoff. Mixing running plays and passes, Cuozzo moved the ball smartly down the field and hit Orr in the end zone for the second time on a post pattern from 23 yards out for a 17–7 lead. The Vikings stormed right back, with Tarkenton scrambling for a 36-yard gain and hitting his favorite target, Paul Flatley, in the end zone to make it 17–14. But Cuozzo was even more impressive on the next drive, going 54 yards in four plays, the last a 29-yard pass that halfback and former flanker Lenny Moore, who had returned from injury, caught over his shoulder at full speed. Again and again this afternoon, Cuozzo delivered crisp passes that reached Orr, Raymond Berry, and Moore going downfield at full stride. That made it 24–14. Then came one of the most shocking and decisive sequences of the season.

Lou Michaels, the Colts' defensive end and placekicker, advanced to the ball on the kicking tee and dribbled it across midfield and to his right for a perfect onside kick. The Colts recovered on the Viking 46-yard line without a Viking anywhere near the play. A draw play to Tony Lorick ripped through the demoralized Vikings for 38 yards, and Cuozzo rolled out left and passed to Raymond Berry for his fourth touchdown and a 31–14 lead. Michaels added a field goal early in the fourth quarter. On the ensuing kickoff, Vikings' rookie Lance Rentzel—later a star receiver for the Dallas Cowboys and San Diego Chargers—fumbled, and the Colts recovered on the Viking 15-yard line. Two plays later, Cuozzo hit young Willie Richardson in the end zone for his fifth touchdown pass—a club record, one more than Unitas had ever managed in a single game, which earned him the choice as NFL Player of the Week. The rout was now 41–14, and Rentzel redeemed himself by running the following kickoff for a 101-yard touchdown—much too little, too late.

The national television audience had seen a great team at its peak. Cuozzo had completed 16 of 26 passes for 208 yards, spread evenly among his wide receivers and Moore, who had 79 yards total offense on the day.

4. The Baltimore Boom

The pass rush had sacked Tarkenton four times as the Colts ran their record to 8–1 and appeared to be unstoppable.

Upton Bell

> Carroll Rosenbloom's money man, Jay Duval Farrar, discovered Cuozzo. He was from Virginia, where Cuozzo went to college, and he told either Weeb Ewbank or Carroll, "You have to take a look at this kid." We signed him as a free agent! He was very intelligent and had a nice touch on his throws.

The drama in Minneapolis-St. Paul did not end on the field. The next morning, Monday, coach Norm Van Brocklin called three reporters into his office and announced that he was quitting the Vikings and football for good. "I thought this team could win the championship," he said. "It's pretty plain that it's not going to do it with me as coach. I've taken the team as far as I can. I can't get the team over the hump. It's been going this way for five years. We come to the big game, and we blow it. I've gone as far as I can go. Maybe another guy can do it." Players, management, and the press all expressed admiration for Van Brocklin and astonishment at his decision.

Then, that evening, Van Brocklin called general manager Jim Finks and asked him to come to his home. When Finks arrived, the Dutchman said he realized he had made a mistake and wanted to be on the job again the next morning to start preparing for the Green Bay Packers. The next morning, Van Brocklin gave a long *mea culpa* to the press and thanked his bosses for taking him back. "I just became depressed," he said, "but I later realized I didn't want to quit. It's the strangest thing that's ever happened to me, and I have no explanation for it." Asked how he thought the whole imbroglio would affect the team, Fran Tarkenton replied that he would prefer to wait to comment until after Sunday's game with the Packers.

Fran Tarkenton

> We were so happy he had quit. We were celebrating. But we had five owners, none of them football people. They talked him into staying! How could you have any respect for a coach that quit when you were five and four?

Vince Lombardi, as it happened, might have been one of the few men in football who could understand Van Brocklin's frustration. He had emerged from his game on Sunday with a victory over the Rams, but one that was anything but reassuring. After scoring just one touchdown in each of its last three games with Dallas, Chicago, and Detroit, his offense—his responsibility and prized possession—had done the impossible. They had gotten even worse.

Tom Moore, for many years the Packers' third running back, opened the game in the backfield and promptly fumbled the ball away, allowing the Rams to open the scoring with a Bruce Gossett field goal. Bart Starr was having a terrible time passing, enduring four sacks, but he got close enough to the Ram end zone for Don Chandler to kick a tying field goal late in the first quarter. That was the end of the scoring until the last few minutes of the game. The Packers managed to rush for 102 yards, but Starr eventually gave way to Zeke Bratkowski in the third quarter, and the two quarterbacks combined to complete just six out of 12 passes. Both defenses were outstanding, and the Rams gained just 142 yards to the Packers' 177. Sacks took both teams out of field goal range on several occasions. With two minutes left, the Rams had the ball in their own territory, and a tie seemed almost certain. But defensive tackle Ron Kostelnik wrapped his arms around Bill Munson and forced a fumble that Lionel Aldridge recovered, and after the Packers barely failed to get the ball into the end zone, Chandler kicked a winning field goal with 1:27 left to make the score 6–3. The Packers remained one game behind the Colts.

Dave Robinson

> Before the game, Willie Davis told the defense, "We know the offense is having trouble. Don't worry about them. If we do our job, we can't lose. If we play a perfect game, we won't lose."
>
> There was a drama within the drama in that game. On our first field goal, Lamar Lundy blindsided Willie Davis. Willie said, "Next time, I'm going to get my revenge." On the second one, he asked me to cover for him while he went after Lundy, and he got him. There's a lot more of that kind of thing in games than you might think.

In Chicago, the Bears renewed their traditional rivalry with the Cardinals, who had left Chicago for St. Louis three years earlier. Emotions still ran high for this game, and both teams were trying desperately to stay in the race for their division title. Gale Sayers, who seemed a little nervous in the midst of his amazing, unprecedented rookie season, had trouble holding on to the ball all day and fumbled it away in the Bears' first series. Charley Johnson promptly struck back with a touchdown pass to Sonny Randle. Sayers proceeded to atone immediately, taking the ensuing kickoff, heading

4. The Baltimore Boom

for the sidelines, faking kicker Jim Bakken out of his jockstrap at the Cardinals' 39-yard line, and making it to the 13-yard line. Jon Arnett scored a few plays later. Three field goals left the Cardinals ahead 13–10 at halftime. Charley Johnson, trying to return from injury, had a miserable day, and the Bears scored the only touchdown of the third period on a naked reverse by Bukich to take a 17–13 lead. Sayers finished off another long drive early in the fourth quarter to make the score 24–13. They added ten more points in the fourth quarter, and fights broke out on three consecutive plays. Butkus got into one with All-Pro guard Ken Gray after running back an interception. In the final minute, with the Bears ahead 34–12, the benches emptied after Bear linebacker Larry Morris began fighting with the Cardinal center, and 70-year-old George Halas ran the length of the field to get close to the action. The Cardinals dropped to two games behind the Browns in the Eastern Conference, while the Bears remained three behind Baltimore and two behind Green Bay.

And in Detroit, the erratic Lions fumbled away a chance to keep ahead of the Bears against the 49ers, dropping their record to 5–4. With John Brodie back in the lineup, the 49ers took the opening kickoff and moved down the field to the Lions' 24-yard line, where Tommy Davis kicked a field goal. On their first play from scrimmage, the Lions fumbled, and 49er linebacker Dave Wilcox ran the ball in for a touchdown. The 49ers' dominance continued through the first half, which finished with Brodie (20 for 32 on the day) hitting Dave Parks in the end zone to make the score 20–0. This was the fourth time in five weeks that the great 49er offense had roared out to a halftime lead, but they had won only two of those games.

The second half began true to form. Milt Plum had now replaced young George Izo at quarterback and led Detroit to a touchdown after the second-half kickoff, helped by two passes to big tight end Ron Kramer. Suddenly, the Lions' defense, which had totally stymied Green Bay the week before, stiffened, and early in the fourth quarter, Plum delivered again, this time with a 22-yard touchdown pass to Pat Studstill to pull within six, 20–14. Then defensive back Bruce Maher intercepted a Brodie pass in Lion territory and ran it back to the 49er 48-yard line. A big-back offense featuring Amos Marsh and Nick Pietrosante carried the ball to the 49er nine-yard line. Then disaster struck.

Quarterback Milt Plum had repeatedly been a bridesmaid rather than a bride for the Cleveland Browns from 1958 when the team was shut out in a 10–0 playoff game against the Giants through 1961. Traded to Detroit in 1962, he had gotten the Lions off to a terrific 3–0 start, tied with Green Bay, where the Lions played the fourth game of the season. In the game immortalized by Vince Lombardi's book *Run to Daylight*—ghosted by W.C. Heinz—Plum had moved the team to a 7–6 lead with just a few minutes left and had tried to run out the clock, only to surrender an interception when receiver Terry Barr slipped on a muddy field, allowing Green Bay to win. Now disaster struck Plum again. He faded back, looking for the go-ahead touchdown, but could not find a receiver or bring himself to throw the ball away. The pass rush reached him, he fumbled, and defensive end Clark Miller grabbed the ball in stride and managed to return it 75 yards into the Lion end zone for a 27–14 lead. The Lions were not done. Another drive got them back within six points, 27–21, and with 4:30 left in the game, cornerback Dick LeBeau intercepted a pass and ran it back to the San Francisco 31-yard line. They reached the 49er 13-yard line, but three straight passes were incomplete, and they surrendered the ball. Tied with the Vikings and Bears at 5–4, they were three games behind the Colts but still one ahead of the mercurial 49ers, who seemed unstoppable on offense but chronically vulnerable on defense.

Week 10

On November 21, 76,251 fans, at that time the largest crowd ever to see a football game in Dallas, packed the Cotton Bowl to see if their young team could close to within two games of the Browns. They nearly did.

The Browns were helpless offensively against the Dallas defense in the first quarter, and although a penalty killed a Dallas drive within easy reach of the goal line, a field goal gave the Cowboys a 3–0 lead. In the second quarter, Ryan moved the Browns down to the Dallas three-yard line and handed the ball to Jim Brown on a sweep left. Brown had to run very wide, and linebacker Dave Edwards slowed him down enough to allow three other Cowboys to surround him. Diving forward so far that he had to put his right hand on the turf to stay on his feet, Brown went under two of their tackles and left the fourth Cowboy sprawling as he went into the end zone.

Don Meredith

> It was the greatest run I ever saw. He went left, and he came back right, and he came back left, and our guys kept hitting him, and they kept falling off. He bounced back and scored. And I'm on the sideline, and I've just never seen anything like this, and I'm saying, "Wow! Go!" And then I realized that I was on the wrong side of the deal.[2]

4. The Baltimore Boom

The Browns took a 10–7 lead in the second quarter and then forced Dallas to punt. Leroy Kelly took just two steps to his left and then shot straight upfield 67 yards for a touchdown and a 17–3 halftime lead. Meredith suffered some bruised ribs in the first half but insisted that he could continue.

Dallas came out of the locker room strong, took the kickoff, and promptly marched 80 yards to a score. Their defense immediately held, and a fine punt return by Mel Renfro got Dallas to the Cleveland 35-yard line. Two plays later, Meredith overthrew an open Buddy Dial near the end zone, and Bernie Parish intercepted. Once again, Jim Brown's sweep to the left appeared to misfire when cornerback Warren Livingston seemed to meet him head-on, but Brown stepped quickly to his left, leaving Livingston in the dirt. Two more Cowboys were directly upfield, and Brown cut back to the right, picked up some impromptu blocking, and went 25 yards to the Cowboy six-yard line. Then Frank Ryan hit Collins on their favorite post pattern to make it 24–10.

In the fourth quarter, Meredith got the Cowboys within a touchdown at 24–17 with a 45-yard pass to Hayes, and the defense promptly held the Browns. The Cowboys took over on their own 29-yard line with more than seven minutes left. Passes to Bob Hayes and the big tight end Frank Clarke promptly got the ball to the Cleveland 12-yard line in just two plays. Then, in a play that foreshadowed the last minutes of the NFL title game just thirteen months later against the Packers in the same stadium, pass interference by Walter Beach gave the Cowboys a first down on the Cleveland one-yard line, just seven points behind.

A year later, trailing the Packers 34–27, four plays and an offside call occurred before Meredith threw an interception in the end zone. This time, Landry sent in a pass play on first down, and the ball was tipped and intercepted by Brown linebacker Vince Costello across the goal line.

That, remarkably, was not the Cowboys' last chance. Jim Brown, who gained 99 yards on the day, promptly fumbled at the Brown 30-yard line, and Chuck Howley recovered at the 40. Meredith connected with Bob Hayes at the Cleveland 23-yard line—and, on the next play, threw another interception to safety Ross Fichtner. Cleveland had essentially wrapped up the Eastern Conference with three games to go.

The next morning, Gary Cartwright of the *Dallas Morning News* opened with a parody of a famous, 40-year-old lead by the legendary Grantland Rice. "Outlined against a grey November sky," he began, "the Four Horsemen rode again Sunday. You know them: Pestilence, Death, Famine, and Meredith." Don Meredith had the misfortune to be a good, but not great, quarterback whose coach often insisted that he execute plays in which he did not believe. On this day, he had passed for 201 yards to Frank Ryan's 75 but ended three drives with interceptions. His next three seasons ended in heartbreaking losses in the NFL Championship to the Packers and in the 1968 playoffs to these same Browns. After that defeat, he retired at the age of 30. Two years later, in 1970, he began a long and very successful career as a broadcaster.

Two days earlier, the Browns, the NFL, and their greatest player had found themselves at the center of the national consciousness. *Time*'s cover story featured a painting of none other than Jim Brown. "Pro football's stars," ran the admiring story, "are the samurai of sport—immensely skilled, brutally tough, corrosively honest mercenaries who respect each other almost as much as they respect themselves. In the critical company of his peers, the Baltimore Colts' Johnny Unitas is considered 'a great quarterback, but if you beat his blockers, you beat him.' Rookie fullback Tucker Frederickson of the New York Giants is 'strong right now, but in a year he'll hit a little less hard.' And Flanker Bobby Mitchell of the Washington Redskins is already 'slowing down fast'—at the age of 30. There is only one player in the game today whose ability on-field commands almost universal admiration, and that is Jimmy Brown." Thanks to Brown, the story noted, Cleveland was the only NFL team relying more on runs than passes.

After dwelling at length on Brown's power-running techniques, the story turned to his background—his first few years on a coastal island in Georgia, his childhood and youth in Manhasset, Long Island, and his years at Syracuse University. He earned 13 letters in five sports in three years in high school and averaged 38 points a game in basketball. He was a B- student and class president. The story zeroed in frankly on racial issues, quoting Brown that when he reached Syracuse, he was seen as "an enemy in the ranks—a potential troublemaker and a threat to Caucasian women." Eventually, as a senior, he had led Syracuse to a 7–1 record and a trip to the Cotton Bowl, where they lost 28–27. Paul Hornung, who had quarterbacked Notre Dame to a disastrous 2–8 season, won the Heisman Trophy, and the Packers took him as the first pick in the draft. In the spring, Brown was an All-American lacrosse player. The story reviewed his pro career, which had blossomed, of course, in the three years since Paul Brown was fired.

"Now Jimmy seems to be shooting for still another title: Most Controversial Athlete of the Year," the story continued. "Flashy, arrogant, casually indiscreet, he drives a red Cadillac Eldorado, brags that he owns so many suits that 'I might lose one in the cleaners and never miss it.'" He admitted to having few friends. The story mentioned that earlier in 1965,

4. The Baltimore Boom

an 18-year-old girl had accused him of assaulting her in a motel room, but that Brown had been acquitted after a brief trial. And he was now a militant Civil Rights leader, the head of his own organization, the Negro Industrial and Economic Union, disdainful of white people who wanted him to be another Martin Luther King, Jr. The story quoted Browns broadcaster John Fitzgerald as having told Brown that he always "admired you as a football player" and "never looked on you as a Negro." "That's ridiculous!" Brown snapped. "You have to look at me as a Negro. Look at me, man! I'm black!" In conclusion, the story mentioned that Brown was talking about retiring, that he had made one movie and was under contract with Fox for three more at $37,000 each (about half his annual salary), and he might run for mayor of Cleveland.[3] In retrospect, the story reads like a fair and advanced piece of journalism for the period and a welcome counterpart to the coverage of *Time*'s sister publication, *Sports Illustrated*, where young Frank Deford discovered that editor Andre Laguerre was worried that black athletes on the cover would cut circulation, and where cover stories on NFL players nearly always seemed to feature white athletes.[4]

The Browns found themselves a full three games ahead with an 8–2 record because the Cardinals, whose season had begun so brightly, also threw away their game, losing to the Giants at home 28–15. Charley Johnson's left shoulder kept him out of the game again, and although Buddy Humphrey passed for 320 yards, he also threw three interceptions while his teammates fumbled twice. Turnovers set up all four of the Giants touchdowns. The last Eastern Conference game was also decided by turnovers. Playing in Pittsburgh, the Redskins won their fourth game, tying them with the Cowboys, their opponent the following week, with the help of four interceptions and three fumble recoveries. The Redskins had led only 10–3 midway through the third quarter, but veteran Ed Brown, subbing for injured Bill Nelsen, completed a pass to Gary Ballman at his own 38-yard line, and Ballman fumbled after the catch. Redskins' safety Paul Krause, later a star with the Vikings, picked it up and ran to the eight-yard line, and Charley Taylor promptly ran the ball into the end zone. Two brilliant punt returns by Rickey Harris led to two more touchdowns. No one could possibly have guessed the role that Ed Brown was going to play later in the NFL season.

Meanwhile, the red-hot Colts entertained the Eagles in Baltimore in a game that turned out to be surprisingly exciting. Gary Cuozzo had been elected NFL Player of the Week after his five touchdown passes in Minnesota, but Johnny Unitas returned to the lineup and began in style, throwing a 52-yard touchdown pass to Lenny Moore. Jerry Logan then intercepted a Norm Snead pass and ran it back 36 yards for a touchdown. But Snead promptly found the key to the Baltimore defense, and by halftime, the score was 17–17. Meanwhile, Colt flanker Jimmy Orr hurt a shoulder, left the game, and went to a local hospital for X-rays. Unitas and the Colts could manage only a single field goal in the third quarter and began the last period trailing 24–20 thanks to a touchdown pass from Snead to Ray Poage. At the hospital, a line of emergency room patients made way for Orr, who didn't wait for the results of his X-rays and headed back for the stadium.

"Men fight best on death ground," the ancient Chinese military theorist Sun Tzu wrote, and no NFL player ever fought better on death ground than Johnny Unitas, whose name had been a byword for last-quarter comebacks since 1958. Alvin Haymond got the Colts off to a good start with a 53-yard kickoff return, and Unitas completed two quick down-and-in passes to his favorite target, Raymond Berry, reaching the one-foot line. Lenny Moore promptly ran the ball in for a 27–24 lead. Snead tried to regain the lead again with another pass to Poage in the end zone, but this time cornerback Bobby Boyd wrestled the ball out of Poage's hands for an interception. As Unitas marched the Colts down the field again, the packed stadium crowd began to roar. The acoustics of the stadium famously tended to amplify their cheers, an effect known to enemy players as the "Baltimore Boom." Jimmy Orr, whose X-rays had proven negative, came on to the field, and the crowd gave him an ovation. Just minutes later, he caught a 22-yard touchdown pass from Unitas in the right-hand corner of the end zone, known as Orrsville, good for a 10-point lead.

Upton Bell

> Union Memorial Hospital was only three blocks away from Memorial Stadium. Otherwise, Orr couldn't have come back. I was sitting in Orrsville myself. The players came out of the locker room through a dugout, and when Orr came out, the fans started *screaming*, and I saw him run onto the field. I can still hear that crowd today. Orr was a borderline Hall of Fame receiver. He had moves that could turn you like a top.

Jimmy Orr

> John threw a sharp pass that came on you quick, but for some reason, was easy to catch. Some balls are softer than others, you know. John had a ball that was so

4. The Baltimore Boom

soft you could catch it and keep on going. You didn't have to concentrate on it. It was a great thing to have, that soft-feeling fastball.[5]

Running their record to 9–1, the Colts remained a full game ahead of the Packers. Moore, who had been hampered much of the year with injuries, had a tremendous day, catching seven passes for 163 yards and rushing for 54 more. Now the Colts had just three days to prepare for their first Thanksgiving Day trip to Detroit to face the Lions.

After four weeks with limited offense, the Packers traveled to Minnesota to face the shaken Vikings, fresh not only from their humiliation on national television but from the resignation and return of Norm Van Brocklin as coach. The Vikings began by moving down within the Packer 10-yard line, but the Green Bay defense, the league's best, held them for five plays. Then, after an interception of a Starr pass, a field goal gave Minnesota a 3–0 lead. Although Paul Hornung missed the game completely, the Green Bay running game finally came to life, with Jim Taylor going over 100 yards for the first time all season, and Starr led the Packers on two drives that gave them a 10–6 lead at the half. The only score of the third quarter was a Tarkenton touchdown pass to Paul Flatley, and as the last period began, the Packers were on pace to continue their four-week string in which they had averaged one touchdown per game. Both Starr and Tarkenton finished the day with mediocre totals of nine completions in 19 attempts.

As the fourth quarter began, the Packers retaliated with some fine running by Taylor and a 55-yard pass from Starr to Dowler, good for a second touchdown and a 17–13 lead. Then, on two successive series of downs, star Viking fullback Bill Brown fumbled, each time leading to a quick Green Bay score. Suddenly, the score was 31–13. The teams exchanged interceptions, and Ron Vander Kelen replaced Tarkenton and fumbled, setting up the Packers' fifth touchdown in the 38–13 win.

The Packers' victory, clearly, was quite a bit less dominant than it looked, and it was only the third relatively easy win the team had throughout the season. Now they had to face the Rams again in Los Angeles the following Sunday—the second year in a row that they did not have to face Detroit on Thanksgiving. Lombardi credited Taylor's and Starr's return to form with the victory, not the defense, and when a reporter asked him if he thought the team had a chance to win the Western Conference title, he bit his lip inwardly and replied that yes, it did.

"The Chicago Bears," *Chicago Tribune* beat reporter George Strickler wrote on Monday morning, "managed to outgain both the Detroit Lions and Referee Bill Downes today in a bizarre exhibition of professional football that ended 17–10.… Detroit not only lost the game and a share of third place to the Bears, it finished third behind Downes in the statistics with 184 yards gained. Downes carried the ball 20 times for 199 yards in penalties, 30 for two remarks he did not feel were exactly complimentary. He also threw Alex Karras, Detroit's star defensive tackle, out of the game in the last minute of play."

The game began like a typical Western Conference thriller when the Lions' Tom Watkins took the opening kickoff 94 yards to the Bears' six-yard line, and big fullback Amos Marsh scored two plays later. Fumbles stalled both teams, however, and things slowed down fast. After recovering a fumbled punt, the Bears evened the score on a 24-yard run by Jon Arnett, and the teams traded field goals in the second quarter to make the score 10–10. Fine running by young Andy Livingston, who returned to the lineup after two weeks of injury, set up the Bears' three-pointer. Gale Sayers, whom no team seemed to be able to contain for a whole game, returned the second-half kickoff 23 yards and kicked off a Chicago drive that ended when he swept the Lions' line and went 20 yards for a score, eluding two of the greatest defensive players in the league, Joe Schmidt and Roger Brown, along the sideline to make the score 17–10. In the last three minutes of the game, the Bears ran 14 plays, ten of which, thanks to penalties, advanced them just 12 yards. The series included five penalties, a fight, a fumble, and the ejection of Alex Karras. The Bears improved to 6–4 and took sole possession of third place, but they could only tie the Colts if Baltimore lost three of their last four games.

Since beating the Rams 45–21 five weeks earlier, the San Francisco 49ers had lost games by scores of 42–41, 34–28, and 39–26. Their pattern was not going to change in their return match against the Rams in San Francisco.

Both teams began moving the ball smartly in the first half, and the score was 10–10 in the second quarter. Then came the worst injury of the NFL season to date. After Ram quarterback Bill Munson got off a pass, he was hit low on his legs by defensive end Clark Miller. The collision tore knee ligaments, and Munson was stretchered off the field and operated on (decades before arthroscopy) that evening. The promising quarterback was lost for the season, and Roman Gabriel replaced him. Although Gabriel completed only seven passes in 24 attempts, one of them was a 40-yard touchdown pass to Jack Snow in the third quarter, and the Rams took a 27–13 lead early in the fourth quarter. Then John Brodie went into his Johnny Units imitation, and San Francisco scored 17 unanswered points for a 30–27 victory. Although the Rams' record fell to a dreadful 2–8, their

4. The Baltimore Boom

offense was coming alive, and they had surprises in store for other teams over the last few weeks of the season.

With four weeks left, the Colts had clearly established themselves as the best team in the league to date. While their defense ranked second in the league behind the Packers, having given up 188 points in the ten games to the Packers' 133, their league-leading offensive point total of 318 was more than 100 points more than Green Bay's 216. The 49ers had scored nearly as many points as the Colts (315), while the Vikings and Bears had 287 and 283, respectively. The Browns' 263 points led the Eastern Conference but would have ranked fifth in the Western Conference, while the Cowboys' 194 points allowed, the best in the East, would have ranked third in the West. That week, *Sports Illustrated* ran a long article by Tex Maule predicting that the Colts would win the title, focusing on the team's new middle linebacker, Dennis Gaubatz.[6] The Colts' defense no longer featured overwhelming athletes like Willie Davis, Dave Robinson, Henry Jordan, and Herb Adderley of the Packers, but they were largely making up for it with numerous defensive deployments that took effect only at the snap of the ball.

Jim Brown had 1,163 yards rushing after the first 10 games, and Tim Brown of Philadelphia was second with 630. Ken Willard, Don Perkins, and Bill Brown had between 500 and 600 yards. Gale Sayers ranked tenth in the league with 441 rushing yards in just 114 attempts—compared to more than 140 for Perkins and Willard and 217 for Jim Brown. The top 10 receivers in the league were Dave Parks of the 49ers (54 receptions), Tommy McDonald of the Rams (46), Raymond Berry of the Colts (45), Pete Retzlaff of the Eagles (45), Tim Brown of the Eagles (41), Bernie Casey of the 49ers (41), Paul Flatley of the Vikings (40), and Bobby Mitchell of the Redskins (39). Jimmy Orr and Gary Collins, tied with 36 receptions, sported the highest per-catch averages, 20.22 and 19.22 yards, respectively. With 90 points from 15 touchdowns, Jim Brown led the league in scoring and was on pace to break Lenny Moore's new record of 20 touchdowns in a season. Sayers was second in touchdowns with 12, and Jimmy Orr was third with 10.

At age 32, Johnny Unitas was having one of his greatest seasons, leading the league with a 61.5 percent completion rate, 2,318 yards passing, 20 touchdowns, and an overall rating of 104.2. He trailed John Brodie in attempts and completions. Unitas had, however, thrown 10 interceptions, while Rudy Bukich had yielded only five, and Bart Starr eight. The top 10 passers in the league, ranked by rating, were Unitas, Bukich, Brodie, Fran Tarkenton, Norm Snead of the Eagles, Starr, Earl Morrall of the Giants, Frank Ryan, Charley Johnson, and Don Meredith, who had completed just 44.2 percent of his passes.

With a three-game lead over the Giants and Cardinals with only four games left to play, the Browns had just about wrapped up the Eastern Conference title. Green Bay, of course, trailed the Colts by only one game. The Bears, winners of six of their last seven games, could tie for the West lead only if the Colts lost three of their four remaining games and the Packers lost two of their remaining games. Chicago would play its last four games against the Giants, Colts, 49ers, and Vikings. Green Bay had the lowly Rams, the Vikings, Colts, and 49ers to deal with, while the Colts had to play the Lions, Bears, Packers, and Rams. And on December 26, if necessary, two of the Western Conference contenders might have to meet in a one-game playoff.

Week 11

Thanksgiving Day had for many years featured a game between the Detroit Lions and Green Bay Packers—a matchup that had become a critical one during the Lombardi era. After 1963, however, the Lions had agreed to host a different team every year, and this year the national television audience was treated to its second look at the red-hot Colts in three weeks. As always, on Thanksgiving, the Lions came to play. For the second time in three weeks, the NFL showed a national television audience how good Western Conference football was.

The Colts had suffered several injuries in their Sunday game with the Eagles, and Jimmy Orr, who had returned from the hospital to score the winning touchdown, did not start the game. The Colts moved smoothly down the Briggs Stadium field after the opening kickoff, and Unitas finished the drive with a touchdown pass to Alex Hawkins, who was subbing for Orr. The Colts got the ball back soon enough, but a Unitas pass toward tight end John Mackey was intercepted by Bruce Maher at midfield and returned to the Colt 28-yard line. A few plays later, Pat Studstill dove to catch a touchdown pass in the corner of the end zone to make it 7–7.

Raymond Berry, the Colts' split end, was an earlier, if larger version of the Oakland Raiders' Fred Biletnikoff—a player with only average speed, but who ran all his moves with extraordinary precision and almost never dropped a ball. Against the Lions, he had to work against cornerback Dick LeBeau. When the Colts began moving the ball down the field again, LeBeau intercepted a pass headed for Berry at the Lion 34-yard line. Berry finished the day with just one reception and Orr with two receptions, as the Lions held Unitas to just 14 completions in 34 attempts.

4. The Baltimore Boom

Dick LeBeau

He caught only one pass? That was a rare occasion! Raymond and Unitas were so damn good together—and Raymond was tall. He had a long reach and could get balls a lot of guys couldn't get to. You got to know the guys in those days, playing them twice a year. The bulk of my interceptions were against Starr and Unitas because of that—for every interception, they got three or four touchdowns. The Colts and the Packers had fantastic defenses, and we knew we wouldn't get too many points.

The Lions now unveiled a new weapon, the big running back Amos Marsh. Marsh had joined the Dallas Cowboys in 1961 and gained an extraordinary 802 yards for them in 1962. He had, however, fallen to about half that total in each of the next two years, and the fans and press had given him a very hard time. The Lions had acquired Marsh in 1964, and this was to be the best day of his NFL career. He finished off this drive with a line plunge, and Detroit led 14–7. The Lions were working the right side of the Colt defense, where both end Ordell Braase and linebacker Don Shinnick were missing with injuries.

With just a minute to go in the half, huge tight end Ron Kramer, formerly of Green Bay, flattened substitute end Roy Hilton as Marsh went off tackle on what looked like a routine play. Instead, Marsh accelerated smoothly through the hole and ran 62 yards for a touchdown without a Colt putting a hand on him. The Lions led 21-10 at the half, and Marsh would finish the day with 146 yards rushing.

Dick LeBeau

Amos Marsh was a big, fast back. He was from the Pacific Northwest. The Ford family owned the Lions, and once or twice, Bill Ford, our owner, let us go to Greenfield Village where Ford unveiled the new cars, and we could order one for the season and turn it in when the season was over. Amos got about $500 worth of parking tickets on his, drove it home to Oregon, and turned it into a dealer there. That was the last time we got those cars. That was the Amos Marsh run I remember best!

In the third quarter, the Lion defense showed the form that had completely stopped the Packers three weeks earlier, and the Colts made only two first downs. A Wayne Walker field goal stretched the Detroit lead to 24–10 as the fourth quarter began. Unitas always noticed the openings a defense gave him but sometimes waited to exploit them until late in the game. Now he suddenly began to move. One drive reached the four-yard line before Tom

Matte fumbled the ball away, but Unitas, whose wide receivers were still shut down by the Lions' cornerbacks, found his great tight end John Mackey for 51 yards and a touchdown in their next possession. A big punt return by Alvin Haymond got the Colts within reach again, and Unitas found Mackey in the end zone once more, this time from 15 yards out with just minutes to play to tie the game 24–24. There was still time for the two teams to exchange punts, and with 28 seconds left, Lion Pat Studstill made a fair catch on the Colt 42-yard line. That opened up a most unusual opportunity for the Lions.

NFL rules allowed a team to attempt a free-kick field goal from the line of scrimmage after a fair catch. Forty-two yards was a long but not impossible distance for Detroit kicker Wayne Walker, who had kicked 10 field goals of 40 yards or more in 23 attempts over the last three years. Detroit coach Harry Gilmer, however, elected to try to use the 28 seconds to try to get the Lions inside the 35, at least, and give Walker an even better chance. For some reason, however, Milt Plum failed to call time out, and after he had thrown one incomplete pass, there were only 11 seconds left. Walker had to try the field goal from the 50-yard line, under normal game conditions, and he missed. Three years later, NFL fans around the country learned about the free-kick rule when the Chicago Bears used it to beat the Packers 13–10 on the last play of a game in Chicago. Don Shula professed himself very happy to have come back from a 24–10 deficit despite the team's injuries, but his lead had shrunk to half a game. Now the team had 10 days to recover before first facing the Bears and then Packers the following week, at home in Baltimore.

On Sunday, November 28, the Browns clinched the Eastern Conference title with a 42–21 romp over the Steelers in Pittsburgh. Picking up where he had left off in Dallas, the fleet Leroy Kelly opened the scoring with a 56-yard touchdown punt return. Later, a fine block by Ernie Green got the Browns' sweep left off to a great start, and Jim Brown ran 67 yards before going down at the Pittsburgh 11-yard line.

Although Ernie Green inevitably played second fiddle to Jim Brown in the Cleveland backfield—and later to Leroy Kelly—he was just as important when they carried the ball as when he did himself. On sweeps, the team depended on his blocks on linebackers or defensive ends to allow the play to develop, and he executed them brilliantly.

Ernie Green

> I grew up as the youngest of seven kids. I could always do what I had to do in the hierarchy of my siblings. We all had responsibilities, and I accepted mine. I

4. The Baltimore Boom

played sandlot baseball on a dirt field. In high school, I played baseball and basketball. I learned early that we all had roles to play. Every person had to understand his role and responsibilities. You don't come off too excited about what you did because others are doing their jobs. I didn't have any issues about being the other guy; I had issues with the role that I had to play. I lived to do my job.

I spent a lot of time blocking, and I took pride in it. It was my contribution. We ran the sweep, one of our key plays. The whole offensive line was moving, and the key block was by me on the defensive end or linebacker. It gave me satisfaction when people talked about the Brown Sweep.

Frank Ryan had to leave the game with an injury, and he and his backup, Jim Ninowski, completed only six of 13 passes combined. Jim Brown rushed for 146 yards, caught two passes for 32 more, and scored four touchdowns to bring his season total to 19, just one shy of Lenny Moore's record with three more games to go. The Cardinals' woes continued as they lost to the Eagles in St. Louis 28-24, their third straight loss, eliminating them from contention. The injured Charley Johnson returned to the lineup but threw five interceptions, and the Eagle offense destroyed the Cardinal defense. Tim Brown rushed for 180 yards on 18 carries and caught three passes for an additional 38 yards, and Norm Snead threw three touchdown passes. The lead changed hands twice in the fourth period.

The Chicago Bears visited New York for the first time since losing the 1956 NFL championship there and cemented their status as the hottest team in the league. Dick Butkus and Gale Sayers took advantage of the opportunity to establish themselves as co-favorites for rookie of the year, as the Giants once again found themselves no match for a Western Conference team. Butkus intercepted his fifth pass of the season and recovered a fumble, both leading to Bear scores, while Sayers scored from 45 and 15 yards out and had a long touchdown pass on a halfback option called back because of a holding penalty. The two touchdowns left him four behind Jimmy Brown with 14 but established a new record for an NFL rookie. Bukich completed 15 of 24 passes for 200 yards, five to Mike Ditka, while Sayers rushed for 113 yards overall. Leading 28–7 in the fourth quarter, George Halas began putting substitutes into the lineup to rest men for the game the following week against the Colts, and the score finished at 35–14. With three games to play, the Bears now found themselves two and one-half games behind the Colts and two behind the Packers. Only a series of miracles could get them into a playoff game—but one such miracle occurred later in the afternoon.

The unstoppable San Francisco 49ers turned in their best game of the season in Bloomington, Minnesota, where the Vikings suffered their third consecutive humiliation at home following their crushing defeats to the

Colts and Packers. This time they could not even put together a good half of football, and the 49ers got off to their customary flying start and never looked back. On a bitterly cold day, John Brodie completed just 10 of 19 passes, but half—five—went for touchdowns. He was not sacked once, and Crow and Willard rushed effectively, as usual. Having blown a 35–21 lead against the Vikings in San Francisco several weeks earlier, the 49ers this time roared out to a 35–10 lead but held on comfortably for a 45–24 final. Brodie, who had never thrown five touchdown passes in a game in his life, told the press that the 49ers would have had at least two more wins and an 8–3 record but for injuries to their linebackers. They still had games with the Bears and Packers remaining.

Things seemed to be going the Green Bay Packers' way as they took the field against the last-place Rams in Los Angeles late on Sunday. After four weeks of dreadful offensive performances against the Cowboys, Bears, Lions, and Rams—weeks from which they had been fortunate to escape with two wins—they had put 38 points on the board the previous week against the Vikings. After a first half of injuries that had forced Lombardi to reshuffle his offensive line, he now had his regular lineup of Bob Skoronski, Fuzzy Thurston, Ken Bowman, Jerry Kramer, and Forrest Gregg in place, with his old favorites Taylor and Hornung in the backfield. A victory against the Rams would keep the Pack's fate in their own hands since they were scheduled to play the Colts in Baltimore two weeks hence. And the game could hardly have begun better. After the Rams took the kickoff, Henry Jordan and Ray Nitschke recovered a fumble on the Ram 16-yard line, and Jim Taylor reached the seven-yard line on the first play from scrimmage. But Taylor and Hornung were stopped for no gain, and Lombardi had to settle for three points. It was an omen of things to come.

Roman Gabriel, who was in his fourth year in the league, had just taken over the starter's job from the injured Bill Munson. Along with rookie wide receiver Jack Snow and tight end Billy Truax, he was one of the future stars of the George Allen-coached Rams, who, beginning in 1967, would remain a league power for four years. Gabriel began well, hitting on four passes during a 10-minute drive that culminated in a touchdown and a 7–3 lead. But the real story was the Ram defense, led by their magnificent front four of Deacon Jones, Merlin Olsen, Rosey Grier, and Lamar Lundy. Starr repeatedly failed to get more than one first down at a time, and in the second quarter, Gabriel completed passes to Jack Snow and Les Josephson, moving from his own 20-yard line to the Packer 18, where Bruce Gossett made the score 10–3. Starr went into an effective two-minute drill but could not get beyond the Ram 38-yard line, and Don Chandler missed from 45

4. The Baltimore Boom

yards out. There were just 15 seconds left, but the Rams gained 38 yards on a single play, and Gossett hit one of the longest field goals of the year, from 49 yards out, for a 13–3 halftime lead.

The Packers got nowhere during the third quarter, and the Rams seemed as if they were about to put the game away early in the fourth when Willie Wood intercepted a pass on his own five-yard line. For the second time this season, Zeke Bratkowski had come into the game, not because Bart Starr was hurt, but because he had failed to move the club. A long Bratkowski pass was immediately intercepted, and the Rams moved close enough for Gossett to hit another long field goal for a 16–3 lead. After the kickoff, Bratkowski was sacked in the end zone for a safety. Gossett then missed yet another field goal, and Bratkowski threw an 80-yard TD pass to Elijah Pitts, who had replaced Hornung, to make the score 18–10. Gabriel promptly moved the Rams down the field again, and Gossett made the score 21–10 from 40 yards out. The Rams outgained the Packers by 344 yards to 254, and the Pack gained just 22 yards rushing. Lombardi was straightforward and gracious in the dressing room, paying tribute to Roman Gabriel and acknowledging that the Rams were much better than their record showed. But, with another second-place finish staring him in the face as the Colts increased their lead to a game and a half, he was beside himself.

In Washington, the 4–6 Cowboys played an extraordinary game with the 4–6 Redskins, the first of five consecutive thrillers that those two rivals put on in three years. When the game was over, Washington had won five of its last six games and was tied for second in the Eastern Conference.

By early in the second quarter, the Cowboys led 21–0 without having generated any offense at all. Jurgensen had fumbled around midfield in the first quarter, and tackle Bob Lilly had returned the ball to the Redskins' six-yard line before halfback Charley Taylor tackled him. Meredith promptly threw a touchdown pass. Taylor fumbled less than a minute later deep in Redskin territory, and cornerback Cornell Green ran the ball in. Then, in the second quarter, Cowboy Mike Gaechter blocked a field goal attempt at the Cowboy 35-yard line, grabbed the ball, and ran 60 yards for the third Dallas touchdown. The Redskins finally got a drive going, and Jurgensen kept it going on fourth and one with a short pass to rookie tight end Jerry Smith. Then Taylor beat double coverage coming out of the backfield and grabbed a 26-yard touchdown pass. The extra point was blocked. Early in the third quarter, another Redskin fumble led to a Cowboy field goal and a 24–6 lead.

Jurgensen finally got the Redskins moving again, pulling up to 24–13 with a long drive that ended with a touchdown pass to their new split end,

NFL 1965

Angelo Coia, whom they had acquired from the Bears. Early in the fourth quarter, more completions to Smith and Taylor—who was converted to a wide receiver in 1966—keyed another long drive for a third touchdown. But Jurgensen threw his only interception around midfield, and Meredith hit his big tight end, Frank Clarke, for a 53-yard score that restored the Cowboys' lead to 11 points, 31–20.

Getting the ball back with just a few minutes left, Jurgensen passed the Redskins down the field again and hit the great Bobby Mitchell in the end zone to draw within four points, 31–27, with 3:28 left to play. The Cowboys managed to move within range of a long field goal, but Danny Villanueva missed from 45 yards, and the Redskins ran the ball back to their own 20-yard line with 1:40 left. Jurgensen immediately fumbled but then picked up the ball and ran for nine yards. An interference call against Jerry Smith earned another nine yards, and Jurgensen passed to Smith—soon to emerge as one of the greatest ever receivers at tight end—for 22 yards to the Cowboy 40-yard line. Then Mitchell got half a step on Cornell Green, and Jurgensen led him with a low pass that Green could not reach at the Cowboy five-yard line. On the next play, Coia caught the ball in the end zone on a post pattern, and the Redskins led 34–31 with 1:12 left.

The drama was not over. Bob Hayes declined to return the kickoff from the end zone, and the defense stopped Meredith and the Cowboys on their first two plays. But Meredith then hit Pete Gent for a first down. Three plays later, Meredith hit Bob Hayes on a short pass, and the Olympian ran 35 yards to the Redskin 37-yard line before safetyman Paul Krause tackled him with seven seconds left. Danny Villanueva came in to try a tying field goal, but Lonnie Sanders managed to block it. Jurgensen finished with 26 completions in 43 attempts, good for 364 yards and three touchdowns.

While only the Cowboys were on the verge of greatness, this game marked the beginning of an exciting but frustrating era for the Redskins. Jurgensen, Mitchell, Smith, and Taylor now gave the team one of the greatest passing attacks in the history of the NFL, and they kept things very interesting for the next two years after Otto Graham had taken over as coach. Sadly, however, their defense—which had ranked seventh in the league in points allowed in 1964 and sixth in the league in 1965—fell to thirteenth in 1966 and eleventh in 1967, and the team never got above .500. Pass defense remained the Cowboys' weakness in this era, and every game between the two clubs became a duel between Jurgensen and Meredith. In their first game in 1966, in mid–November, it was Meredith who led the Cowboys down the field in a last-minute drive to win 31–30 in Washington. One month later, in the Cotton Bowl, Sonny turned the tables, leading

4. The Baltimore Boom

the Redskins to 10 points in the last few minutes and a 34–31 victory on a last-second field goal. The Cowboys appeared to be beaten 14–10 with less than a minute left on October 8, 1967, but Meredith threw a 36-yard touchdown pass to halfback Dan Reeves to win the game. In the rematch in the Cotton Bowl six weeks later, Jurgensen threw for four touchdowns, and the Redskins earned a 27–6 lead in the fourth quarter and hung on to win 27–20.

Both the NFL and the AFL held their drafts over this weekend. The class of 1966 turned out, in the long run, to be much less impressive than that of 1965, although the Packers landed fullback Jim Grabowski to go with Donny Anderson, whom they had drafted a year early, and the Rams got offensive lineman Tom Mack and defensive lineman Diron Talbert, who had fine careers ahead of them. The bidding war between the two leagues began at once, with 28 picks signed immediately by NFL teams. The top pick in the league went to the new Atlanta Falcons, who chose Tommy Nobis, the highly touted middle linebacker from Oklahoma. No one knew that the two leagues were drafting separately for the last time.

Week 12

Any remaining drama had now gone out of the Eastern Conference race, even though the Giants, Redskins, Cowboys, and Cardinals were still fighting for second place and a berth in the Playoff Bowl in Miami. Yet the teams were still taking their games seriously. Boosted by their five wins in six games, the Redskins traveled to Cleveland and nearly upset the Browns.

In another game dominated by turnovers, the Redskins opened the scoring in the first period after recovering a fumble on the Cleveland 15-yard line, but Cleveland blocked the extra point try. Cleveland promptly put a long drive together—Jim Brown gained 141 yards on the day—and it finished with Ryan throwing yet another touchdown pass to Gary Collins in the end zone for a 7–6 lead. The Redskins promptly retaliated with a long drive of their own, finishing with a Jurgensen touchdown pass, and late in the half, a Sam Huff interception set up a field goal for a 16–7 lead at the half. Cleveland added a field goal for the only tally of the third quarter and trailed by six points.

On the first play of the fourth quarter, Vince Costello intercepted a Jurgensen pass deep in Washington territory, and Ryan quickly threw a 14-yard touchdown pass to reserve end Tom Hutchinson for a 17–16 lead. Neither team could move the ball effectively for the rest of the quarter, and with 3:30 to go, end Bill Glass forced Jurgensen to fumble while trying to pass, and Jim Houston recovered the ball. Jim Brown promptly scored his 20th touchdown of the season, tying Lenny Moore's record with two games to go. The game was safe with an eight-point lead and 1:41 to go, but Jurgensen got the Redskins within striking distance again with a long pass to Bobby Mitchell. Another interception killed that drive. Jurgensen outdueled Ryan, 155 yards passing to 124, but the Browns rushed for 200 yards compared to 63 for the Redskins. Not until 1969, under Vince Lombardi, would the Redskins develop an effective running game.

In the first of two battles of also-rans, the Giants played their best game of the season and unpacked the Pittsburgh Steelers 35–10 in Yankee Stadium, running their record to 6–6 and earning them second place in the conference. The Steelers made only 13 first downs and surrendered the ball six times on turnovers, while Tucker Frederickson scored three touchdowns in quick succession during the second quarter. In Dallas, the surging Philadelphia Eagles scored on their first play from scrimmage, a 65-yard halfback option pass thrown by Earl Gros, but never managed to get the ball into the Dallas end zone again. Don Meredith ran for a touchdown and threw two passes for others, and the Eagles drove down the field looking for a win in the last few minutes, trailing 21–19. A pass interception near the Dallas goal line saved the game for the Cowboys, who improved to 5–7, one game behind the Giants. The struggling St. Louis Cardinals, meanwhile, found themselves entertaining the Rams fresh from their conquest of the Packers. Finally matched against the Eastern Conference in the season's twelfth week, the Rams destroyed the once-fancied Cardinals 27–3 for their third victory of the year. Charley Johnson was helpless against the Fearsome Foursome, and in the second quarter, faced with a chance to close the score to 14–10, he fumbled when Lamar Lundy hit him and had to watch Merlin Olsen return the ball 59 yards. Soon the score was 17–3 on a Gossett field goal. Roman Gabriel had another fine day, and the Rams even scored a touchdown on a fake field goal. The Rams now had Cleveland and Baltimore—the two conference leaders—to play at home in the last two weeks of the season.

The Green Bay Packers had endured a major crisis on Tuesday, November 30, after returning from their Los Angeles loss. The trouble had begun on the plane back from Los Angeles when Lionel Aldridge—following in the footsteps of Yankee infielder Phil Linz, who had enraged his manager, Yogi Berra, by playing the harmonica after a loss in the summer of 1964—broke into song. Having seen his team fall to a game and a half behind the Colts with three left with another dreadful offensive performance, Vince Lombardi

4. The Baltimore Boom

was beside himself and determined to whip his team into shape. On Tuesday, he had begun by questioning Aldridge's ancestry, as reserve center Bill Curry later recalled, and then dismissing the assistant coaches from the team meeting. "Goddammit," he shrieked, "you guys don't care if we win or lose. I'm the only one that cares. I'm the only one that puts his blood and his guts and his heart into the game. You're nothing! I'm the only guy who cares if we win or lose."

Curry heard a stirring near the back of the room and turned around. The All-Pro tackle (and sometime reserve guard) Forrest Gregg was on his feet, red in the face, with two other players holding him by the arms to keep him from assaulting the most famous coach in the NFL. "'Scuse me, Coach," he said furiously, "but it makes me sick to hear you say something like that. We lay it on the line for you every Sunday. We live and die the same way you do, and it hurts." Before Gregg could break loose and reach Lombardi, his fellow tackle and offensive captain, Bob Skoronski, joined in. "That's right," he said. "Dammit, don't you tell us that we don't care about winning. That makes me sick. Makes me want to puke. It's our knees and our bodies out there that we're throwing around."

Lombardi paused for a moment and then characteristically managed to turn the situation around. "Now *that's* the kind of attitude I want to see!" he yelled. "Who else feels that way?" And one by one, the Packers all said that they did.[7]

The problem, of course, was not the Packers' lack of dedication, but their aging offense, for whom Lombardi had failed to design game plans that would enable them to score more than one touchdown on five of the last six Sundays. Now they had to beat the Vikings for the second time in three weeks to give them a chance of overtaking the Colts in Baltimore. This, with some key help from the officials in front of the hysterical Green Bay crowd, they managed to do.

The day began poorly for the Packers during the warm-up when Bart Starr was taking snaps from reserve rookie center Bill Curry while he warmed up his passing arm.

Bill Curry

As I was about to snap the ball to Bart, the ball boy rolled another ball over to me, and it hit the one I was about to snap. I hesitated a split second, then snapped it anyway. Bart was already pulling his hands back, and the ball hit him on the end of the middle finger of his right hand. He cried out in pain, and it immediately swelled up. It looked like a long week for me. When something went wrong on Sunday with the Packers, I could never sleep Sunday or Monday night, worrying about what Lombardi would say in the films.

The Vikings received the kickoff, but star halfback Tommy Mason was hit hard by linebacker Dave Robinson and Curry at the Viking 27-yard line, and the Packers recovered his fumble. Starr immediately passed to Dowler for a touchdown.

Packer luck continued. Lance Rentzel, who had fumbled one kickoff and returned another for a touchdown against the Colts a few weeks earlier, fumbled this one. The Packers quickly moved inside the five-yard line, but the Vikings stiffened, and when Lombardi ordered them to try for a touchdown on fourth and one, Starr and Tom Moore botched the handoff, and the Vikings recovered the ball. That was the end of Starr's game.

Bill Curry

I thought I had redeemed myself forcing the fumble, but after that fumble, Starr ran right to Lombardi. "I'm out. I can't go," he said. "Get Zeke ready."

Bratkowski played the rest of the game. The teams exchanged punts, but then fine running by Tommy Mason took the Vikings down the field 80 yards for a tying touchdown, and Fred Cox soon put them ahead 10–7. Two critical interceptions of Bartkowski's passes led to two more Viking field goals and a 16–7 lead, and with 39 seconds left in the half, Cox tried yet another one from 59 yards out. The kick was short, and Willie Wood grabbed it at the Packer 21-yard line and returned it 71 yards. The Packers were now playing a new receiver corps, including Bob Long at flanker and Bill Anderson at tight end, and Long was interfered with at the three-yard line. Elijah Pitts brought the score to 16–14 with just a few seconds left.

Another Cox field goal opened the scoring in the third quarter, but the Packers got a fine kickoff return from Moore and Bratkowski put together their best drive of the day for a 21–19 lead. They stretched it to 24–19 with the help of a long option pass from halfback Elijah Pitts to Anderson. The Packers had held the Viking offense through the third quarter, but Tarkenton now took the club down the field on a long drive. He appeared to have put the team back in the lead with a touchdown pass to Tom Hall, but the officials called pass interference on Hall against Herb Adderley. Highlight film shows Adderley and Hall running stride for stride as the pass arrives, with no sign of contact. If interference had occurred earlier, it hadn't kept Adderley out of position.

4. The Baltimore Boom

Then, on the Vikings' last play, Tarkenton scrambled, pirouetted away from Willie Davis when he appeared completely trapped on the sideline and connected with Red Phillips, who had run a turnout in the end zone. Coming back for the ball, Phillips appeared to catch it as he dove to the ground right at the front corner of the end zone. Another Viking trailing the play threw his arms up in the touchdown sign in jubilation, but one of the officials behind him apparently ruled that Phillip's leg was touching the sideline as he caught the ball. Only replays from multiple angles could have resolved this one for sure. The Vikings were so incensed that they eventually drew a 15-yard penalty for unsportsmanlike conduct as the game came to an end.

Bill Curry

> Van Brocklin was furious. I was walking behind him on the way into the dressing rooms, and a fan started mouthing off at him from the stands. He was so angry he started into the stands after him. I grabbed him and said, "Come on, Coach, let's go on in." "OK, kid," he said, and we did.

"We were overrunning everything in the first half," Lombardi told the press after the game. "It was the highest I've seen my team in a long time—two or three years." The Packers had not managed a dominating performance. The Vikings had outgained them 336 yards to 266, but they had thrown three interceptions and lost two fumbles, while Green Bay had only one very costly fumble, though Bratkowski had thrown three interceptions. In this extraordinary year, the Packers had outgained their opponents in total yards only four times in twelve games, but they would finish the season with 50 combined interceptions and fumble recoveries, compared to just 26 for their opponents. Their fate was back in their hands as they prepared to face the Colts.

The Chicago Bears had arrived in Baltimore with only the slimmest chances of making it into the NFL Championship—but with a corresponding determination to prove how good they really were. "The Bears, over the years in which I've been playing," said John Unitas in a pregame interview, "have been one of the toughest teams on us physically. In 1960, I recall that we beat them in the last few seconds of the ball game, but in so doing, we lost about four key players. They do beat you up pretty badly physically."[8]

CBS, not surprisingly, chose the contest as the nationally televised doubleheader game. George Allen, their defensive coach, had devised a plan to contain the Colts, and from the opening whistle, it worked to perfection. Meanwhile, the depleted Colt defense, which had failed to stop Amos Marsh on Thanksgiving, had just as much trouble with Gale Sayers. The Bears moved 69 yards down the field in their first possession, reaching the Colt 14-yard line. A trap play opened a huge hole through the middle for Sayers, but a collision on the goal line with his teammate Ronnie Bull jarred the ball loose, and the Colts recovered in the end zone. The Colts could not move the ball, however, and had to punt. On second down from the Bears' 39-yard line, Rudy Bukich pitched out to Sayers, going right behind two pulling guards. Cornerback Bobby Boyd came up fast, and Sayers feinted to his right, then cut left and left Boyd sprawled on the ground as he turned up the sideline. A great downfield block by one of the guards on end Lou Michaels, pursuing, sprung him through a sideline crowd, and Sayers outran the rest of the Colt secondary for a 7–0 lead.

Upton Bell

> I was on the sidelines, and Alex Hawkins came off the field after the touchdown. "He went like the wind," he said.

On their next possession, the Bears moved the ball very well behind Bukich's passing to Dick Gordon and Mike Ditka, but Roger LeClerc missed a field goal. Dick Butkus, who had another outstanding game, forced Lenny Moore to fumble on the next series. Fine completions over the middle to Ditka and Johnny Morris got the Bears down to the Colt 20-yard line. On fourth and one, Sayers was stopped off left tackle around the Colt 10-yard line, and the Colts took over. Butkus promptly stripped the ball out of fullback Tony Lorick's hands for a first down on the Colt 10-yard line. On third and goal, Bukich went back to pass, was smothered, and coughed up the ball himself. The Colts recovered.

Then, in the second quarter came the biggest play of the season.

The customs and officials of the NFL in 1965 did not protect quarterbacks, and the Bears clearly used assaults on enemy signal callers as part of their strategy. In the 1963 NFL title game, linebacker Larry Morris had sent Y.A. Tittle to the sidelines limping on an injured knee with a low hit late in the first half, and although Tittle returned for the second half, he was ineffective. Earlier this year, the Bears had sent both Bart Starr and Johnny Unitas to the sidelines. In the second quarter in Baltimore, Unitas, who had completed only three of eight passes, faded back on third down. He had already gotten the pass off deep toward John Mackey when big Earl Leggett,

4. The Baltimore Boom

already approaching on the run, hit him high. Tackle Stan Jones was on the ground against Unitas's leg, which had no room to move. He had to limp off the field. Double coverage on Mackey had broken up the pass. The hit had torn ligaments in Unitas's right knee, and he underwent surgery and put on a cast that night. Johnny Unitas's 1965 season—so far, one of his greatest—was over. Gary Cuozzo had to come in.

Cuozzo started brilliantly in his first series with a great scramble, a quick-opener to Lenny Moore, and an excellent pass to Jimmy Orr to the Bear 26-yard line. Unfortunately, he fumbled the snap on the next play and the Bears recovered for the third turnover of the half. The Baltimore crowd, by reputation the league's noisiest, was silenced, and two fights broke out before the end of the half. Near the end of the half, Cuozzo threw an interception to Richie Pettibon at the Colt 32-yard line, and Sayers promptly went 17 yards on a sweep. Roger LeClerc kicked a field goal, and the Bears led 10–0 at the half. Alex Hawkins and Bivins got into a fistfight on the ensuing kickoff, and both were ejected.

Cuozzo had proven against the Vikings that he could, on his day, lead the Colts as well as Unitas, but this day belonged to the Bears. They eventually won the game 13–0 after one more field goal, but they could easily have won by much more. Bukich completed 14 of 24 passes, and the Bears outgained the Colts 418 yards to 222. LeClerc missed two other makeable field goals, and another drive was halted on downs on the Colt seven-yard line. Meanwhile, Cuozzo completed just 12 passes in 30 attempts and was sacked four times for 33 yards worth of losses. In the fourth quarter, Cuozzo seemed for a moment to have gotten the Colts back in the game with a 48-yard touchdown pass to Jimmy Orr, but a tripping penalty nullified the play. "This has to rank among the great Bear victories," said George Halas, "because we defeated a truly great Baltimore team." George Allen explained that Butkus had shifted to the Colt strong side to try to keep receivers from getting downfield, and both Bear safeties had been detailed, in effect, to watch John Mackey, who had single-handedly tied the Lions on Thanksgiving.

Don Shula pronounced the game the worst his offense had played all year—an easy call—but praised the defense, which had played without veteran linebacker Don Shinnick or Ordell Braase, their right end and probably their best defensive lineman. "We have 100 percent confidence in Gary Cuozzo as Unitas's replacement," Shula said. "He filled the bill in the second half of the first Bear game, and look what he did going all the way against the Vikings. He's not a rookie. I definitely think he can do the job, and so does everyone else on the team." Cuozzo also welcomed the challenge. "I haven't made up my mind. In fact, I haven't started to think about a backup quarterback," Shula continued. "We have Tom Matte who can go in, and a band [taxi] squad member, Haffner, we could activate. But I will have to look around. Haffner has never played." Neither Shula nor the Colt beat writer, apparently, could remember Haffner's first name.

Late that afternoon in San Francisco, two strong but inconsistent teams, the 49ers and the Lions, played a tight, hotly contested, seesaw game that gave no hint that both teams were entirely out of the race. Detroit got off to a strong start, scoring twice to lead 14–3 at the half, and the third period was scoreless. After Kermit Alexander intercepted a Milt Plum pass in 49er territory in the fourth period, John Brodie caught fire. He hit Bernie Casey for 20 yards and then connected with Dave Parks, the league's leading receiver, for a 34-yard touchdown pass. It took two possessions for San Francisco to get going again. Helped by an offside penalty, they got within the five-yard line, and Ken Willard took it from there to make it 17–14. With their second close victory over the Lions this season, the 49ers improved their record to 7–5 with two games to go—against the Chicago Bears, now generally recognized as the strongest team in football, and at home to the Packers in the season finale, a game that could clearly be decisive in the chase for the Western Conference title.

5

The Climax

Standings

Eastern Conference	W	L	T	PCT	PF	PA
Cleveland	10	2	0	.833	329	259
New York	6	6	0	.500	223	290
St. Louis	5	7	0	.417	259	255
Washington	5	7	0	.417	212	260
Dallas	5	7	0	.471	260	247
Philadelphia	4	8	0	.333	288	311
Pittsburgh	2	10	0	.167	175	315

Western Conference	W	L	T	PCT	PF	PA
Baltimore	9	2	1	.818	342	225
Green Bay	9	3	0	.750	250	173
Chicago	8	4	0	.667	331	231
San Francisco	7	5	0	.583	377	317
Detroit	5	6	1	.455	215	238
Minnesota	5	7	0	.417	330	379
Los Angeles	3	9	0	.250	210	304

The season-ending injury to Johnny Unitas, the reigning NFL MVP who had ligaments repaired and cartilage removed from his right knee on Sunday night, led the nation's sports pages on Monday and Tuesday. Interviewed on Monday, both Unitas and Coach Don Shula insisted that the team could beat Green Bay with Cuozzo at quarterback. Tom Matte, who had played quarterback for Woody Hayes at Ohio State, was announced as Cuozzo's backup. With Unitas gone, the Colts had the option of adding a new player to their roster, but this week was the last week they could sign such a player and have him eligible for postseason play. As it turned out, they activated veteran linebacker Don Shinnick, who had been injured for several weeks, instead of looking for a new quarterback.

The Western Conference race now had three possible outcomes. If the Colts could beat Green Bay on Sunday, December 12, they would repeat as champions, 1½ games ahead of the Packers and at least two games ahead of the Bears with just one game to play. They could also win by tying the

Packers in Baltimore and beating the Rams in Los Angeles, finishing at 10–2–2 while the Packers went (at best) 10–3–1. If they lost the game in Baltimore, they could regain the lead in the final week if they beat the Rams and Green Bay lost to the 49ers. If the Packers beat the Colts and the 49ers, they would win by at least half a game over the Colts and two games over the Bears. They could conceivably tie the Colts, forcing a playoff on December 26, if they beat the Colts in Baltimore but tied the 49ers while the Colts beat the Rams. The Bears had only one hope. If they could beat the 49ers and then the Vikings, they would finish at 10–4, potentially overtaking the Colts if they lost both their last two games and tying the Packers if they lost to the 49ers. That would force a playoff between Chicago and Green Bay. On Monday, coin flips in Pete Rozelle's New York office awarded the home field advantage to the Packers for a playoff with either the Colts or the Bears.

The Packers also had a quarterback problem—the injury to Bart Starr's finger sustained when reserve rookie center Bill Curry was snapping the ball to him before the Viking game. It had kept him out of most of that game, but he was hopeful that he could recover. Lombardi now decided to take an extraordinary step to help the team prepare. All the Green Bay fields were frozen solid, and late Monday afternoon, he flew the whole team to the Washington, D.C., area. They spent the week in Gaithersburg, Maryland, on an old Redskins practice field, getting ready to face the Colts in Baltimore. Without any distractions, the offense and defense met from 9:30 to 11:30 every morning, practiced on the field at 11:30, and watched films of Colts games in the afternoon and evening. On Friday, the team moved to Baltimore.

The nation's attention now turned to Gary Cuozzo, a rather unusual athlete. A Phi Beta Kappa graduate of the University of Virginia, Cuozzo came from a family of New Jersey dentists and was in the midst of dental studies himself in the off-season at the University of Tennessee. The Colts had signed him in 1963 after no one had taken him in the draft. He had played late in many games but had started only once, the Vikings game three weeks earlier in which he had thrown a team-record five touchdown passes. "I have learned a lot from Don Shula, Unitas, and Raymond Berry," he said. "This week," he told the AP, "I have to learn everything because so much is at stake."

Going into what looked like the decisive game of the season, the two teams' performance had diverged more than in 1964. The Colts had scored 342 points, second in the league behind the amazing 49ers (377), while the Packers ranked ninth in the league with just 250 points. The Packers were

5. The Climax

first in defense and the Colts second—but the Packers had allowed only 137 points and the Colts 225. The Packer defense, of course, was also responsible for a great many of the points the team had scored, and they led the league with 42 takeaways, evenly split between fumble recoveries and interceptions. Thus, the Packers, ninth in the league in points scored, ranked just eleventh in the 14-team league in yards gained. The Colts had lost nine fumbles and given up 19 interceptions (all thrown by Unitas), while the Packers had lost the ball 10 times on fumbles and eight on interceptions. The Bears point differential now narrowly trailed the Colts and Packers, with 331 points scored and 231 allowed.

The Packers had their whole starting lineup ready to go, with Taylor and a refreshed Hornung in the backfield, Boyd Dowler at split end, Carroll Dale at flanker, and Bill Anderson now the starting tight end. With the single, massive exception of John Unitas, the Colts did as well. Lenny Moore and Jerry Hill would be the running backs behind Cuozzo, with the great John Mackey at tight end, Raymond Berry at split end, and Jimmy Orr, in the midst of a remarkable year, at flanker. Ordell Braase had returned on defense, but although Don Shinnick had been activated, he had only just removed a cast on his broken arm. Tom Matte was now officially the backup quarterback, and the team was even experimenting with some running plays for him. In the midst of the Colts preparation, baseball took over page one of the Baltimore sports sections when the team announced that it had acquired slugging outfielder Frank Robinson from the Cincinnati Reds in exchange for pitcher Milt Pappas and two reserve players. It turned out to be one of the most fateful trades in baseball history.

The nation tuned in to the game of the year at 2:00 Eastern Time, but the viewers found their screens shrouded by a thick fog that lasted the whole game. The game got off to a very nervous start. The Packers received the kickoff, and Bart Starr's second pass was intercepted by the Colts' quick cornerback Leonard Lyles and run back to the Packer 11-yard line. Cuozzo, however, couldn't move the team very far, and Lou Michaels opened the scoring with a field goal.

A new Packer team took the kickoff and set off down the field, with Taylor and Hornung rediscovering their 1961 form. Both ran well and caught passes on a six-play, 80-yard drive. On the next to last play, Taylor took a pass on the right from a rapidly retreating Bart Starr and broke four different tackles on the way to the two-yard line. Hornung went in from there for a 7–3 lead. After the Colts stalled and kicker Tom Gilburg got off an 18-yard punt, Starr, on third and two, faked to Taylor, who put a tremendous block on Shinnick blitzing, and found Hornung in the clear with a pass on the left side. The Colt coverage had broken down, and Hornung caught the ball spinning and raced 50 yards untouched for his second touchdown. Early in the second period, the Colts got on the board again with a remarkable 46-yard field goal by Lou Michaels and found themselves right back in the game after Elijah Pitts fumbled the kickoff and Lyles recovered on the Packer 22-yard line. A nice pass to Raymond Berry over the middle and three fine running plays got the Colts into the end zone, with Lenny Moore carrying the ball in from the three-yard line to make the score 14–13, Green Bay.

Now came the decisive minutes of the 1965 season. Late in the half, Cuozzo marched the Colts from his own 29-yard line to the Green Bay 42. On third down, he found Ray Berry open on the 18-yard line—but the great receiver dropped the ball. Michaels had to try for the lead again from 49 yards and could not make it. On the first play from scrimmage, Jim Taylor fumbled after a good gain, and cornerback Bobby Boyd grabbed the ball on the Packer 18-yard line and ran it back to the four-yard line. Today it was the Packers, not the Colts, who had surrendered the ball twice deep in their own territory, and with only a minute left, Baltimore seemed certain to go into the locker room with a 20–14 lead, ready to receive the second-half kickoff.

On first down, Jerry Hill got the ball to the Packer two-yard line. Then Cuozzo, going for the score, called a play-action pass to Hill in the right flat. He expected the Packers to be in a goal-line 6–1 defense, with outside linebackers Leroy Caffey on his left and Dave Robinson on his right blitzing—or, at the very least, stepping toward the middle in response to his fake to Lenny Moore, who had already scored once. After appearing to glance toward Mackey, who was not yet in the secondary, Cuozzo looked further rightward toward Hill, who was moving into the right flat.

Dave Robinson

> John Mackey was lined up opposite me. Every time he was, I had to hit him at the line of scrimmage to slow him down. Otherwise, he would beat our safety, Tom Brown. Mackey was a friend of mine—we had played each other in college when I was at Penn State and he was at Syracuse. He would say to me, "Let me off the ball one time clean!" He told me later that Cuozzo didn't realize I was a cover linebacker on that play. I was watching Jerry Hill.

Mackey had driven Robinson back a step. Tackle Ron Kostelnik had slipped around a trap block by Jim Parker and was nearly on top of Cuozzo,

5. The Climax

who probably could not even see Robinson as he lofted the ball toward a wide-open Hill. That gave Robinson time to get into the ball's path with several giant strides after stepping around Mackey. A great athlete who had played offensive and defensive end in college, Robinson leaped several feet into the air, came down with Cuozzo's lofted pass between his outstretched hands, and broke upfield. Escorted by several Packers, he looked on his way to a touchdown, but Cuozzo managed to make him change direction, and Lenny Moore—who had begun the play faking into the line—caught the much bigger Robinson at the Colt 10-yard line. Starr promptly hit Dowler in the back of the end zone, and the Packers went into the locker room ahead 21–13, not down 20–14.

Worse was to come for the Colts. On the first series after the second-half kickoff, Cuozzo went back to pass, set up, and was grabbed around the chest by Willie Davis, who slammed him onto the ground so hard that he dislocated his left shoulder. The unthinkable had happened—Unitas's talented backup had not made it through a single game. The injury happened on third down, and Gilburg got off another short punt that left the Packers on the Colt 38-yard line. Five plays later, Hornung scored on the fabled Packer sweep around left end, and Green Bay led 28–13.

Tom Matte, who had hardly had time to speak to his teammates, now came into the game for his first-ever stint as a pro quarterback.

Tom Matte

> I had moved from halfback to quarterback my last two years at Ohio State for Woody Hayes. I had small hands, and when he asked me to do it, I was afraid of fumbling. I was a running back playing quarterback there.

In his senior year, Matte rushed for 682 yards in 161 attempts, second on the team, and completed 50 of 95 passes as Ohio State finished 7–2. He finished seventh in the Heisman Trophy voting, and the Colts made him their first pick in the 1961 draft.

Tom Matte

> I couldn't figure out what the hell the Colts were going to do with me—they had Unitas! It turned out they wanted me as a sixth defensive back as well as a running back since we all played defense in college too. Eventually, I became a pass receiver out of the backfield. Unitas had a lot of confidence in me to read the

defenses, to read them the same way he did. I would line up, look at the linebackers, and figure out where to go to be open. Unitas would figure it out the same way, and when I turned around, there was the ball.

In 1965, they had started working me out at quarterback a little even before Unitas's injury, just taking snaps, handing the ball off, throwing a few passes.

The Colts were known for their relaxed atmosphere and sense of humor, and it served them well in this absurdly catastrophic situation. Matte ran on to the field undaunted, determined, as he explained six years later to then-teammate George Plimpton, to shock the Packers by starting with a pass. He immediately looked at flanker Jimmy Orr—his roommate—and asked, "Jimmy, whatcha have over there?"—how quarterbacks asked receivers how they might best get open. "Well," replied Orr, "I'm on the wide side of the field, and I doubt you could throw the ball that far. So, the answer is, I don't have anything for you." Raymond Berry answered similarly and suggested that Matte call a running play, the Ride 38. "That play's on the other side of the field from you!" Matte replied. "You don't have to do anything—you don't even have to block." "I don't feel like blocking right now," Berry replied.[1] "We can't punt yet, Tom," lineman Dan Sullivan told Matte after he ran his first running play.

Properly chastened, Matte moved the team to the Packer 44-yard line on the ground, including a run he began to his right before completely reversing his field. Then he tried a pass, and it bounced off receiver Jerry Hill's hands and into those of Packer safety Tom Brown, who returned it to midfield. The Packers moved quickly to a fifth score, with Hornung doing the damage again from three yards out and led 35–13 as the third period ended.

With his left shoulder full of Novocaine, Cuozzo came back onto the field after the kickoff and led his team to a touchdown. Key to the first drive was a pass interference call on Doug Hart against Berry in the end zone. Aroused, the Colt defense stopped the Packers again, and after a punt, Cuozzo found his Minnesota form. First, Raymond Berry made a great leaping catch on a slant out toward the left sideline. Then passes to Mackey, sub Alex Hawkins, and Berry again got the ball down to the Green Bay three-yard line. On third down, Cuozzo hit Berry again in the back of the end zone, and the Baltimore crowd went wild. He finished the game with 20 completions in 38 attempts. It was 35–27 now, with 5:33 to play, and it looked possible for the Colts to get back into the game.

The Colts stopped the Packers on the first two plays after the kickoff, and Starr faced third and 10 on the Packer 35-yard line. He faded back and found Hornung slanting up the middle. Colt safety Jerry Logan tried for a

5. The Climax

leaping interception and missed the ball completely. The Green Bay wide receivers had spread the rest of the secondary out, and Hornung took this one in stride and sprinted 55 yards into the end zone for his fifth touchdown. It was 42–27 now, and the game was effectively over.

Lombardi's week of cloistered preparation had paid off. Taylor, who said after the game that he had been injured in preseason, and Hornung, who had hardly practiced all week, had recovered the form of their prime. Taylor finished with 115 yards total offense, Hornung with 176 yards—115 of them on the two long touchdown passes. Starr had 10 completions in 17 attempts. With Unitas absent, the Packers, not the Colts, had delivered the big plays. The Colts had 21 first downs to the Packers' 18 but were outgained, 366 yards to 264—and outscored 42–27. Lombardi had pulled off one of the greatest coaching weeks of his career, Paul Hornung had turned in the greatest game of his life, and Green Bay was back in first place.

And while the Packers were taking the Colts apart, the Chicago Bears and Gale Sayers put on a record-breaking performance on a wet Wrigley Field in Chicago against the mercurial San Francisco 49ers. The game began routinely, as first the Bears and then the 49ers failed to move the ball and had to punt. On his second series, the Bears' Rudy Bukich missed two passes but then threw a screen pass to Sayers on the right. Taking the ball in stride with one blocker in front of him, Sayers cut diagonally to his left to avoid one tackler. A second 49er was closing in on him from his left a few steps later, but he cut left again, moving directly across the field and forcing the 49er to overrun him completely. Then he picked up another block, cut to his right up the left sideline, and made his way into the end zone without another 49er coming anywhere near him. The Bears missed the extra point but led 6–0. The 49ers once again failed to move the ball after the kickoff, and Bukich led his team down the field in 14 plays, finishing with a touchdown pass that Mike Ditka caught at full stretch to make the score 13–0. However, John Brodie now briefly took charge, moving down the field with passes to Parks and Willard and a fine scramble of his own inside the 10-yard line. A touchdown pass to his leading receiver, Parks, made it 13–7.

The veteran Jon Arnett—who was playing most of the half at halfback in place of Sayers—took the ensuing kickoff, ran off a block by Sayers, and returned it 77 yards to the 49er 21-yard line before cornerback Jim Johnson stopped him. Sayers promptly took the ball for a beautifully executed trap play off left tackle, accelerated, and made it into the end zone, diving over a desperate last-second tackle by Jim Johnson to get to 20–7.

NFL 1965

Johnny Morris

Sayers had quick legs, and he could change directions like no one else. He could change direction in midair by throwing his leg over instead of planting his foot like most guys. He was going straight down the field and then could throw down his foot to one side, instead of pushing off.

The 49ers fought back again, and Brodie found John David Crow with a touchdown pass. Kicker Tommy Davis missed his first extra point ever after 234 consecutive successes, and Chicago led 20–13. On the next Chicago possession, Bukich completed a 51-yard pass play to Jimmy Jones to get the ball to the San Francisco 16-yard line with less than a minute left in the half. Sayers gained seven more yards on a pass over the middle and then took a pitchout to the right. A great block from pulling guard Bob Watuska opened up a lane into the end zone, and Sayers accelerated as he cut upfield and went in untouched for his third touchdown. The Bears led 27–13 at halftime.

The Bears stopped the 49ers to open the second half and moved the ball to midfield. With the help of great blocking by fullback Ronnie Bull, tight end Mike Ditka and flanker Johnny Morris opened up a big hole for Sayers on the right side, and he slipped by one possible tackler, accelerated again, and left the whole San Francisco team behind, streaking down the field for his fourth touchdown. The next 49er drive came to an end when Rosie Taylor cut in front of Parks for an interception at the Bear 11-yard line. A 54-yard option pass from Ronnie Bull to Jim Jones set up Sayers' fifth touchdown, a short line plunge, making it 40–13 after another missed extra point. Then George Halas took Sayers out of the game. Brodie and Bukich traded long drives for touchdowns with fine passing—including a 58-yarder from Bukich to Morris—and the score was 47–20. George Mira replaced Brodie and failed to move the ball, and Halas sent Sayers in to return the punt.

Sayers took the punt on the Bear 15-yard line, cut right, cut left, cut right again, and left the whole 49er punting unit behind. Looking around at the 49er 30-yard line and finding himself all alone, Sayers literally trotted into the end zone for his sixth touchdown of the day, tying the NFL record held by Ernie Nevers (1929) and Dub Jones (1951). His six broke Lenny Moore's new record for touchdowns in a season, with 20 to Moore's 19, and leap-frogged over Jim Brown, who scored his 19th on the same day, for the season lead. An interception by Bennie McRae set up a final touchdown by Jon Arnett, and the final score was 61–20.

The game exemplified the spectacular offensive football that

5. The Climax

dominated the NFL in 1965. Brodie and Mira combined for 23 completions in 44 attempts, while Bukich went 16 for 32. Dave Parks caught nine passes for 129 yards, and Johnny Morris caught five passes for 95 yards. Even Andy Livingston got into the game late and showed flashes of brilliance. All eyes, however, rested on Sayers, whose performance left an indelible impression on everyone who was there.

Ken Willard

> Before that game, Gale and I were the top candidates for Rookie of the Year.[2] As it turned out, he touched the ball sixteen times, gained 336 yards, and scored six touchdowns. I rushed ten times for 24 yards and caught three passes for 22 more yards. That was the end of the argument about Rookie of the Year. I was on our punting unit, and on his last touchdown, the punt return, you can see me miss him.[3]

Dick LeBeau

> I was a great student of films. I watched that whole game, and that was the most stunning individual performance that I have ever seen. The field was wet, and Sayers was superhuman—nobody else could keep up with him, nobody else could run.

In George Plimpton's second classic of pro football reporting, *Mad Ducks and Bears,* Alex Karras described "the greatest thrill that ever happened to me" in a pro football game. It was in the Pro Bowl, and the East ran a sucker play—what Karras called the "Oh shit!" play—right at Karras, pulling the guard opposite him to get him to pursue and leave a hole for Jim Brown. The East didn't know that Karras and his neighbor, defensive end Gino Marchetti, had just had a late night out and weren't likely to run unnecessarily, and both of them hit Brown head-on, clearly stunning him and driving him back a couple of steps. They hesitated, savoring what they had done as other defenders closed in—and then stood open-mouthed in awe as Brown righted himself and took off on an 86-yard touchdown run.

"I can understand that," said guard John Gordy. "In professional football, you often ask yourself, *What am I doing on the field with these great athletes?*"[4]

That was the awe I also heard in the voices of Ken Willard, Dick LeBeau, and other contemporaries when they talked about Gale Sayers.

The Bears had avenged their opening day rout by the 49ers and looked like the strongest team in the league. Yet because of their bitterly controversial loss to the Colts in week eight, they now depended on San Francisco and Los Angeles for a chance to prolong their season. Only if the Rams beat the Colts, the 49ers beat the Packers, and the Bears once again beat the Vikings in their season finales could the Bears face the Packers in a playoff.

The Vikings, as it happened, came to life, snapping their four-game losing streak with a decisive 29–7 win over the Lions in Detroit. The Viking defense stopped the Lions cold, and three Viking interceptions helped them to victory. In the Eastern Conference, the Giants retained possession of second place with a strong 27–10 victory over the Redskins, who crashed and burned after their amazing win against the Cowboys. Washington started the day with a chance to finish second in the East and jumped off to a 10–0 lead, but then collapsed. The game was extraordinarily rough, with two Redskin receivers and one Giant being forced out of the game with injuries. The Giant attack featured two bombs of 72 and 74 yards from Earl Morrall to Giant receiver Homer Jones, while the Redskins lost three fumbles and rushed for just 74 yards. Dallas, meanwhile, stayed one game behind the Giants (6–7) with a dramatic 27–13 victory against the Cardinals, featuring two touchdown passes from Don Meredith in the fourth quarter, who threw for 326 yards and no interceptions on the day, while Charley Johnson and Buddy Humphrey shared the quarterbacking for the preseason favorite Cardinals. Dallas now had to face the Giants in New York in a game that would decide who finished second and went to the Playoff Bowl. And in Philadelphia, the resurgent Eagles blitzed the Steelers with 27 unanswered first-quarter points and routed them 47–13 as Pittsburgh quarterbacks Bill Nelsen and Tommie Wade threw nine interceptions between them.

The third noteworthy result of the week occurred in Los Angeles, where the Rams—fresh from victories over the Packers and the Cardinals—entertained the Eastern Conference champion Browns. Roman Gabriel, the 6'4", 225-pound quarterback who had only become the starter when Bill Munson was hurt, had a day to rival Gale Sayers, throwing for five touchdown passes and scoring another one himself as the Rams, mired in the middle of the Western Conference pack, demolished the reigning champion Browns 42–7. Jim Ninowski replaced Frank Ryan for this game, but the Fearsome Foursome utterly throttled Jim Brown and the Browns' rushing game, which managed just 80 yards overall, 40 of them by Brown. Only an interception allowed the Browns to get on the board at all, as Brown scored his 19th touchdown.

5. The Climax

Roman Gabriel

At the time Munson got hurt, they had been talking about using me as a receiver. I looked at the schedule when I took over, and we were facing four playoff teams—St. Louis, Green Bay, Cleveland, and Baltimore. I said to myself, *Well, I have nothing to lose. I'm going to call my own game.* I depended on my creative juices, and the offense really responded to me.

Gary Collins

Well, we had the title wrapped up. We were really there to party! I was trying to break Sammy Baugh's record for punting average for a season. I could have tied him with two punts of 54 yards each and an average of 51. But it was rainy, and I had to punt 11 times, averaging 45 yards each.

John Wooten

Gary didn't miss very many parties.

The Rams' victory ran the Western Conference's record against the Eastern Conference to 12–1 with one week to play. Having beaten the Packers and the Browns in successive weeks, the Rams now faced a finale in the Coliseum the following Saturday against the Colts. Another victory would eliminate Baltimore and give the Bears a slim chance for a tie against the Packers, but in that case, the Packers would go into the title game against Cleveland unless they lost to the dangerous 49ers in San Francisco on Sunday.

Week 14

On Monday, December 13, the Baltimore Colts announced that Gary Cuozzo, who had returned to the game against the Packers and moved the team for two touchdowns in the fourth quarter on Sunday, was having surgery on his injured left shoulder and would be unavailable for the final game of the season on Saturday. Cameron Snyder, the beat writer for *The Baltimore Sun*, noted that the Colts would need a 49er win over the Packers, which he regarded as nothing short of a miracle, to get them into the title game for a rematch with the Browns. Don Shula announced that he was activating George Haffner from the "band squad," or taxi squad, for Saturday's game, but no new man could be added to the roster for post-season play. With the game scheduled for Saturday, the Colts had a short week to prepare, and things got even worse on Wednesday. "Can you throw the ball?" coach Don Shula asked a middle-aged reporter as Wednesday's practice began. "If you can, we'll give you a uniform. We might need you." Matte, he explained, was crippled with diarrhea and a stomach virus, making it very possible that Haffner, who had never played in a pro game of any kind, might have to start in Los Angeles. That explanation, it turns out, was not entirely true. Matte managed to practice for an hour, working intensively on patterns with Raymond Berry before he fled to the locker room and Haffner took over. The team flew to Los Angeles that evening.

Tom Matte

> I had ulcers—sometimes they would bleed. Shula looked at some old films of mine from Ohio State—Woody Hayes had given them to me. He came over to my house every night, and he and [offensive coach] Don McCafferty designed the offense around what I could do. After the season was over, they operated on me for the ulcers and took a good piece of my stomach out.

On Wednesday evening, the Colts organization sprang a surprise on the football world. Earlier in the week, they had persuaded owner Art Rooney of the Steelers to put his third-string quarterback, ten-year veteran Ed Brown, on waivers, allowing the Colts to claim him for $100. George Halas, however—still hoping for Baltimore and Green Bay defeats on Saturday and Sunday that might allow him to tie the Packers—had initially put in a claim of his own. Halas had now dropped his claim, but that meant that Brown would have just one day of practice on Friday in Los Angeles to get used to his new teammates. Neither Brown nor Haffner, however, would be eligible for any post-season competition because they had not been on the final season roster the team had to submit before the Packer game. Matte, meanwhile, had gotten over his stomach problems by Thursday, but end Raymond Berry was limping so badly that he was doubtful. So was middle linebacker Dennis Gaubatz, who was nursing a sprained ankle. The Rams—having just beaten the Packers, Cardinals, and Browns over the last few weeks by a combined 90–20 score—were favored by 6½ points, and no one in Baltimore seemed to be holding out much hope for the game. *The Baltimore Sun* repeatedly rehashed the various possibilities that might come true over the weekend—but without ever mentioning the one that was destined, with fateful consequences, to take place.

5. The Climax

The country gathered around television sets at 1:00 Pacific Standard Time to watch the Colts try to stay alive against the red-hot Rams. Among the viewers were the Chicago Bears, who needed a Colt defeat to give them a chance of tying the Packers with a 10–4 record if they could beat the Vikings the next day while the 49ers beat Green Bay. Adjusting to his desperate circumstances, Don Shula had designed a defensive game plan. His defense, coached by Charlie Winner, was supposed to play aggressively, blitzing much more than usual in an attempt to get the ball, and the offense was supposed to keep it. With Matte and Brown alternating at quarterback, the Colts ran the ball 47 times for 214 yards—99 of them by Matte himself—and attempted just seven passes, five of them by Brown. Years later, Matte, who stood less than six feet tall, recalled that he could hardly see into the secondary over the Rams' massive front four when he lined up over center.[5] The Rams, meanwhile, gained just 57 yards in 25 rushing attempts, although Gabriel completed 16 of 30 passes for 253 yards. It was a traditional defensive battle, and the teams punted sixteen times between them. Matte played with a special accessory on his wrist.

Tom Matte

> That was the famous wristband with all the plays written on it. My wife actually wrote it; she had better penmanship! It's in the Hall of Fame now. I needed the numbers so they could signal the plays with hand signals from the bench.
>
> The great thing about the scenario was the way the whole team rallied to protect my ass—the defense and the offense. The line really protected me, and I wasn't sacked once.

Neither team could move the ball in the first quarter, with the Rams punting three times and the Colts adding a missed field goal attempt and two punts of their own. Early in the second period, Alvin Haymond returned another Ram punt to near midfield. Jerry Hill picked up five yards through the line, and after the ball was advanced to the Ram 43-yard line, Lou Michaels kicked a field goal from 50 yards out to open the scoring. On the next series, Bobby Boyd, the Colts' left cornerback, stepped in front of Tommy McDonald and intercepted a Gabriel pass at the Ram 36-yard line, and after one more play, Lenny Moore recovered his old form, found a hole off right tackle, cut outside, and outran the whole Los Angeles defense for a touchdown and a 10–0 lead. The Colts, who blitzed on half the Rams' offensive plays, contained the Rams for most of the rest of the half, but Gabriel eventually led them 80 yards in ten plays for a touchdown, finishing with a pass to Tommy McDonald. The Rams trailed 10–7 at the half.

Gabriel picked up where he had left off early in the third quarter, beating a blitz and hitting the fleet rookie Jack Snow for 60 yards and another touchdown, his seventh TD pass in two weeks, and a 14–10 lead. As the fourth quarter opened, Los Angeles was threatening to stretch the lead to 21–10, but the Colt defense stopped the Rams at the Colts' four-yard line, and the Rams settled for a field goal to make it 17–10 early in the fourth quarter.

Roman Gabriel

> Jack Snow was one of the great ones. He was fearless. If we had thrown as much then as they do now, he would be in the Hall of Fame. He made one-handed catches 50 yards down the field.

With Raymond Berry limping and ineffective, Shula decided to go to big John Mackey, the tight end. The Colts drew the play on the ground in their huddle for the benefit of their new quarterback, Ed Brown. Jimmy Orr, flanked right outside Mackey, took off down the field and persuaded right safety Ed Meador to move toward him to help. Mackey moved behind the Ram linebackers, took a quick pass at full stride from Brown, and ran through Meador's tackle when he came back to get him. He kept going for 68 yards, and Michaels' kick tied the score 17–17. The Colts stopped the Rams again and took over the ball at their own 15-yard line with Matte at quarterback. One running play after another—including a 23-yard gain by Matte from a deep drop—took the Colts down the field in good 1930s fashion, and they didn't face fourth down until they had gotten inside the 20-yard line.

Tom Matte

> That was a delayed draw—we gave the linebackers time to drop back, and then I took off. The Rams were trying to get me out of the game.

Then Lou Michaels kicked another field goal for a 20–17 lead. After the game, the Colts gave special credit to right guard Alex Sandusky and right tackle George Preas. Both were long-time veterans who had decided to make 1965 their last season, and this was likely to be their final game. They had contained Merlin Olsen and Deacon Jones, two of the greatest defensive linemen in the history of the NFL.

5. The Climax

In his fourth year in the league, Roman Gabriel had gotten a chance to show what he could do. His performance in this last month of 1965 launched him on a path to a winning season in 1966 and two frustrating trips to the postseason in 1967–69 that established him as one of the league's best. He wasn't through now, and after the Colts kicked off, he passed to Tommy McDonald and Marlon McKeever to take the Rams down the field and inside the Colt 10-yard line—second and goal at the seven-yard line—with a little over a minute left. Over his four games as a starter against four of the league's best teams, Gabriel had averaged 16 completions in 30 attempts for 257 yards, two touchdowns, and just one interception per game. He wasn't going to keep the ball on the ground and settle, if necessary, for a field goal that would have tied the game and given the Colts only the slightest of chances to survive the next day's play. He wanted to beat them, and under pressure from the Colt defense, he tried to hit McKeever in the end zone. Bobby Boyd got in front of McKeever, reached up, and came down with his 11th, league-leading interception of the year and second of the game to preserve the 20–17 victory.

Andy Livingston

The Rams were close enough to have kept that ball on the ground! That was the end of our hopes.

Roman Gabriel

Bobby Boyd was a smart one. Not that fast, but very smart.

The Colts were still alive in the title race, and the Packers now had to beat the 49ers the next afternoon to meet the Browns for the title on January 2 in Green Bay.

Sunday's early East Coast games featured one between Cleveland and St. Louis that back in September had looked like one of the climatic contests of the season and a game between Dallas and New York that decided who would represent the Eastern Conference in the Playoff Bowl in three weeks. As things had turned out, the Cardinals, now hopelessly out of contention, were trying to snap a five-game losing streak while the Browns were coming off their humiliation in Los Angeles. The game, though meaningless, turned out to be a thriller.

The Cardinals finished the season without Charley Johnson, who, like Gary Cuozzo, was now out for the season's count with shoulder surgery, but saw the return of their remarkable free safety Larry Wilson, who had missed the whole last month with hand injuries. The Browns began strongly, repeatedly intercepting Cardinal backup quarterback Buddy Humphrey's passes and running up a 14–0 lead on a pass from Frank Ryan to Gary Collins and a short plunge by Jim Brown, which tied Gale Sayers for the touchdown lead (and new NFL single-season record) with 21 touchdowns. Shortly thereafter, however, while blocking on a pass play, Brown got into an altercation with Cardinal defensive lineman Joe Robb, and despite their protests, both were ejected from the game. Brown had already rushed for 74 yards and finished the season with a total of 1,544, easily leading the league for the eighth time in his nine-year career. Collins also left the game in the first half with bruised ribs. A field goal gave Cleveland a 17–0 lead at the half.

Larry Wilson took over the game and nearly won it for the Cardinals. The Browns were driving for a score late in the half when he intercepted a pass on the Cardinal five-yard line and returned it 95 yards for a touchdown. New quarterback Terry Nofziger did well, and after Wilson got his second interception on the Brown 35-yard line, the Cardinals ran the ball over to make it 17–14 before their home crowd. Jim Bakken kicked a field goal to tie the game at 17, and a third Wilson interception got the ball back deep in Cleveland territory again. Nofziger passed to Bill Triplett for a touchdown that gave the Cardinals the lead. Cleveland clawed back with another field goal, however, and another Cleveland interception allowed Frank Ryan to regain the lead, 27–24, with a touchdown pass. With less than two minutes left, the Browns tried to extend the lead with another field goal, but Pat Fisher blocked it, picked it up, and ran to the Cleveland 23-yard line. On third down, tight end Jackie Smith dropped a pass on the goal line, eerily foreshadowing the most famous play of his career in the Super Bowl 14 years later for Dallas. Like the Rams the day before against the Colts, the Cardinals scorned a tying field goal and tried to end the season with a win. They failed, and the Browns had squeaked through, leaving them with two weeks to rest before the championship.

In New York, the Cowboys began the day one game behind the Giants in the race for second place. They could earn their trip to the Playoff Bowl with a win because it would mark their second victory of the season over New York. They began well with a long touchdown pass from Meredith to Bob Hayes and a field goal, good for a 10–0 lead. Tom Landry's flex defense contained the Giant running attack all day, but pass defense remained the Cowboys' weakness, as the Redskins had shown three weeks earlier.

5. The Climax

Morrall's passing closed the gap to 17–14 early in the fourth quarter. Then, in another wild play, the Cowboys blocked a Giant field goal attempt on the Cowboy 42-yard line, and Obert Logan, a Cowboy reserve, picked it up and raced 60 yards for a touchdown and a 24–14 lead. Morrall quickly drove the Giants down the field for another touchdown, but the extra point was missed. Leading 24–20, Don Meredith, who had had so many downs and ups during the year, now had his finest hour. Running and rolling out, he finished a long drive with a touchdown pass to veteran Buddy Dial, giving the Cowboys a 31–20 lead with just four minutes to go. A Giant fumble led to yet another score, and the Dallas Cowboys of Tom Landry and Tex Schramm reached post-season play for the first of nine consecutive seasons.

In Washington, the 5–8 Redskins met the 2–11 Steelers and closed out the season with a 35–14 win, the first time in their last 11 tries—and the second in their last 20—that the Redskins had won a game in December. Although Jurgensen threw two touchdown passes, the Redskin defense dominated with four interceptions and a fumble recovery. The Redskins played without defensive back Johnny Sample, who had been suspended on Saturday for not returning a series of weekly defensive playbooks. As it turned out, the Redskins let the talented but uncontrollable Sample go after the season, and he caught on with the New York Jets in the AFL. In January 1969, he played against his original team, the Baltimore Colts, as the Jets won the third Super Bowl. And in Philadelphia, much-maligned quarterback Milt Plum of the Detroit Lions had by far his best day of the season, completing 18 of 31 passes for 218 yards and three touchdowns, and the Lions closed out their disappointing season with a 35–28 win. It was the Western Conference's 13th victory in 14 interconference games in the 1965 season.

The Bears, eliminated on Saturday from title contention by the Colts' victory, took the field at home against the Vikings with one last chance to confirm that they were, in fact, the strongest aggregation in the NFL and had been since the fourth week of the season. The Vikings, who, like the Cardinals, had fallen so far short of their pre-season hopes, were playing for pride and a chance at a 7–7 record.

The Bears had evidently suffered a letdown after their elimination from the race by the Colts the day before, and they squandered three big opportunities in a scoreless first half. Early in the third quarter, Ronnie Bull scored for the Bears on a 20-yard sweep left, but the Vikings soon made it 7–3. Then Sayers began moving, and on the opening play of the fourth quarter, he plunged a few yards into the end zone to pass Jim Brown, now through for the day, with his 22nd touchdown and a 14–3 lead. They added a field goal, but Fran Tarkenton got hot and threw two touchdown passes, tying the game at 17. With less than two minutes left, Rudy Bukich, who finished the season as the NFL's leading passer, tried to hit Sayers on a screen under heavy pressure and underthrew the ball. Sayers finished his magnificent season chasing Viking linebacker Rip Hawkins into the end zone with the interception that gave the Vikings a 24–17 win and dropped the Bears to a record of 9–5. No one could have guessed that neither Sayers nor Butkus would ever play on a team that good in the remainder of their careers.

At 4:00 Eastern Time, the Packers took the field against the 49ers needing a victory to clinch Lombardi's fourth Western Conference title after a two-year hiatus. Having whipped his club into an entirely new shape during a week's practice away from home around Washington, D.C., Lombardi had flown the team directly from Baltimore to San Francisco to begin preparation for the final game on Tuesday. The team exuded confidence all week. On Wednesday, tackle Forrest Gregg, who had also played guard early in the season, and four defensive Packers—Willie Wood, Herb Adderley, Willie Davis, and Ray Nitschke—were named as first-team all-pros, the most of any team in the league. But they knew they were facing a tough opponent, led by John Brodie, who had completed 60 percent of his passes and had not once been sacked trying to pass in his last five games. While 49er quarterbacks had gone down only 18 times all year, Starr and Bratkowski had been sacked a combined 42 times. Although doubleheader games were now a fixture of CBS's schedule, the NFL inexplicably failed to put the Packer-49er game on national television. They did arrange a closed-circuit broadcast at the local Baltimore CBS affiliate so that the Colts, fresh from their flight back from Los Angeles, could watch it. No one could have predicted the almost unbelievable outcome.

The first quarter was scoreless. A 34-yard punt return by Kermit Alexander put the 49ers deep in Packer territory, but the 49ers promptly fumbled it back. Brodie, however, was on his way to one of the greatest days of his remarkable season, completing 26 of 34 passes for 295 yards. He drove the team down the field early in the second quarter with two great passes to Dave Parks, and Tommy Davis kicked a 21-yard field goal. The Packers came alive in response, moving into the end zone on just four plays, including an option pass from Tom Moore to Carroll Dale and a 49-yard touchdown on a play-action pass from Starr to Boyd Dowler for a 7–3 lead. Then, late in the second quarter came another amazing twist in this unbelievable season.

Brodie passed twice to Dave Parks and once to Bernie Casey, and John

5. The Climax

David Crow's fine running got the 49ers to the Packer 14-yard line and a chance to take the halftime lead. Brodie called a pitchout to the left to Crow. The ball appeared to go through Crow's hands, bouncing, and Willie Wood picked it up in full stride. Easily rounding Brodie, Wood cut back twice and made it to the end zone. Just as in Baltimore the previous week, the Packer defense seemed to have turned a probable halftime deficit into a comfortable halftime lead. But as the teams lined up for the extra point, John Brodie came running back onto the field holding a rule book. The pitchout, he explained to the referee, was a lateral—as indeed it was—and the rules forbade advancing a recovery of a lateral rather than a fumble. The issue was whether Crow had ever had possession, and the surviving film, although inconclusive, certainly looks as if he didn't since he does not appear to have lost the ball because of contact with a Packer. An enraged Vince Lombardi ran onto the field in his camel's hair coat and black fedora to scream at the official, to no avail. The half finished with the 49ers trailing 7–3. Paul Hornung, last week's hero, had left the game with bruised ribs. The 49er defense played all afternoon as if they, not the Packers, were fighting to reach the championship.

The second half began with the 49ers wasting another fantastic return from Kermit Alexander on the opening kickoff when much of his 60-yard run was nullified by a clipping penalty, and Green Bay promptly forced a punt. Starr moved the ball into 49er territory with play-action passes until 49er cornerback Jim Johnson came up with a brilliant leaping interception just in front of a flying Carroll Dale on the ten-yard line.

Ken Willard

> Jim Johnson was one of the greatest athletes I ever played with. That's not surprising—his brother was Rafer Johnson, the Olympic decathlon champion.

Packer Doug Hart, normally a weak link in the Green Bay secondary, returned the favor almost immediately, stealing a deep pass from Dave Parks. Don Chandler missed a subsequent field goal, but then the Green Bay defense came through again. Deep in his own territory after a penalty, Brodie threw a short pass toward Bernie Casey, and Herb Adderley cut in front of him and ran the interception into the end zone, the third time in the season that he had made this play. The Packers now led 14–3, but Brodie was just getting started.

Passes to Parks and tight end Monte Stickles moved the 49ers past midfield. From more than 40 yards out, Brodie hit John David Crow in full stride at the Packer 10-yard line, and Crow broke two tackles, one by Dave

Robinson, to score and make it 14–10. Then the 49ers stopped the Packers a yard shy of a first down and took over after a punt on their own 34-yard line. A short pass to Ken Willard, who ran right through a necktie tackle by Ray Nitschke, was good for 28 yards. A pass to Dave Parks and a tremendous piece of running by John David Crow on a draw play got the 49ers inside the 10-yard line, but a blown screen pass left them with a third and 12. On a broken play, Brodie hit Parks in the end zone and put the 49ers ahead 17–14 with five minutes gone in the fourth quarter. Suddenly, the Baltimore Colts were on track to host a rematch with the Cleveland Browns in Baltimore two weeks' hence. The Packers were on death ground with ten minutes left.

Responding like champions, they moved 55 yards on 10 plays after Herb Adderley returned the kickoff 33 yards and regained the lead 21–17. A 34-yard pass to reserve end Bob Long was the big play, and Taylor finished the drive with a sweep. Then Willie Wood picked up yet another interception off of John Brodie's underthrown pass on the 50-yard line. The fired-up 49er defense gang-tackled Elijah Pitts for no gain on a sweep, but a 15-yard penalty for piling on put Green Bay in field goal range, and Chandler made it 24–17 from 31 yards out. San Francisco had one more chance with just two minutes left in the game.

The Packers gave Brodie a bit of a head start on the kickoff when one of them grabbed Kermit Alexander's face mask, and the penalty moved the ball up to the 49er 44-yard line. Brodie ran four plays, all passes. Dave Parks caught the first over the middle for 13 yards. Gary Lewis took the second in nearly the same spot for six more. Then Parks caught the third on a down and out, moving the ball down to the Packer 17-yard line with 1:12 left. Tight end Monte Stickles was hurt on the play, and Vern Burke—who during the previous week's game in Chicago had caught his first pass of the season—replaced him. Brodie faded back again with Parks at tight left end, and both Burke and Bernie Casey split to the right. With Crow and Parks running short patterns on the left, Burke beat safety Tom Brown on a slant to the left at the edge of the end zone and caught the touchdown pass that tied the game 24–24 with 1:07 left. The play had been brilliantly designed, and there wasn't another Packer within 10 yards of the catch. In Baltimore, the assembled Colts rose to give the 49ers a standing ovation.

Upton Bell

> You couldn't believe that room. Usually, players just watch, but this time they were like a bunch of kids, rooting for the 49ers. That's when we came together as a team.

5. The Climax

The Packers weren't through. They ran the kickoff back to the 32-yard line, and Starr got a quick first down on the 42 with 52 seconds left. Then his luck ran out, and he missed two consecutive passes. On third and 10, he appeared to have Max McGee open on a crossing pattern from the left, but at the last second, Kermit Alexander closed to within a yard of McGee, leaped, and batted the pass away around the 49er 10-yard line. The Packers had to punt to try to save the tie with 24 seconds left. Their special teams had been strong all year, but Alexander made a fantastic punt return from the 16-yard line to the Packer 46. There were just seven seconds left, and the 49ers were already close enough to try for a long field goal that could win the game and send Green Bay home for the season. Brodie tried one sideline pass but overthrew Burke, who had to catch it out of bounds. The clock had presumably stopped, but the gun went off after the 49er kicking team came on the field, leaving them enraged. Two days later, the league explained that the official time—which was kept on the field, not on the scoreboard—had expired during that last play. In the Baltimore studio, linebacker Don Shinnick ran to the screen and kissed it. The Colts would be playing the Packers again in Green Bay on the following Sunday. The unbelievable had happened: the two great teams had finished with identical records of ten wins, three losses, and one tie.

No team has produced more books and television documentaries than Lombardi's Packers, and the game in San Francisco evidently has a special place in all their hearts—it was simply too painful to remember. Bill Curry, in *One More July*, told the story of Lombardi's confrontation with Forrest Gregg and Bob Skoronski after their loss to the Rams and added that they hadn't lost for the rest of the season. That was technically true, but the tie against the 49ers forced them into a playoff that a win would have avoided. In his acclaimed biography of Lombardi, *When Pride Still Mattered*, David Maraniss managed to tell the story of the 1965 season without mentioning the final regular season contest at all. The team that eventually became legendary for winning when it had to had failed to do just that. John Brodie had thrown three interceptions, but he had also passed for three touchdowns to three different receivers and extended his streak without a sack to six games. The teams of the Western Conference had proven all year that any of them could beat any other, and the 49ers had come through with their part in this amazing play.

The playoff between the Packers and the Colts was the first scheduled since 1958, when the New York Giants had beaten the Browns 10–0 one week after winning over the same Browns 13–10 on Pat Summerall's long field goal in the snow in Yankee Stadium. In a Western Conference playoff in the previous year, the Lions had come from way behind in the second half against the 49ers, turning a 24–7 halftime lead for San Francisco—playing at home—into a 31–27 victory. This matchup pitted the Colts, who had won successive championships in 1958–59, faded for four years, but returned to the top of the division in 1964, against the Packers, who had won the Western Conference in three straight seasons, 1960–62, and the NFL championship in the last two of those. But the Colts were the first team to reach the playoffs without a real quarterback. Fighting the odds, the team had caught the imagination of the American public, and Tom Matte was suddenly the most famous athlete in the United States.

6

The Playoff
(December 26, 1965)

The Packers and the Colts had the nation's sports pages almost to themselves during the week before Christmas as they prepared for their third clash of the season. Sunday evening, after the Colts watched the Packer-49er tie, Don Shula explained that the team was going to ask permission to activate Ed Brown, Saturday's hero, to have at least some backup for Matte for the playoff. If the league office refused—as they did—the backup would be cornerback Bobby Boyd, Saturday's other hero, who, like Matte, had not played the position since college. The Colts had not expected to practice until Wednesday, 10 days before the NFL Championship, if the Packers had lost, or until at least another week after that, for the Playoff Bowl, if Green Bay had won. Now they prepared to work out Tuesday and fly to Green Bay on Christmas Day, Saturday, for the extra game.

On Monday, the NFL owners met in New York with Commissioner Rozelle to discuss negotiations with CBS for a new TV contract. They also turned down the Colts' request to allow Brown to play, in violation of the existing rule, which limited post-season play to players who had been on the active roster for the last two weeks of the season. On Tuesday, the Associated Press announced its selections for the All-Pro team. The offensive line featured center Mick Tingelhoff of the Vikings, and Forrest Gregg of the Packers joined Colt Jim Parker at offensive guard, where Gregg had spent most of the season. The tackles were Dick Schafrath of the Browns and a newcomer, Bob Brown of the Eagles, and the Eagles' Pete Retzlaff beat out John Mackey and Mike Ditka at tight end. Jimmy Orr edged out Gary Collins at flanker, 49er Dave Parks was the split end, Johnny Unitas was the quarterback, and Gale Sayers and Jim Brown were the running backs—surely as distinguished a group as the NFL ever fielded.

On defense, ends Willie Davis of the Packers and Deacon Jones of the Rams joined tackles Bob Lilly of Dallas and Alex Karras of Detroit. The linebackers were Joe Fortunato and rookie Dick Butkus of the Bears, who edged out Ray Nitschke, and Wayne Walker of the Lions. Herb Adderley and Bobby Boyd, who would meet the following Sunday, were the cornerbacks, and Willie Wood and Paul Krause of the Redskins were the safeties. The next day, George Halas, whose Bears had just gotten started a little too late, was named the NFL Coach of the Year, and Gale Sayers, to the surprise of no one, won NFL Rookie of the Year. John Brodie got the Comeback Player of the Year award the next day.

Tom Matte, getting into the swing of his new role, had an impressive practice in Baltimore on Wednesday, hitting Raymond Berry on numerous passes. "He has a strong arm and throws well," said Shula. On that same day, the first post-season firing of a coach struck down Harland Svare of the Rams. John McKay of USC, former Lions coaches George Wilson and Buddy Parker, and Bears assistant George Allen were listed as the prime candidates to succeed him, with Allen eventually being chosen.

The Colts arrived in Green Bay in time for a quick workout on Saturday, Christmas Day, December 25, and Tom Matte told the press that they wanted to win the game for Don Shula. The team seemed relaxed and loose, knowing that they were 7½ point underdogs.

The Packers, on the other hand, who had had so many more downs, ups, and narrow escapes during the season, felt relatively fortunate to be facing a crippled Colts team for the Western Conference title. "If we can't win a must-win game against a team as handicapped as the Colts," Willie Davis told a Green Bay fan club lunch on Tuesday, "then we don't deserve to win the championship." They knew that they had to prepare to stop Tom Matte's running plays. "Psychologically, the Colts have something going for them," Lombardi said the next day. "They've been reprieved. This has got to give them, psychologically at least, a little bit of an edge." A full statistical comparison of the regular season, however, gave a clear edge to the Packers. The Colts' superiority, of course, lay in their offense, which had outgained the Packers' 4,598 yards to 3,601—but they had gained most of those additional yards in the air, where they could not figure to gain too many without a true quarterback. They had scored 369 points to the Packers' 314 but given up 284 to the Packers' 224. The Colts also had a secret weapon, second-year back Alvin Haymond, who had gained an extraordinary 1,017 yards on kickoff and punt returns during the season. And they had the better field goal kicker, Lou Michaels, who had scored 101 points. The Colts had pioneered the use of special teams and even had a captain for theirs, Alex Hawkins, who gave a weekly award of a fifth of whiskey to the outstanding special teams player. The recipient, invariably, was Alex Hawkins.[1]

6. The Playoff (December 26, 1965)

At 1:00 p.m. Central Standard Time on Sunday, December 26, the Colts and the Packers took the field in Green Bay. The temperature was slightly below freezing, but the field had been well cared for all week, covered with hay and a tarpaulin. Lambeau Field was, of course, packed with rabid rooters. The Packers won the toss and elected to receive. Lou Michaels's kickoff went deep into the end zone, and Tom Moore returned it to the Packer 20-yard line, where Bart Starr took over the offense. What happened then was surely one of the most dramatic starts to any major sporting event ever. It compared, in the long experience of this writer, to only two other games. One was the World Cup Final of 1974, when Holland, facing West Germany, passed the ball around for one minute before the great Johan Cruyff dribbled past his defender, reached the penalty area, and was tripped, yielding a penalty kick and a 1–0 lead before the Germans had touched the ball. Just five months later, the second occurred in an NFL playoff game between the favored Oakland Raiders and the two-time Super Bowl champion Miami Dolphins, when Miami's Nat Moore returned the opening kickoff for a touchdown that upset all the odds makers' calculations. Neither play was more of a shock than the Packers' first play from scrimmage.

The team lined up in standard formation with Taylor as a lone setback, Bill Anderson at tight left end, and Paul Hornung in a slot right. The Colts did not blitz on the first play, and although Starr faked a draw to Taylor, the offensive line quickly set up to pass block. Starr looked left and found Anderson, who had evidently left Colt linebacker Don Shinnick at the line of scrimmage and was open on a quick down and out. Anderson caught the pass in the open, but the Colts' right cornerback, the lightning-quick Lenny Lyles, came up quickly and crashed into his mid-section with a low tackle that jarred the ball loose just inside the Packer 25-yard line. The ball bounced toward the sideline, and linebacker Shinnick, trailing the play, scooped it up in full stride and headed for the goal line escorted by Lyles and middle linebacker Dennis Gaubatz. Bart Starr, headed for the sideline, sensed Fuzzy Thurston right behind him and decided to try to break up the interference inside the five-yard line. He collided violently with reserve strong safety Jim Welch as Shinnick crossed into the end zone and raised the football in triumph. Then Starr limped off the field with a bruised back that left him unable to raise his right arm above his shoulder. Two devastating hits by the Colt defense had given them a 7–0 lead and taken away the Packers' starting quarterback for the rest of the game. The impossible suddenly looked possible. Lou Michaels kicked the extra point.

NFL 1965

Dave Robinson

We were stunned. Why did Bart try to make the tackle?

Zeke Bratkowski, who had played a key role in the first Colt-Packer game back in September, took over after the kickoff. He began well with two first downs, but then another hard hit at midfield jarred the ball loose from Hornung, and the busy Lyles recovered it. Matte gave the ball to Lenny Moore on a sweep right on his first play from scrimmage, and Willie Davis and Herb Adderley returned the favor with a hit that forced a fumble recovered by safety Tom Brown. The Packers couldn't move the ball very far in three plays, and Chandler tried a field goal from the Colt 47-yard line. He missed to the right.

The defenses took over the game for the next fifteen minutes as Chandler and Colt punter Tom Gilburg each punted three times. The Packers lost a great opportunity when a pass play to Hornung, good for about 50 yards, was called back because of an ineligible receiver downfield. Midway through the second quarter, after a gutsy Alvin Haymond was tackled quickly after refusing to call for a fair catch, the Colts took over on their own 24-yard line. The Packers would not have minded putting yet another Colt quarterback out of action and forcing them to use cornerback Bobby Boyd, and Willie Davis ran into Matte after he had already been tackled on a sweep around right end, drawing a 15-yard penalty. Then came Matte's finest hour.

Dropping back to pass, the quarterback-in-training found himself retreating at full speed as Packer ends Willie Davis and Lionel Aldridge closed in on him from both sides. Yet he managed to flip the ball over them while facing the sideline, reaching a wide-open Lenny Moore, who played off a great block and made it down the sideline to the Packer 40-yard line before Dave Robinson, coming over from the opposite side of the field, forced him out of bounds. A great block by Jim Parker on Henry Jordan allowed fullback Jerry Hill to reach the Green Bay 29-yard line, by far the deepest penetration of either offense so far. After two more solid running plays, blocks by the Colts' guards and center opened a big hole for Lenny Moore and got the ball down to the Packer nine-yard line. Then the Packer defense rose to the occasion, and the drive stalled. With 5:29 left in the first half, Lou Michaels drilled the ball through the uprights for a 10–0 lead.

Tom Matte

I was asking the offensive line what to do, what play would work. Shula would send in the play, and if they didn't like it, we'd change it. He wasn't very happy about that.

6. The Playoff (December 26, 1965)

Eager to get back into the game before the half ended, Bratkowski completed passes to Carroll Dale and Paul Hornung, both of whom were immediately hit hard by Colt defenders. Then he went for broke from the Colt 36-yard line, looking for flanker Bob Long on a deep sideline pattern. Safety Jerry Logan was in good position and appeared to strip the ball out of Long's arms, but an official trailing the play signaled for pass interference on the Colt nine-yard line.

On first down, Bratkowski threw a down and out to Anderson to his left, and Anderson took the pass as he ran out of bounds on the one-yard line. On second down, Bratkowski called the same play that Bart Starr scored on in the 1967 NFL Championship against Dallas, a wedge behind Jerry Kramer, but middle linebacker Gaubatz anticipated it perfectly, stepping to his left at the snap, and he and Lou Michaels stopped the play for no gain. The Colts got up quietly, with no celebration, to prepare for two more plays. The ball was now on the one-foot line.

On third down, rather than go straight ahead again, Bratkowski handed off to Hornung on a slant off left tackle, but Gaubatz anticipated the play perfectly once again and stopped the Golden Boy a full yard shy of the goal line. Lombardi disdained a field goal on fourth and one, and the teams lined up for another play. The Colts were in a new 5–1 defense, with their defensive tackles lined up in the gaps between center Ken Bowman and their two guards and Gaubatz facing Bowman at middle linebacker. The play appeared to be designed to go off right tackle, and this time Gaubatz's first step took him in the wrong direction. Jim Taylor failed to run to daylight inside Forrest Gregg, and Lou Michaels met him head-on. Gaubatz reversed field, slipped around Jerry Kramer, and piled into Taylor, forcing a fumble shy of the goal line. A jubilant, leaping Jerry Logan signaled the first down for Baltimore, and the defense ran off the field after one of the most amazing goal-line stands in NFL history. Taking over on his own one-yard line, Matte ran five good running plays and got all the way out to his own 20-yard line as the gun went off, and the Colts went into the locker room ahead 10–0.

Upton Bell

> I thought we had probably lost our chance for the title when Unitas went out. But when we got to 10–0 in the playoff, I really thought we could win—maybe 10–3 or 10–7. I thought, *We're actually going to win.*

The Colts got a fine return from Alvin Haymond on the second-half kickoff but could not move the ball and had to punt from their own 35-yard line. So far, their offense had certainly done as well as might have been expected, while their defense had magnificently risen to the occasion. Now, ironically, their special teams—one of their comparative advantages—let them down. On the punt, the snap from center Buzz Nutter was so high that Tom Gilburg had to leap for it, and by the time he got the ball under control, there was no chance to get the punt off. He tried to run but was forced out of bounds on his own 35-yard line. Bratkowski promptly found Carroll Dale, who had left Bobby Boyd for dead, open on a post pattern, and Dale's diving catch took him down just shy of the goal line. This time, excellent blocking took Hornung into the end zone on the second try, and the lead was down to 10–7 with most of the half left.

Packer defensive coach Phil Bengtson had apparently put halftime to good use, and the Colts failed to move the ball again after the kickoff. The Packers had the momentum now, and crisp Bratkowski passes to Hornung and Anderson accompanied by a determined run by Jim Taylor got the ball down to near midfield. But then Bratkowski, under pressure from a Colt blitz, threw a long, off-balance pass behind Dale up the middle of the field, and Bobby Boyd grabbed it untouched at his own 20-yard line to end the Packer drive. Once again, however, the Colts failed to make a first down and had to punt.

Dave Robinson

> We played the entire game in a goal-line defense. We figured they would be trying to win on the ground.

Looking for the big play, the Colt defense was frequently blitzing, and Bratkowski had found the appropriate answer in quick passes after a very short drop back. He hit Boyd Dowler on a quick slant over the middle, where he was immediately tackled by safety Jerry Logan, then hit Hornung on the left, where Hornung was immediately tackled by Shinnick at the Colt 33-yard line. Hornung gained eight yards on a sweep. But then, Bratkowski threw the ball behind Boyd Dowler, and it bounced off Dowler's hands into those of Jerry Logan, ending the second straight Packer drive with an interception as the Colt defense came up with the big play yet again.

Taking over on the 20-yard line, Matte promptly dropped back and hit John Mackey with a perfect pass good for 15 yards. He could not, however, move the ball any further. The game was now well into the fourth quarter as the Colts punted yet again. The Packers took over on their own 28-yard line and began one of the most controversial drives in NFL history.

6. The Playoff (December 26, 1965)

Bratkowski promptly hit Boyd Dowler for 12 yards and Hornung for another eight. Once again, Hornung was hit hard by the linebacker Gaubatz, and this time he had to leave the game, never to return. Then came the first of two critical plays. Bratkowski dropped back to pass and was unable to find a receiver, and Colt tackle Billy Ray Smith, coming from the quarterback's left, felled him with a forearm to the helmet. The official threw a flag and signaled a penalty, turning an eight-yard loss into a 15-yard gain. During the heated argument that followed, the official repeatedly pantomimed a facemask penalty. Perhaps the forearm to the helmet could have been ruled unnecessary roughness, but Smith clearly had not grabbed Bratkowski's facemask.

Bratkowski snapped right back. A quick slant over the middle by Anderson beat another Colt blitz for a short gain. Another pass to Anderson on the left side took the ball to the Colt 20-yard line. Then, once again, the Packer attack stalled, this time with just two minutes left. On fourth down, with the ball on the Colt 15-yard line. Don Chandler came on for what looked like the Packers' last chance to tie the game. Bart Starr, holding as usual, set up right on the right hash mark, and rookie center Bill Curry snapped the ball back. Chandler kicked. He missed. The ball, rising very high, began moving toward the right upright but then drifted out. As it did so, Chandler turned away from it in disgust and horror, knowing it was no good. The film of the kick, shot from the end zone and readily available on YouTube today, clearly shows the ball passing to the side of the upright. But the official behind the goalposts signaled that it was good.[2] The game was tied 10–10.

Dave Robinson

I was on the field blocking on the right side of the line. If that goal post had been higher, the ball would have hit it.

Dan Sullivan

We got screwed.

The Packers might have gotten another chance even if the kick had been called correctly. As it was, the Colts went nowhere with the ball after the kickoff, and Green Bay got it back on a punt with 27 seconds left on their own 38-yard line. On the second play, Bratkowski hit Jim Taylor on a swing pass, and he crossed midfield. As he went down amidst a swarm of Colts, he fumbled, and the Colts recovered. The officials, however, wrongly insisted that the play had been blown dead.[3] Then time ran out.

Seven years earlier, in 1958, the Colts had played the Giants and won the first sudden-death overtime game in NFL history. Now they were in the second. The captains met for the coin toss, and the Packers won and chose to receive.

Now it was the Colt defense's turn to revive the team, and they stopped the Packers cold and forced a punt. Once again, the Colts could not move the ball and returned the favor. The game had become a defensive classic worthy of the early days of football. Bratkowski was sacked on the next series, and the Packers had to punt again. Alvin Haymond took the ball on his 22-yard line and showed his stuff, moving the ball to the Colt 41-yard line.

Matte ran a beautiful quarterback draw, scooting through a huge hole and finding his way across midfield. Then he did it again and made it to the Green Bay 40-yard line. Trying to catch the Packers looking inside, Matte sent Moore around right end, but the play went nowhere. Neither did another quarterback draw. On fourth down, Lou Michaels and holder Bobby Boyd trotted onto the field to try a game-winning field goal from 47 yards out. In the last two seasons, Michaels had made eight of 16 attempts from 40 to 49 yards.

For the second time in the game, Buzz Nutter's center snap was a little off, hitting the ground right in front of Bobby Boyd. Boyd handled it well and set it in place, but Michaels's timing was inevitably affected. He missed badly, and Green Bay took over on their own 20-yard line.

Bill Curry

My heart went out to Buzz Nutter. I was doing our long snaps on kicks myself.

Bratkowski promptly hit Bill Anderson cutting over the middle yet again for 20 yards. Two running plays took the ball across midfield, and then Carroll Dale survived a hard hit from Bobby Boyd on a sideline pattern down to the Colt 26-yard line. The Packer line sprung Elijah Pitts up the middle, and he reached the Colt 18-yard line. Then they stalled again, and with just 4:02 left in the first overtime, Chandler came on to kick once more, this time from 18 yards out in the middle of the field.

The kick was good. The Packers had won the Western Conference playoff 13–10.

6. *The Playoff (December 26, 1965)*

"Well, gentlemen," a jubilant Lombardi told the press after the game, "you can't say we don't give the world a thrill.... The game was typical of the season. We did what we had to do."

Matte—whose amazing emergence as Colt quarterback made him something of a celebrity for the rest of his life—was remarkably gracious in the locker room. Shula, he explained, had called "about 90 percent of the plays.... Maybe we should have passed more," he mused. He had not felt lonely. "It's not lonely when you know the guys are behind you. And they were behind me 100 percent. And our coach has been behind us 1,000 percent. He's the greatest coach I've ever been with. He's done a great job keeping us in there the last couple of weeks." Shula declined to mention the officials' calls, but Colt owner, Carroll Rosenbloom, was less restrained. "I was never more proud of any team I've had," he said. "We didn't deserve to lose. There was no justice out there today."

Shula made no excuses and spoke the last word with class. "We figured we would have to play a hell of a defensive game," he said. "Our only offensive weapon was Matte's running. We couldn't throw. We had to win with defense and field position. We had to contain the Packers so well that every time they gave the ball up, we would be in a good position to attack. It didn't quite work out, but I've never had a club that gave more than this one did. But I guess if you can't beat a team once in three tries, you don't deserve to be in the championship game, and we couldn't beat Green Bay."

Matte had completed just five passes—two to Lenny Moore, three to John Mackey, and none to Berry or Orr—in 12 attempts, good for 40 yards. He tied with Jerry Hill for the team lead with 57 yards rushing, and Moore added 33 more. The Packers rushed for 112 yards on 39 carries, with Taylor leading them with 60 yards. Bratkowski's passing was the difference, with 22 completions in 39 attempts for 248 yards—but also with two interceptions. Anderson led the team with eight receptions, followed by Dowler with five, Hornung with four, and Dale with three. Thanks to those passes, the Packers had moved the ball far better than the Colts, but the Colt defense had repeatedly come up with the big play, most notably, of course, in the first-half goal-line stand. And in fact, the Packers had won thanks only to the last critical officials' call, which, as Don Chandler confirmed decades later, had awarded his team the tying three points for a field goal that had drifted wide.[4]

7

The Championship

The nation's fans had focused on the game between crippled Baltimore and already legendary Green Bay for the last week. The Packers had come away the winners, but their season was anything but over. They now faced the Cleveland Browns, who had comfortably won the Eastern Conference with a record of 11–3, who still featured the single most powerful offensive force in football—Jimmy Brown—and who had shocked the heavily favored Colts 27–0 with almost exactly the same team a year ago. No one could be certain, obviously, of beating such a team, and the Packers initially were not even sure that Bart Starr would return from injury in time to play quarterback.

On the one hand, the Browns' record reflected the weakness of their division. Their three defeats had come at the hands of the Cardinals (49–13 in the second week of the season), the Vikings (27–17), and a humiliating rout at the hands of the Rams (42–7 after they had clinched the Eastern Conference title). In earlier years, they had played Lombardi's Packers three times without success, losing by a humiliating 49–17 in 1961, 40–23 in the Playoff Bowl after the 1963 season, and a much closer 28–21 in November of 1964, the previous year. Over the course of the 1965 season, they had outscored the Packers 363 points to 316 and outgained them with 4,398 yards to 3,601. Led by Jimmy Brown, the Browns had outrushed the Packers 2,331 yards to 1,488, although the Packers narrowly edged them out in passing yards, 2,113 to 2,067. Although Taylor and Hornung each had a few fine games during the year, Brown and Green clearly seemed superior now. Paul Warfield, who was now healthy after missing most of his second year with a broken collarbone, and Gary Collins, the hero of the 1964 championship game, certainly looked to be at least the equal of any pair of Green Bay receivers. The Packers had beaten the Browns 28–21 late in the 1964 season, but Warfield and Collins had combined for 11 catches and 295 yards in that game. The Packers had a massive advantage on defense, where they had given up 100 fewer points against a much tougher schedule, allowed 743 fewer yards passing, and taken the ball away on fumbles and

7. The Championship

interceptions 50 times to the Browns' 32. Still, Cleveland had had a whole week to rest while the Packers were dealing with the Colts, and they had done the impossible the year before.

On Wednesday, December 29, the NFL announced it had signed a new two-year contract with CBS guaranteeing $18.8 million a year, compared to the current $14.1 million. The agreement also allowed CBS to televise one game a week in markets whose team was playing at home, allowing New Yorkers, for instance, to see a Western Conference game on the same day that the Giants were playing in Yankee Stadium. The league already planned to continue doubleheader games throughout the 1966 season and added the expansion Atlanta Falcons, who would play a swing schedule against the other 14 teams, reducing the number of interconference games to one per team.

A coin flip had placed the Colts-Packers playoff in Green Bay, but the NFL championship had always been slated to take place in the stadium of the Western Conference champion. The weather on January 2, 1966, was cold, and snow had fallen—snow that would melt during the game, leaving the players with very muddy uniforms by the time the game was over. The Browns' team bus crawled along the highway for the 30 miles from their motel in Appleton, Wisconsin, to the stadium, and when they finally arrived, they hardly had time to get dressed, much less loosen up on the field.

Ernie Green

> The day before was clear and cold. On game day, it was snowing, and the Packers had electric coils under the field to keep it warm. It melted the snow and turned it into mush.

The Packers won the toss, and Tom Moore received the kickoff and returned it to the 22-yard line. Hornung gained four yards through the line on the first play, but Lombardi and Starr had no intention of relying on their ground game. Starr threw to Hornung on second down, but the halfback dropped it. On third down, Taylor circled left out of the backfield, Starr got great protection, and Taylor snagged the pass for a first down on the 36-yard line before Galen Fiss hit him.

Taylor, keeping his feet and finding a new hole, gained four more yards on first down. Starr promptly called the same pass over the middle that Hornung had dropped, and this time the Golden Boy took his time making the catch before immediately being tackled at the 47-yard line for another first down. A hole opened behind Fuzzy Thurston and Bob Skoronski on the next play, and Taylor went through it for five more yards. On second down, Starr went back quickly and looked left. Carroll Dale, split wide, was drawing double coverage from cornerback Walter Beach and safety Ross Fichtner, but Starr went for him. He appeared to underthrow the pass slightly, and when the two defenders tried to come back for an interception or make the tackle, both of them slipped and fell, letting Dale take off down the field untouched. He made it into the end zone, and Chandler kicked the point for a 7–0 lead. The Packers had avoided the Colts' pitfall of the year before and jumped out ahead.

The Browns got off to a good start when Chandler's kickoff came down around the Cleveland 15-yard line, where Charley Scales, who had toiled in obscurity for several years as Jim Brown's backup, grabbed it and ran it back to about the 34-yard line. Not to be outdone by Starr, Frank Ryan faded back, looked right, and hit Jim Brown coming out of the backfield on a slant. The great Dave Robinson was trying to cover Brown, and the pass was slightly underthrown, but the great fullback made the catch, left Robinson in his wake, and kept on running to the Packer 36-yard line for a 30-yard gain.

Dave Robinson

> I picked up Brown from Ray Nitschke when he came over to my side, but I jumped too soon.

Turning to the other side of the field, Ryan found Paul Warfield, who had easily beaten Doug Hart on a slant into the middle, and he went to the Packer 17-yard line. The third play from scrimmage was another pass play—the coup de grace. Gary Collins, flanked right, was known for his post pattern, and Herb Adderley was looking for it. But Collins took another cut for the corner of the end zone instead, leaving Adderley several yards behind him, and caught Ryan's pass a few yards inside the sideline.

Gary Collins

> I owned Herb Adderley. He was a great cornerback, but not against me. He would admit that. Just a few years ago, he was signing autographs at Harrisburg, and my son came up to him and said, "Gary Collins is here." He said, "Where is he? I want to touch him!" On that touchdown, he was playing the post, and we ran a flag pattern.

7. The Championship

Three quick passes to three different receivers had produced a touchdown. Neither quarterback had yet been threatened by a pass rush. Now came the second big break of the game. Lou Groza had not missed an extra point all year, but the snap from center bounced in front of the holder, Bobby Franklin. Groza picked up the bouncing ball, and Franklin broke cleverly into the right flat. Groza completed the pass well short of the goal line, and Franklin quickly went down. With less than four minutes gone by, the Packers still led 7–6.

The kickoff bounced into the end zone for a touchback, and the Packers took over on the 20-yard line. The Packers failed to block end Paul Wiggin on first down, and he nailed Hornung for a two-yard loss. On second down, Starr went for Boyd Dowler on the left sideline, but the pass was overthrown and incomplete. On third down, Starr could find no one, and Jim Kanicki and Bill Glass dumped him on his own eight-yard line. Chandler punted, and Leroy Kelly signaled for a fair catch on the Packer 39-yard line.

For the first time, the Browns unsheathed their biggest weapon, but a pitchout to Brown gained only three yards before the pursuit got him. Ryan faded back and found Paul Warfield on a quick hook pattern to the left, and Warfield caught it and took the ball down to the Packer 24-yard line for a first down. Ryan went back to Brown, who cut to his right when the hole on the left failed to materialize and gained four yards. On second down, Ryan faded back behind good protection but suddenly appeared to see a large, empty space to his right and took off around end. He seemed to have room to make the first down but slipped before he could be tackled. On third and three, Ryan faded back again. Warfield beat Hart on a post pattern, and the pass appeared to go perfectly over his shoulder, but the receiver couldn't handle it. The venerable Lou Groza kicked a 24-yard field goal, and the Browns led 9–7.

Groza kicked off for the third time, and Tom Moore brought it back to the 23-yard line. Excellent Cleveland penetration threw Taylor for a two-yard loss on the first play. Starr's next pass missed Hornung, but middle linebacker Vince Costello was called for holding, giving the Packers a first down on their own 27-yard line. Hornung took the ball on a sweep left, got a good block from Kramer pulling, broke a tackle, went into high gear, and ran the ball thirty yards to the Cleveland 39-yard line. Starr threw a quick pass to Carroll Dale on the left, good for another 10 yards when Walter Beach missed the tackle. An excellent block by Hornung sprang Taylor off left tackle for another six yards to the 22-yard line. A second handoff to Taylor earned a first down on the 17-yard line. Lombardi had evidently decided that the right side of Cleveland's defense was the weaker, and Hornung gained another four yards in that direction on the next play.

Taylor ran strongly to the nine-yard line, making it third and two as the first period ended. Hornung made the first down on the next play, but the Packers stalled after first and goal on the eight-yard line. Chandler kicked a 14-yard field goal, putting Green Bay in the lead 10–9. Meanwhile, the Browns were missing their great tackle Dick Schafrath, and Ernie Green had to leave the game.

Ernie Green

> The weather was horrible. It had snowed, and Green Bay had a coil underneath the field to melt the snow. The coil turned the snow into slush. It was the worst experience I ever had, falling and having to sit in the slush. I fell down early in the game making a block, and it was awful. On top of that, I hurt my foot, and I had to spend a couple of days in the hospital after the game.

Cleveland took over after the kickoff, and Ryan began passing again. The Packers, however, had replaced Doug Hart with young Bob Jeter at right cornerback, and Jeter broke up a zig-out along the sideline to Paul Warfield when the ball was slightly underthrown. Then came disaster. Fading back again, Ryan passed the ball to a streaking Leroy Kelly, in for Ernie Green, coming directly out of the backfield on the right side. Linebacker Dave Robinson had followed tight end Brewer toward the sidelines, and Kelly appeared to be all alone, but the tremendous free safety Willie Wood anticipated the play, ran and jumped in front of Kelly, grabbed the ball with outstretched fingertips, and ran it back to the Cleveland 10-yard line.

The Packers failed to take full advantage of the break. Hornung was called for illegal procedure on first down, and Starr, who seemed nearly as pass-happy as Ryan, threw three incompletions in a row. Chandler kicked another field goal from the 23-yard line, and the score was now 13–9.

Prodded, perhaps by Blanton Collier, Ryan returned to the basics after the kickoff. Great blocks from guards Gene Hickerson and John Wooten allowed Brown to gain nine yards on a sweep left. Then center John Morrow pulled right, took Herb Adderley out of the play with a fine block, and sprang Brown for another 14 yards. A third consecutive carry was good for eight more yards. But the drive stalled, and on third and two, the Packers dropped Brown for a loss. Gary Collins, one of the league's best punters, dropped the ball out of bounds just shy of the Packer goal line.

The Cleveland defense stiffened again, and Starr tried a play-action

7. The Championship

pass to Hornung on third and three. He overthrew it to the left, and Walter Beach atoned for his earlier slip with an interception at the Packer 30-yard line. Once again, it was anyone's game with time running out in the first half. Ryan went for broke on first down, throwing to Collins on a post pattern, but the Packers had switched to a zone defense, and Bob Jeter and Tom Brown converged on him. They hit Collins as he attempted to catch the ball, but the official did not call interference in front of the raucous Green Bay crowd, as another official had against Bobby Boyd a week earlier. On the next play, Nitschke and Robinson, blitzing, dropped Ryan for a loss. On third and long, Ryan completed a pass to Brown coming out of the backfield, but he was stopped one yard short of the first down on a great tackle by Jeter. Collier decided to play it safe. Groza kicked a field goal from 28 yards, and the teams went into the locker room with the Packers leading 13–12.

The Browns couldn't move the ball after the kickoff, and a botched punt return by Elijah Pitts left the Packers on their own 10-yard line. Then followed one of the most classic Green Bay drives of the season, a series of well-executed running plays that culminated in Hornung's 13-yard touchdown on a sweep left and used up all but five minutes of the quarter—the kind of drive the Browns never managed to mount. The Packers led 20–12.

With 20 minutes of football left, the Browns had no need to panic. A Ryan scramble, a roughness penalty on linebacker Leroy Caffey, and two carries by Brown, good for a first down, reached the Green Bay 35-yard line. A short pass to Collins got the ball to the Green Bay 28-yard line. Then Ryan went for broke on a post pattern to Brown. The great fullback appeared to have two defenders beaten under the goalposts, but the pass was slightly underthrown—perhaps to avoid hitting the crossbar—and he slowed and then dropped the ball. On the next play, the ball slipped out of Ryan's hand as he tried to pass, and although he retained possession, Lionel Aldridge dropped him on the spot. Once again, Groza lined up for a field goal, but this time Henry Jordan broke through and blocked it.

The Green Bay attack resumed, and with 9:28 left, Chandler kicked another field goal to make the score 23–12, effectively a two-touchdown lead. Seconds later, Leroy Kelly almost got one of them back with a great kickoff return, but Packer kicker Chandler, the last man with a chance at him, saved the day on the Packer 47-yard line. There were nine minutes left—but Ryan decided to pass three times in a row. The first pass, delivered against a strong rush, missed Collins; the second reached Brown, but he was stopped for no gain; the third never was thrown, as Willie Davis tackled Ryan. Once again, Collins punted, this time down to the Green Bay seven-yard line, but now there were less than eight minutes left.

Rising to the occasion, the Cleveland defense stopped the Packers cold. An all-out rush attempted to block Chandler's punt but just failed to do so and resulted in a roughing the kicker penalty instead. The Packers promptly made one first down, and there were only two minutes left when Chandler punted the ball. On the first play from scrimmage, Ryan overthrew Collins, and Herb Adderley atoned for his early mistake and intercepted. The Packers ran out the clock. The game and the championship belonged to them, 23–12, and for the first time in three years, they carried Vince Lombardi off the field.

Taylor, Hornung, and the Packers' offensive line had risen to the occasion. Hornung had rushed for 105 yards and Taylor for 96, easily their best joint performance of the whole season. Hornung's 105 totaled more than one-third of his entire rushing yardage for the year. Aging and often injured, he had saved two outstanding performances for the games in which they were needed most, against the Colts in Baltimore and in the NFL Championship. Starr, meanwhile, had completed 10 of 18 passes for 147 yards and a touchdown—47 of those yards on the opening score to Dale, who had managed to keep his feet when Beach and Fichtner couldn't.

John Wooten

> The day before the game was cold and dry. We were staying at the Holiday Inn in Appleton, 30 miles away. It snowed overnight, the road was full of snow and ice, with accidents everywhere. It took so long they almost had to delay the game. We lost that game sitting on the bus, and Frank Ryan had his worst game ever.

Paul Warfield

> We certainly had opportunities to win the ballgame. I refuse to acknowledge the fact that the field was any worse for us than it was for them. We both had to play on it.[1]

Frank Ryan, apparently, had felt it was his destiny to repeat his brilliant three-touchdown performance of 1964. In that 27–0 victory over the Colts, he had completed 11 of 18 passes for 197 yards and three touchdowns, but meanwhile, Jim Brown had rushed 27 times for 114 yards, and the team had 142 rushing yards overall. This year, in the third title game of his career, Jim Brown had carried the ball just 12 times, good for 50 yards, while Ryan

7. The Championship

finished with eight completions in 18 attempts. Brown was a better back than Hornung or Taylor, and the Cleveland offensive line in 1965 was probably as good as the vaunted Packers—but he had carried the ball only a dozen times. No one knew that Jim Brown had played his last game for the Cleveland Browns. The team's strategy had cost him the chance to go out a winner.

The Packers had risen to the occasion, less spectacularly than in Baltimore on December 12, when they won 42–27, but well enough. Lombardi told the press after the game that the team was not the most talented he had ever had but had perhaps the most character. "A lot of things happened to us this season," he said, thinking perhaps of the nearly violent revolt he faced after the loss in Los Angeles, "but the players closed their mouths and never said a word to the press or anyone. They kept their mouths shut. Everything that was said was said here in the dressing room." Not for nearly ten years did reserve center Bill Curry tell the story of Lombardi's meltdown after the loss to the Rams and the team's response.

The Packer defense—coached by Phil Bengtson, not Lombardi—had been outstanding all season and had won the team several key games, beginning with the 20–17 win over the Colts the second week of the season and including their 13–3 and 6–3 victories over the Cowboys and Rams. The offense had struggled but had come to life in key games against the Vikings and Colts. The team had been unable to advance smoothly to the championship by beating the 49ers on the last day of the season, and they had beaten the crippled Colts only with critical help from the official who had ruled Chandler's missed field goal good to tie the game at 10–10 with two minutes left. They were probably not the equal of the Colts with Unitas, or perhaps even with Cuozzo, and they had been beaten 31–10 midway through the season by the Chicago Bears. But they had won—and a similar mix of greatness and luck gave them two more championships in the next two years.

Two games remained on the NFL schedule.

The Playoff Bowl in Miami now looks like the ancestor of the Super Bowl—the first annual postseason game in a neutral warm-weather site—but it had aroused more negative than positive comments since its inception in 1960. The Detroit Lions had won the first three iterations against Cleveland, Philadelphia, and Pittsburgh after the 1960–62 seasons, establishing a strong claim to the status of second-best team in the league after the Packers. Then Lombardi, who notoriously hated the very idea of a game for second-place teams—"A hinky-dink game for hinky-dink football players," he once wrote—had won once (against the Browns) and lost once (to the Cardinals). This year was different. The Cowboys, declared the second-place team in the East by virtue of their record in two games with the Giants, were making their first post-season appearance—as it turned out, the first of ten consecutive such trips. The Colts, on the other hand, had something to prove after their heartbreaking loss to the Packers, and since the game meant nothing, they could afford to relax, take some chances, and have some fun. They might as well have—the winners stood to earn $1,200 each and the losers $500. Shula, mindful of his team's bitterness over the playoff outcome, let them spend most of the time with their families.

Meanwhile, Shula gave no hint to the press of how he planned to play the game. Press attention focused on two of the Cowboys' young stars: Bob Hayes, who had finished the season with just over 1,000 yards gained receiving and a 20-yard per reception average, and tackle Bob Lilly, who would face off against Colt all-time great Jim Parker. To counter Hayes, the Colts inserted their speedy kick returner Alvin Haymond at free safety to help Lenny Lyles and Bobby Boyd contain him. The Cowboys and the Packers were among the first teams to flip wide receivers from one side of the field to the other.

The Cowboys were four-point favorites over the Colts when the teams took the field on Sunday, January 9, 1966. The game started according to plan. Although Matte tried a couple of passes in the Colts' first series, he could not move the team, and Dallas took over on their own 49-yard line after a short punt. Don Meredith quickly passed to Hayes for 20 yards. But on the next play, a Colt blitz got to Meredith as he let his pass go, and strong safety Jerry Logan intercepted. The teams traded the ball for most of the period, but then the Colts took over on their own 21-yard line and drove the ball to the Cowboy six-yard line on the ground, led by fullback Jerry Hill and Matte. There they stalled, and Shula—who was calling nearly all the plays—resorted to trickery. Bobby Boyd, the field goal holder, picked up the ball to pass but missed Jerry Hill, who was wide open in the end zone. The Colts appeared to have squandered a rare opportunity.

The Colts continued to contain the Cowboy offense, however, and in the second quarter, a new Colt team took over the ball on the Colt 35-yard line. Dropping back in the best John Unitas style, Matte found Raymond Berry open on a quick hitch for a first down. Then, a few plays later, he delivered the ball 20 yards upfield to John Mackey in full stride behind the Dallas secondary, and Mackey was tackled from behind on the Dallas eight-yard line. A beautifully executed trap play opened a hole for Lenny Moore, and he scored to make it 7–0. Dallas finally got going late in the period and moved the ball to the Colt four-yard line, but the Baltimore

7. The Championship

defense put up another inspired goal-line stand and forced the Cowboys to settle for a field goal.

When the Colts started again from their own 33-yard line, Matte dropped back and found Hill—the fullback—wide open on what appeared to be a fly pattern down the middle of the field. His pass was perfect, finding the receiver in full stride, and Hill went 52 yards to the Dallas 15-yard line. Two pitchouts to Hill around the right side—away from George Andrie and Bob Lilly—got the ball into the end zone for a 14–3 lead. The half was almost over, and the Colts got the ball back once more when Alex Hawkins made a fair catch of a punt at his own 43-yard line. This time the Colts took advantage of the rule allowing for a free-kick field goal after a fair catch—the rule that the Lions had failed to use against them on Thanksgiving Day. Michaels was long enough, but the kick was wide right. Matte finished the first half with three completions good for 103 yards.

The second half began with a turnover when Dallas fullback Don Perkins fumbled on his own 25-yard line. It took just five plays for Jerry Hill to make it into the end zone for the Colts' third touchdown. Meredith was sacked more than once by young end Roy Hilton, subbing for Ordell Braase, and when the Colts got the ball back again in good field position, Matte finished yet another drive with a 15-yard pass to a wide-open Jimmy Orr in the end zone, and the Colts led 28–3. In the fourth quarter, the Colts put together another great drive featuring fine runs by Jerry Hill and rookie fullback Mike Curtis—who was destined to become a star linebacker. Matte finished that drive with the same rollout and corner pattern to Orr in the end zone. The Colts had destroyed the Cowboys 35–3, and the Western Conference's record against the East now stood at 15–1. The Colts had 21 first downs to the Cowboys' 13, and Matte outgained Meredith in the air 165 yards to 159. Meredith was sacked three times, and Matte completed his third game in a row without being dumped trying to pass. He finished his NFL quarterback career as the game MVP. "Maybe we should have passed more," Matte had commented two weeks earlier after the loss to the Packers. Apparently, he was right.

"I can't help being proud of them when they hit like this," Don Shula said. "I have gained so much respect for Tom Matte. I don't know what to say. I respected him before, but the way he took over and did the job, he will have to keep his tape with the plays on his wrist." Today, that tape is in the NFL Hall of Fame. The Colts had proven themselves at least the second-best team in the NFL. For the Cowboys, a whole new era lay just ahead.

A week later, Vince Lombardi and Blanton Collier faced off again in the Pro Bowl in Los Angeles. With Unitas injured and Bart Starr left off the roster, John Brodie and Fran Tarkenton quarterbacked the Western Conference team, with Frank Ryan calling the signals for the East. Lombardi was already worrying that his team's success might go to their head.

Ken Willard

> We practiced in Dodger Stadium. Leroy Caffey was on the team, and he made a mistake in practice. "Leroy," Vince said, "you are so stupid. You did that all year." He never let up.
>
> Vince picked me to start, but I pulled my hamstring in the last carry in practice. The doctor gave me a shot on game day, but I couldn't run. My job was to stay with Vince on the sidelines. Gale Sayers dropped the first couple of punts, and Vince said, "He doesn't have it."

The West, not surprisingly, were seven-point favorites—but they never had a chance. Six minutes into the first quarter, Redskin safety Paul Krause intercepted a Brodie pass, and Jim Bakken of the Cardinals opened the scoring with a field goal. A 51-yard pass from Ryan to Sonny Randle set up a two-yard plunge by Jim Brown—who always enjoyed the nationwide television audience and the competition among the best—and when Gale Sayers fumbled a fair catch near the goal line in the second quarter, Brown scored again. He scored his third touchdown after Detroit linebacker Wayne Walker was called for pass interference in the end zone, and the East led 23–0 at the half. In the second half, the magnificent Sayers showed his stuff with kickoff returns of 51 and 48 yards, but additional interceptions of Brodie passes by Maxie Baughan and Cornell Green stopped two Western Conference drives. Brodie threw yet another interception into the arms of Mel Renfro deep in his own territory, and Renfro ran it in for a touchdown. In the final quarter, Brodie ended by far his worst performance of the season with a touchdown pass to Tommy McDonald. Although the East made only 19 first downs to 16 for the West, gaining 141 yards rushing and 127 passing, they emerged with a 34–7 victory. Somewhere, the late, legendary commissioner Bert Bell must have been smiling, as the unpredictability of the league he had created had proven out once again. Humiliated 15–1 in the first sixteen games between the conferences, the East had some revenge. Now the most significant offseason in the league's history got underway.

Epilogue

On May 16, 1966, the NFL announced at its annual meetings that its goalposts would now rise a full 20 feet above the crossbar, twice as much as previously, to make it easier for officials to judge whether a kick was good. The league denied that this decision had anything to do with the dispute over Don Chandler's tying field goal in the playoff against the Colts five months earlier.[1]

Two days later, on May 18, the nation's sports pages reported the opening salvo in an all-out war between the two professional leagues. The New York Giants, struggling to improve after their 7–7 season, fired the shot. They had lacked any real field goal kicker all season, and they broke all precedents by signing Pete Gogolak of the Buffalo Bills. Gogolak, whose family had come to the U.S. in 1956 as refugees from the Hungarian Revolution, had grown up playing soccer and adapted the soccer style of kicking to football at Cornell. After Gogolak graduated, the Buffalo Bills had signed him to a one-year contract for 1964, and he had played out his option in the 1965 season, in which the Bills won a second straight AFL title. This was the first time that a team in either league had raided a player in mid-career under these circumstances. Giants' owner, Wellington Mara, wanted to destroy the AFL, not least because the New York Jets had just put themselves on the city's map with their highly publicized signing of Joe Namath to an expensive contract, and Namath had just finished an uneven but promising rookie season. Pete Rozelle, who seldom took on powerful owners, had ten days to try to block the contract and took no action.

Al Davis, a 36-year-old Brooklynite who had been serving as head coach and general manager of the Oakland Raiders, had just replaced Joe Foss as commissioner of the AFL. Davis was Sonny Corleone to Foss's Tom Hagen, determined to end the battle between the two leagues with total victory, using a new strategy of stealing away established NFL stars. On May 27, Davis's old team, Oakland, announced that they had signed Rams quarterback Roman Gabriel, who had come on strong during the second half of the season after Bill Munson's injury, to a big three-year contract. The

Epilogue

Rams replied that Gabriel had already committed to two more years with them and promised a court battle, but several other NFL stars, including defensive back Irv Cross and running back Tim Brown of the Philadelphia Eagles and guard John Gordy of the Detroit Lions, were quickly reported to be negotiating with AFL teams. The AFL teams were offering contracts that would begin in 1967, after their new players had spent 1966 playing out their current team's option. Two other extremely influential NFL executives, Vince Lombardi and George Halas, criticized the Gogolak signing publicly in the first week of June, and Lombardi expressed the hope that the two leagues might discuss peace. John Brodie, meanwhile, opened negotiations with the AFL Houston Oilers. On June 5, their owner, Bud Adams, said that he had offered Brodie $750,000 but that the contract hadn't been signed because "some things had taken place since then." The 49er owners were among Wellington Mara's allies in their opposition to the merger.

The public did not know that Mara and Davis were trying, in effect, to disrupt peace talks between the two leagues that had begun in late February or early March of 1966. Three AFL owners—Ralph Wilson of Buffalo, Lamar Hunt of Kansas City (the richest and probably the most powerful owner in the league), and Billy Sullivan of Boston had opened up merger negotiations with Tex Schramm of the Cowboys. Joe Namath's contract, in particular, had convinced many owners that the bidding war had to stop before it bankrupted them all. Rozelle evidently had known about the talks, but Davis had not. The signing of Gogolak had struck directly at Wilson.

Upton Bell

> Carroll Rosenbloom was also involved in the merger talks. When Davis started signing the NFL quarterbacks, he said, "We can't go on paying this kind of money." But I was told that Rozelle was against it. He had an NFL background himself and didn't want to take them in.

On June 7, *The New York Times* broke the story of the talks. Davis pooh-poohed the reports, while Rozelle had no comment. The next day, the two leagues announced a merger. Rozelle would immediately become sole commissioner, the leagues would hold a common draft in January 1967, and the two league champions would play the first Super Bowl in the same month. The leagues would remain separate for the next three years. The AFL teams would have to pay the NFL about $2 million each over the next 18 years—a great deal less than the $50 million that Rozelle had demanded in informal contacts a year earlier. $10 million of that money went to the

Epilogue

New York Giants and $8 million to the San Francisco 49ers to indemnify them for having to share their markets with the Jets and the Raiders, respectively. The Giants also received an extra first-round draft pick. Neither of those concessions, as it turned out, enabled New York to reach postseason play again for many years.[2]

Al Davis, whose job had ceased to exist under the merger terms, attacked the deal, claiming that the new league "had the NFL on the run." He returned to the Raiders as their general manager and remained a bone in Rozelle's throat for many more years, most notably when he moved the team to Los Angeles.

Another huge story broke about ten days later. Jim Brown was now filming his second movie, *The Dirty Dozen*, in London, and the huge production had fallen behind schedule because of bad weather. By mid-June, it was clear that Brown would have to miss at least a month of training camp, and Cleveland owner Art Modell announced that Brown, who was paid his yearly salary on a 12-month basis, would incur a heavy fine if he were late, and that his role on the team would come into question. On July 14, Brown called a London press conference to announce his retirement from football at the age of 30. He had not missed a single game in nine years with the Browns and had led the NFL in rushing in eight of them. The career of the most dominant player in NFL history was over.

As it turned out, the 1965 season kicked off a second round of Packer domination that lasted for two more years. The 1966 season was the last in which two divisions played a whole season to produce two title contenders. Green Bay won the Western Conference quite easily, finishing three full games ahead of the disappointing Colts, whom they beat two more times. The two teams met in the season opener on a Saturday night, and Unitas, returning from injury, threw three interceptions, two of them for touchdowns, as the Packers won 24–3.

In the Eastern Conference, the Cowboys won an exciting three-team race against Cleveland and St. Louis, thanks largely to another key injury to Charley Johnson of the Cardinals, who had led the conference until they lost their last three games without him. Leroy Kelly, replacing Jim Brown in the Cleveland backfield, turned in a great season for the Browns, but they fell short nonetheless. In 1966, the Green Bay offense improved considerably as Bart Starr turned in a fine year, increasing from 316 points—eighth in the league—to 335, good for fourth in the league, but the defense remained the stronger part of the team, allowing a league-leading 163 points, a 61-point improvement from 1965. Losing only to the 49ers and Vikings, the pack finished with a 12–2 record. They got a terrible scare in the championship

Epilogue

game against Dallas, in which they jumped off to a 14–0 lead before the Cowboys had run off a single play, only to see the Cowboys tie the game before the end of the first quarter. A wild, seesaw battle followed, and with less than two minutes to go, the Cowboys found themselves on the Green Bay two-yard line thanks to a pass interference call, first and goal, trailing 34–27. On their second play, however, an offensive lineman moved too quickly, and the ball went back to the six-yard line. The Cowboys reached the two again on third down, but Don Meredith had to throw while locked in the arms of Dave Robinson on the final play after Bob Hayes, who should have been removed from the game, failed to block Robinson. Tom Brown intercepted the pass and saved the victory. The Packers went on to win the first Super Bowl against the Kansas City Chiefs easily 35–10.

Dave Robinson

> I was *very* surprised to see Bob Hayes line up opposite me on that play. Bob Hayes couldn't block me if he had his twin brother along to help.

In 1967, the league added a 16th team, the New Orleans Saints, and split into four divisions of four teams each, adding a second round of playoffs. That alone enabled the Packers to reach postseason play, win another NFL title, and add a second Super Bowl. With the league's ninth-best offense and third-best defense, the Packers went 9–4–1, good enough to win their division against Detroit, Minnesota, and the disappointing Bears. Meanwhile, in the Coastal Division, the Colts and the Los Angeles Rams—now in their second season under George Allen, who had quit Halas and the Bears after 1965—finished second and first in both points scored and points allowed and ended the year with identical 11–1–2 records. Both teams had won single games against the Packers, and they had tied in their first meeting. They met for the second time in the last game of the season, and the Rams won in a very impressive rout, 34–10, giving them the division championship based on the total points scored in the teams' two games and earning them the right to play the Packers again in Milwaukee the following week. Lombardi now worked an even bigger miracle than the one he had pulled off in Baltimore two weeks before the season's end in 1965, utterly dominating the Rams and winning the game 28–7.

The Packers won the NFL Championship the following week against the Cowboys in the Ice Bowl, 17–14, in a finish fraught with irony. This time it was the Packers who found themselves on the Cowboy one-yard line trailing 14–10 with less than a minute left, and Bart Starr called his own

Epilogue

number on a wedge behind Jerry Kramer. Kramer admitted in his account of the season, *Instant Replay*, that he might have been offside on the play, and film eventually showed that he was.[3] But this time, the officials did not call the offside, and Starr scored the winning touchdown. Every dynasty in every sport probably gets more than its share of breaks from the officials, and for the second time in three years, an officiating failure had given Green Bay an NFL title. The Packers won the Super Bowl again against Oakland. Lombardi retired, and the aging team fell to 6–7–1 the following year under Phil Bengtson.

Don Shula's Colts run of bad luck continued for three years. They definitely fell off the Packers' pace in 1966, finishing 9–5, and then, as we have seen, failed to make the playoffs in 1967 despite losing just one game. Johnny Unitas began 1968 with a badly injured elbow, and veteran Earl Morrall took over. The team had an extraordinary season, finishing a close second in points scored and an easy first in fewest points allowed, and lost just one game. They destroyed the Cleveland Browns in the NFL title game 34–0—and lost the third Super Bowl to the New York Jets 16–7 in the biggest upset in the history of the league. After an off year in 1969, Shula's last with the team, they turned in another fine season behind Unitas and new coach Don McCafferty in 1970, when they joined the American Football Conference and edged out the Cowboys 16–13 in an error-filled Super Bowl. They had the best won-loss record of any NFL team in the second half of the 1960s. Don Shula won two Super Bowls with the Miami Dolphins, remained their coach for 25 years, and retired as the winningest coach in the history of the NFL.

The Chicago Bears had looked like the best team in the NFL during the last six weeks or so of the 1965 season. Gale Sayers and Dick Butkus were two of the most impressive rookies in league history, and the Bears' future appeared bright. It didn't turn out that way.

In the opinion of Dick Butkus, the Bears' dreams of glory went down the tubes before the 1966 season even started when George Allen, his mentor as Bear defensive coach, left the team over the strenuous objections of George Halas to take over as head coach of the Rams. Halas was now well into his seventies and might easily have given Allen the Bears head coaching position instead, but he wound up staying on for two more years.[4] Although Sayers had a tremendous 1966 season, leading the NFL with 1,231 yards rushing and catching 34 passes for 447 additional yards, Rudy Bukich could not repeat his great 1965 season, and the offense as a whole was mediocre. They opened 1966 with 14–3 and 31–17 losses to the Lions and the Rams, reached .500 with the help of a victory over the Colts, but then won just one of their next five games, tying two, and finished the year at 5–7–2. Overall, their offense fell from more than 400 points to just 234. Poor quarterbacking hurt them in 1967, although they improved to 7–6–1. The team got off to a 1–4 start in 1968, but won three in a row, culminating in a 13–10 win over the Packers in which Sayers gained more than 200 yards for the only time in his career. After eight weeks, Sayers had gained 824 yards and appeared certain to lead the league again. However, the next week he tore knee ligaments against the 49ers and missed the rest of the season. The team finished at 7–7. Sayers returned after lengthy rehab in 1969 and carried the ball 236 times for a league-leading 1,032 yards, although his longest gain from scrimmage was just 28 yards, compared to an average of 63 yards in his first four seasons. That, however, turned out to be the end of his career. He suffered more knee injuries, played just two games each in the following two years, and retired. It took much longer for the Bears to return to the top of the league.

Meanwhile, the Rams picked up where they had left off in 1965 under Allen as they beat the Colts and the Bears once each during 1966, and finished the year 8–6, with better to come. They were nearly unbeatable in 1967, as we have seen, before crashing against the Packers in Milwaukee in the first round of the playoffs. After a slight slump in 1968 left them behind the Colts, owner Dan Reeves announced that he was firing George Allen, but a players' revolt forced him to keep the highly independent coach for two more years. The team won its first 11 games in a row in 1969 to clinch a playoff spot, lost the next three, and lost a cold-weather thriller in Minnesota 23–20 in the first-round playoff game.

After finishing at .500 in 1965, the promising Vikings slipped to 4–9–1 and then lost the two men who had defined the team for the first six years of its existence.

Fran Tarkenton

> During 1966, we played the expansion Falcons in Atlanta. I was a Georgia boy, and Van Brocklin benched me for the game, and we lost. With four weeks left in the season, he said to me, "You and I have to get on the same page. We can be a winning team." Then he never spoke to me again for the rest of the season. Our offensive coach, Lew Carpenter, and I put together the offense on our own. I decided I'm not going to play for Van Brocklin anymore.
>
> In January, I met with Van Brocklin for four or five hours and told him I had no respect for him, and I didn't want to play for him anymore. He wouldn't accept that. The next day, Jim Finks, the general manager, called me and said,

Epilogue

"Van Brocklin says you had a great conversation, and everything is fine!" I said, "No, I won't play for him anymore. I can quit and go into business." The next day, Finks called me to say they had fired Van Brocklin and asked me to stay. I said I wouldn't stay. They traded me to the Giants [who had just gone 1–12–1] for three number-one picks and two number-two picks. With those picks and their own, they got tackle Ron Yary, defensive tackle Alan Page, halfback Clint Jones, and receiver Gene Washington, and that made them a winning team. I played my best football in New York from 1967 through 1971, but we never made the playoffs. Then I came back to the Vikings, and we went to three Super Bowls.

After one year as the general manager of the Packers in 1968, Vince Lombardi returned to coaching with the Washington Redskins, who had fired Otto Graham after two very disappointing seasons. The team's main assets were still Sonny Jurgensen at quarterback and his remarkable receivers. Lombardi coached the team to a 7–5–2 record, its first winning season in more than a decade. Then, during training camp in 1970, he was diagnosed with terminal colon cancer.

Sonny Jurgensen

Playing for Lombardi was the highlight of my career. The first time I met with him, he didn't say a word about my weight. I couldn't believe it—every other coach had. I asked him about that later, and he said, "I figured that if you could get through my practices, you'd be in shape." And he was right! I had nine different coaches, and he was the only one who *simplified* the game of football. That was fun.

In training camp, he told me not to pass so quickly. "Let the play develop!" he said. At the end of the year, he stopped me in the office and said, "You had a good year! You completed 66% of your passes!" "Yes," I said, "but look how many times I got sacked!" "You knew the personnel better than I did," he said.

In the spring of 1970, when he got diagnosed, we were working out at Georgetown University before camp. He was in Georgetown Hospital, and he would sit out on the porch. After the workouts, I would go and give him a report. About two weeks before he died, I stopped over, and he said, "I was thinking about the 3–4 defense that all these AFL teams play. We're going to have a problem with that because we key the middle linebacker on our backs' divide pass, and they don't have one. I think I've figured out what to do. If we could use a flood pattern, we can get the fullback through on the weak side, and we'd have Brown and Taylor on the strong side." I said, "That makes sense." I was just amazed that he was still thinking about football plays.

After 1970, when the AFC and NFC merged their schedules, NFL fans accustomed themselves to a new rhythm. Now one team in each conference

Epilogue

qualified for postseason play via a wild card. Some teams often had an easy road to the playoffs thanks to a weak division, and the postseason often included aggregations that fell well short of championship caliber. For a while, the Baby Boomer generation provided an ample flow of new talent into the league, but as it continued to expand and birth rates fell, eventually, the size of the league outran the available talent pool. Meanwhile, the playoffs have continually expanded to keep more teams in contention, from two teams out of 15 in 1966, to eight teams out of 27 in the fully merged leagues in 1970, to 14 out of 32 teams in 2020. Every individual regular-season game, clearly, has become far less important.

The amazing 1965 season was a crossroads in many ways: the last season of Jim Brown, the first season of telecast doubleheaders, the last season before the merger, and the next-to-last season in which contending teams knew that to reach the NFL championship game, they had to play every game as if they absolutely had to win it. They did—and they left behind a story for the ages.

Chapter Notes

Chapter 1

1. On Unitas see Tom Callahan, *Johnny U: The Life and Times of Johnny Unitas* (New York: Crown, 2006).
2. Many friends and teammates of Lipscomb refused to believe that he had voluntarily injected heroin.
3. George Plimpton, *One More July: A Football Dialogue with Bill Curry* (New York: Harper and Row, 1977), p. 45.
4. Callahan, *Johnny U,* pp. 109, 131.
5. David Maraniss, *When Pride Still Mattered* (New York: Simon & Schuster, 1999), pp. 362–3. On the afternoon of her daughter's eighteenth birthday, she drank too much and swallowed too many pills and had to be taken to the hospital.
6. Plimpton, *One More July,* pp. 25–6.
7. Paul Hornung as told to Al Silverman, *Football and the Single Man* (New York: Doubleday, 1965).
8. For another account of Hornung's lifestyle, see Maraniss, *When Pride Still Mattered,* p. 278.
9. "Pro Football 1965," *Sports Illustrated,* September 13, 1965, p. 46.
10. George Plimpton, *Paper Lion: Confessions of a Last-String Quarterback* (New York: Harper and Row, 1965), p. 59.
11. Dick Butkus and Pat Smith, *Butkus: Flesh and Blood* (New York: Doubleday, 1997), pp. 1–119.
12. Gale Sayers with Fred Mitchell, *Sayers: My Life and Times* (Chicago: Triumph, 2007), pp. 127–144, 155–164.
13. Jim Brown with Myron Cope, *Off My Chest* (New York: Doubleday, 1964), pp. 47–74.
14. Roger Gordon, *Blanton's Browns, The Great 1965-69 Cleveland Browns* (Kent, OH: Kent State University Press, 2019), p. 8.

Unless otherwise indicated, these indented quotes come from my own interviews.

15. On Landry see the detailed biography, Mark Ribowsky, *The Last Cowboy* (New York, 2014).
16. *Sports Illustrated,* September 13, 1965, p. 40.
17. Neely wound up with the Dallas Cowboys via the Oakland Raiders of the AFL, who initially signed him.
18. "Football Rights Bought by NBC," *New York Times,* January 30, 1964, p. 59.
19. The AFL is the subject of a wonderful oral history, Jeff Miller's *Going Long: The Wild 10-Year Saga of the Renegade American Football League in the Words of Those Who Lived It* (New York: McGraw-Hill, 2003).

Chapter 2

1. Sayers with Mitchell, *Sayers,* p. 61.
2. *Chicago Tribune,* October 14, 1965, p. E4.

Chapter 3

1. Maraniss, *When Pride Still Mattered,* p. 371.
2. *Sports Illustrated,* November 1, 1965.
3. *Chicago Tribune,* November 1, 1965, p. C2.
4. Plimpton, *One More July,* pp. 33, 85.

Chapter 4

1. Jerry Kramer, *Instant Replay: The Green Bay Diary of Jerry Kramer* (New York: Doubleday, 2006), pp. 179–80.
2. Quoted in Gordon, *Blanton's Browns,* p. 19.

Chapter Notes

3. *Time*, November 26, 1965, pp. 80ff.
4. Frank Deford, *Over Time: My Life as a Sportswriter* (New York: Atlantic Monthly, 2012), p. 245.
5. Callahan, *Johnny U*, pp. 28, 205–6.
6. "Heroes without Headlines," *Sports Illustrated*, November 29, 1965, p. 30.
7. Plimpton, *One More July*, pp. 28–30.
8. From the ABC documentary, *Portrait of a Team*, released in November 1966—copy in author's possession.

Chapter 5

1. Plimpton, *Mad Ducks and Bears*, p. 280.
2. After 12 games, Willard led Sayers in rushing, 745 yards to 672.
3. Indeed one can, around the Bears' 37-yard line.
4. Plimpton, *Mad Ducks and Bears*, pp. 24–5.
5. Plimpton, *Mad Ducks and Bears*, p. 280.

Chapter 6

1. Plimpton, *One More July*, p. 47.
2. The ABC documentary *Portrait of a Team* artificially extended the goal post upward, confirming that the ball passed outside it. The camera angle would if anything have made the kick look closer to being good than it was.
3. Film in the ABC documentary *Portrait of a Team* shows unequivocally that Taylor fumbled before he hit the ground.
4. "Chandler's admission helps take sting out of 31-year old bad call," *Baltimore Sun*, November 3, 1996, https://www.baltimoresun.com/news/bs-xpm-1996-11-03-1996308165-story.html.

Chapter 7

1. Gordon, *Blanton's Browns*, p. 26.

Epilogue

1. "Rozelle Declares NFL Hasn't Chosen City," *Corpus Christi Caller-Times*, May 17, 1966, p. 44.
2. The best account of the merger is in Miller, *Going Long*, pp. 189–205.
3. Kramer, *Instant Replay*, p. 217. An ESPN documentary, *The Ice Bowl*, includes the film of the offside: https://www.youtube.com/watch?v=vGjg7j-qTvw&t=8s.
4. Butkus and Smith, *Butkus*, pp. 169–71.

Bibliography

Periodicals

Baltimore Sun
Chicago Tribune
Cleveland Plain Dealer
Corpus Christi Caller-Times
Dallas Morning News
Detroit Free Press
Green Bay Press Gazette
Los Angeles Times
Minneapolis Star-Tribune
New York Times
Sports Illustrated
Washington Post

Books

Brown, Jim, with Myron Cope. *Off My Chest.* Garden City, NY: Doubleday, 1964
Butkus, Dick, and Pat Smith. *Butkus: Flesh and Blood.* New York: Doubleday, 1997.
Callahan, Tom. *Johnny U: The Life and Times of Johnny Unitas.* New York: Crown, 2006.
Deford, Frank. *Over Time: My Life as a Sportswriter.* New York: Atlantic Monthly, 2012.
Gordon, Roger. *Blanton's Browns: The Great 1965–69 Cleveland Browns.* Kent, OH: Kent State University Press, 2019.
Hornung, Paul, as told to Al Silverman. *Football and the Single Man.* New York: Doubleday, 1965.
Kramer, Jerry. *Instant Replay: The Green Bay Diary of Jerry Kramer.* New York: Doubleday, 2006.
Maraniss, David. *When Pride Still Mattered.* New York: Simon & Schuster, 1999.
Miller, Jeff. *Going Long: The Wild 10-Year Saga of the Renegade American Football League in the Words of Those Who Lived It.* New York: McGraw-Hill, 2003.
Plimpton, George. *Mad Ducks and Bears: Football Revisited.* New York: Random House, 1973.
_____. *One More July: A Football Dialogue with Bill Curry.* New York: Harper and Row, 1977.
_____. *Paper Lion: Confessions of a Last-String Quarterback.* New York: Harper and Row, 1965.
Ribowsky, Mark. *The Last Cowboy: A Life of Tom Landry.* New York: W.W. Norton, 2014.
Sayers, Gale, with Fred Mitchell. *Sayers: My Life and Times.* Chicago: Triumph, 2007.

Interviews

Upton Bell
Gary Collins
Bill Curry
Roman Gabriel
Dennis Gaubatz
Ernie Green
Charley Johnson
Sonny Jurgensen
Dick LeBeau
Andy Livingston
Tom Matte
Johnny Morris
Dave Robinson
Dan Sullivan
Fran Tarkenton
Ken Willard
John Wooten

Index

Adams, Bud 144
Adderley, Herb 15, 17, 31, 34, 39–41, 44, 96, 118–20, 124, 126, 134, 136, 138
Aldridge, Lionel 15, 31, 76, 94–95, 126, 137
Alexander, Kermit 18, 100, 118–21
Allen, George 32, 36, 90, 97, 99, 146–48
Ameche, Alan 7
American Football League (AFL) 1, 5, 18–20, 26, 28, 33, 59, 93, 117, 143, 151
Anderson, Bill 68, 96, 103, 125, 127–31
Anderson, Donny 93
Andrie, George 26, 67, 141
Arnett, Jon 48, 53, 60, 63, 77, 84, 107–8
Atkins, Doug 19, 38, 59, 71
Atlanta Falcons 93, 133

Baker, Terry 38
Bakken, Jim 77, 116, 142
Ballman, Gary 61, 81
Baltimore Colts 1–3, 6–10, 15–17, 20, 24, 30–35, 39–40, 42–43, 47, 55–56, 60, 63–65, 70–76, 80–91, 95–99, 101–7, 110–18, 121–31, 138–41, 146–48
Barnes, Erich 37
Barr, Terry 17, 36, 54, 64, 68, 78
Bartkowski, Steve 96
baseball 1, 5, 18, 20, 27, 29, 103
basketball 80, 89
Bass, Dick 43
Baugh, Sammy 111
Baughan, Maxie 142
Beach, Walter 31, 37, 79, 134–35, 137
Bears 38–39, 43–44, 47–49, 51–53, 62–65, 70–71, 76–78, 84–86, 88–90, 97–99, 101–3, 107–11, 117–18, 123–24, 146–48, 152–53
Bell, Bert 9, 61, 142
Bell, Upton 2, 9, 56, 75, 82, 98, 120, 127, 144
Bengtson, Phil 12, 54, 69, 128, 139, 147
Benz, Larry 41
Berra, Yogi 94
Berry, Raymond 7, 9, 40, 60, 64–65, 70–71, 74, 82, 85–86, 102–4, 106, 112, 114
Biletnikoff, Fred 32, 86
Bivins, Charlie 99
Bledsoe, Hal 34, 59

Boston Patriots 22
Bowman, Ken 14, 90, 127
Boyd, Bobby 8, 98, 104, 113, 115, 123–24, 126, 128, 130, 137, 140
Braase, Ordell 8, 39, 70, 87, 99, 103, 141
Bratkowski, Zeke 40, 76, 91, 96–97, 118, 126–31
Briggs Stadium 86
Brodie, John 35, 42–43, 47, 49, 51, 59, 64–65, 67, 77, 84–85, 90, 107–9, 118–21, 142, 144
Brown, Bill 15, 43, 51, 62, 73, 85
Brown, Jim 23, 25, 41, 48, 50–51, 65–66, 73, 78–80, 85, 88–89, 93–94, 108–9, 134, 138–39, 150–51
Brown, Paul 11, 21–22, 31, 80
Brown, Roger 36, 39, 53, 68–69, 84
Brown, Roosevelt 9
Brown, Tim 26, 41, 66, 85, 89, 144
Brown, Tom 104, 106, 120, 137, 146
Buffalo Bills 18, 28, 33, 143
Bukich, Rudy 36, 38–39, 44, 48–49, 51–52, 59–60, 62, 71, 77, 85, 89, 98–99, 107–9
Bull, Ronnie 51–53, 63, 98, 108, 117
Burk, Adrian 37
Burke, Vernon 120–21
Burson, Jim 50
Butkus, Dick 19, 28, 32, 36, 38, 49, 52, 60, 65, 89, 98–99, 147, 151–53

Caffey, Leroy 14, 43, 62, 104, 137, 142
Callahan, Tom 151–53
Carpenter, Lew 148
Carpenter, Preston 62
Carr, Henry 73
Casey, Bernie 18, 35, 47, 59, 64–65, 67, 85, 100, 118–20
Chandler, Don 38, 40, 44, 47, 53, 58, 76, 119–20, 126, 129–31, 134–38, 143
Chicago Bears 43, 47, 60, 83, 88–89, 97, 100, 107, 113, 139, 147
Christiansen, Jack 42
Cincinnati Reds 103
Civil Rights Act 5
Civil Rights Movement, modern 31
Clarke, Frank 26, 31, 79, 92

155

Index

Cleveland Browns 1, 6, 11, 21, 61, 66, 132, 139, 147, 151, 153
Coastal Division 146
Cogdill, Gail 17
Coia, Angelo 35, 92
Collier, Blanton 21–23, 32, 136–37, 141
Collins, Gary 22, 24, 35, 37, 41, 45, 49, 79, 111, 116, 132, 134, 136–38
Concannon, Jack 56
Conrad, Bobby Joe 25, 45, 67
Cope, Myron 151, 153
Corleone, Sonny 143
Costello, Vince 93, 135
Cotton Bowl 67, 78, 80, 92–93
Cox, Fred 35, 39, 96
Crenshaw, Willis 31, 37, 53
Cross, Irv 144
Crow, John David 18, 25, 35, 64, 90, 108, 119–20
Cruyff, Johan 125
Cuozzo, Gary 35, 56, 70, 73–75, 81, 99, 101–6, 111, 116, 139
Currie, Dan 14
Curry, Bill 2, 9, 11, 13–14, 95–97, 102, 121, 129–30, 139, 151, 153
Curtis, Mike 32, 141

Dale, Carroll 14, 28, 47, 55, 103, 118–19, 127–28, 130–31, 134–35, 138
Dallas Cowboys 3, 24, 26, 30, 32–33, 36–37, 45–46, 58, 67–68, 73–74, 78–79, 90–94, 116–17, 139–41, 144–47
David, Jim 27
Davis, Tommy 59, 77, 108, 118
Davis, Willie 11, 15, 58–59, 62, 71, 76, 118, 123–24, 126, 137, 143–45
Dawson, Len 33
Deford, Frank 81, 152–53
Denver Broncos 19
Detroit Lions 2, 6, 8, 14, 16, 18, 36, 41, 83, 86, 139, 144
Dial, Buddy 79, 117
Ditka, Mike 19, 48, 51, 60, 89, 98, 107–8, 123
Dodger Stadium 142
Donovan, Art 7–8
Dowler, Boyd 13–14, 40, 62, 103, 118, 128–29, 135
Dowling, Tom 11
Downes, Bill 83–84
Dudley, Bill 18

Eastern Conference 24–25, 36–38, 45–46, 49–51, 56, 58, 72, 77, 79, 85–86, 88, 91, 93–94, 110–11, 132
Edwards, Dave 78
Eller, Carl 15, 39
Evey, Dick 70
Ewbank, Weeb 6, 8, 75

Fearsome Foursome 18, 51, 94, 110
Fichtner, Ross 41, 79, 134, 138
Finks, Jim 75, 148–49
Fisher, Bill 18
Fisher, Pat 37, 46, 50, 116
Fiss, Galen 133
Flatley, Paul 59, 74, 83, 85
Fleming, Marv 14, 31, 68
Ford, Bill 87
Fortunato, Joe 19, 123
Foss, Joe 143
Franklin, Bobby 135
Frederickson, Tucker 28, 32, 49, 61, 65, 80, 94

Gabriel, Roman 2, 18, 43, 48, 84, 90–91, 94, 110–11, 113–15, 143–44
Gaechter, Mike 91
Galimore, Willie 19
Gambrell, Billy 25, 67
Gaubatz, Dennis 2, 10, 64, 71, 85, 112, 125, 127, 129
Gent, Pete 50, 68, 92
George, Bill 19, 153
Gifford, Frank 28, 32
Gilburg, Tom 103, 105, 126, 128
Gilchrist, Cookie 18
Gilmer, Harry 63, 88
Glass, Bill 94, 135
Gogolak, Pete 28, 33, 143–44
Gordon, Dick 48, 98
Gordon, Roger 151
Gordy, John 109, 144
Gossett, Bruce 38, 60, 76, 90–91
Grabowski, Jim 93
Gray, Ken 58
Green, Cornell 31, 91–92, 142
Green, Ernie 2, 23, 31, 35, 41, 45, 53, 73, 88, 133, 136
Green Bay Packers 1–3, 9–17, 23–25, 30–32, 38–40, 42–45, 47, 52–55, 58–60, 62–65, 68–72, 75–80, 83, 85–91, 93–97, 100–107, 110–13, 118–26, 128–41, 145–49
Gregg, Forrest 11, 14, 53, 90, 95, 118, 121, 123, 127
Grier, Roosevelt "Rosey" 18, 27, 31, 90
Griese, Bob 9
Gros, Earl 94
Groza, Lou 28, 37, 135, 137

Haffner, George 100, 111–12
Halas, George Stanley 2, 19, 21, 36, 52–53, 60, 71, 108, 112, 147
Hall, Tom 96
Hall of Fame 9, 31
Hanburger, Chris 32, 42, 57
Hanner, Dave 32
Harris, Rickey 81

156

Index

Hart, Doug 15, 106, 119, 134, 136
Hart, Leon 27
Hawkins, Alex 86, 98–99, 106, 124, 141
Hayes, Bob 20, 26, 31, 36–37, 45–46, 49, 67–68, 73, 79, 92, 140, 146
Hayes, Woody 101, 105, 112
Haymond, Alvin 82, 88, 113, 124, 126–27, 130
Heisman Trophy 38, 80, 105
Hickerson, Gene 23, 136
Hill, Jerry 7, 103–4, 106, 113, 126, 131, 140–41
Hill, King 41, 46, 50, 56, 61
Hilton, Roy 87, 141
Hollow, Cooper 48
Hornung, Paul 10–13, 15, 17, 23, 80, 83, 90, 103–7, 125–29, 131–33, 135–39, 151, 153
Houston, Jim 94
Houston Oilers 144
Howley, Chuck 26, 67, 73, 79
Huff, Sam 26–28, 35, 56, 93
Humphrey, Buddy 57, 81, 110, 116
Hunt, Lamar 20, 33, 144
Hutchinson, Tom 93

Izo, George 63, 77

Jefferson, Roy 32, 34, 45, 49, 67
Jeter, Bob 63, 136–37
Johnson, Charley 24–26, 37, 44–46, 49–50, 57, 66, 76–77, 81, 85, 110, 115
Johnson, Jim 18, 47, 107, 119
Johnson, Pres. Lyndon 5, 37, 45, 49, 67
Johnson, Rafer 119
Jones, Clint 149
Jones, David "Deacon" 18, 31, 60, 90, 114, 123
Jones, Dick 62
Jones, Homer 50, 110
Jones, Jimmy 38, 108
Jones, Stan 19, 99
Jones, William Augustus "Dub" 108
Jordan, Henry 11, 15, 39, 71, 85, 90, 126, 137
Josephson, Les 90
Jurgensen, Christian Adolf "Sonny" 2, 24–26, 28, 35, 42, 55–57, 62, 67, 72, 91–94, 149

Kanicki, Jim 135
Kansas City Chiefs 1, 20, 33, 146
Karras, Alex 7, 12, 16–17, 36, 39, 53–55, 68–69, 84, 109, 123
Kelly, Leroy 45, 66, 79, 88, 135–37, 145
Kezar Stadium 36
King, Martin Luther 81
King, Phil 73
Kostelnik, Ron 15, 43, 76, 104
Kramer, Jerry 10–11, 14, 54–55, 69, 90, 127, 135, 147, 151–53
Kramer, Ron 14, 53, 55, 77, 87
Krause, Paul 26, 67, 81, 92, 124

Lambeau Field 31, 125
Landry, Tom 11, 26–27, 32–33, 46, 50, 58, 79, 116–17, 151, 153
Lane, Bobby 27
Lane, Dick "Night Train" 17, 60
Larsen, Gary 15
Lary, Yale 17, 32
LeBaron, Eddie 46
LeBeau, Dick 2, 14, 17, 47, 54, 78, 86–87, 109
LeClerc, Roger 98–99
Leggett, Earl 98
Lemm, Wally 58
Lewis, Dan 62, 67
Lewis, Gary 35, 120
Lilly, Bob 26, 67, 91, 123, 140–41
Linz, Phil 94
Lipscomb, Gene "Big Daddy" 7–9, 151
Livingston, Andy 20–21, 25, 44, 48, 51–53, 62–63, 65, 79, 84, 109, 115
Livingston, Warren 20, 31, 53, 67, 79
Lockhart, Spider 32
Logan, Jerry 8, 35, 81, 106, 127–28, 140
Logan, Obert 117
Lombardi, Vince 1–2, 10–14, 26–27, 34, 39–40, 54–55, 63, 68–70, 90–91, 94–97, 107, 118–19, 138–39, 141–42, 144, 146–47, 149
Long, Bob 44, 47, 55, 96, 120, 127
Looney, Joe Don 10, 36
Lorick, Tony 7, 40, 64, 70, 74, 98
Los Angeles Coliseum 63
Los Angeles Dodgers 46
Los Angeles Rams 2–3, 30–31, 36, 38–39, 43, 47–48, 51–52, 60, 63–64, 75–76, 83–86, 90–91, 93–94, 110–16, 123–24, 139, 146–48
Luckman, Sid 37
Lundy, Lamar 18, 31, 76, 90, 94
Lyles, Lenny 8, 40, 42, 103–4, 125–26, 140

Mack, Tom 93
Mackey, John 7, 9, 40, 70–71, 86, 88, 98–99, 103–6, 114, 123, 128, 131, 140
Maher, Bruce 77, 86
Mantle, Mickey 1
Mara, Wellington 143–44
Maraniss, David 11, 121
Marchetti, Gino 7–9, 32, 109
Marsh, Amos 39, 77, 84, 87, 98
Marshall, Jim 15
Mason, Tommy 15, 48, 59, 65, 72–73, 96
Matte, Tom 2, 7, 9–10, 40, 87–88, 100–101, 103, 105–6, 112–14, 122–24, 126–28, 130–31, 140–41
Maynard, Don 33
Mays, Willie 1
McAfee, Ken 52
McCafferty, Don 147
McCaffrey, Don 10, 112
McCord, Darris 17, 68

157

Index

McDonald, Tommy 38, 49, 85, 113–15, 142
McElhenny, Hugh 32
McGee, Max 14, 40, 121
McKeever, Marlon 115
McMillan, Ernie 31, 58
McPeak, Bill 35, 42, 45, 50–51, 55
McRae, Bennie 19, 39, 60, 62, 108
Meador, Ed 114
Memorial Stadium 34, 82
Meredith, Don 26, 45–46, 50, 61, 67–68, 73, 78–79, 85, 91–94, 110, 116–17, 140–41, 146
Miami Dolphins 147
Michaels, Lou 8, 28, 64, 74, 98, 103–4, 113–14, 124–27, 130
Miller, Clark 78, 84
Miller, Fred 8
Miller, Jeff 151
Milwaukee County Stadium 31
Minnesota Vikings 2–3, 15–17, 31–32, 34–35, 39, 43, 46, 48–49, 51–52, 59, 62, 64–65, 70–75, 85–86, 89–90, 95–97, 99, 110, 117–18, 148–49
Mira, George 64, 67, 108
Mitchell, Bobby 25, 28, 46, 49, 55, 57, 72, 80, 85, 92, 94
Mitchell, Fred 151, 153
Modell, Art 21, 145
Moore, Lenny 7–9, 40, 42, 74, 81–83, 85, 94, 96, 98–99, 103–5, 108, 126, 130–31
Moore, Tom 55, 76, 96, 118, 125, 133, 135
Morrall, Earl 28, 36, 38, 41, 50, 61, 67, 73, 85, 110, 117
Morris, Johnny 2, 19, 38, 49, 51, 60, 71, 98, 108–9
Morris, Larry 70, 77, 98
Morrison, Joe 38
Morrow, John 136
Morse, Arthur 19
Morton, Craig 32, 46, 50, 58
Muhammad, Elijah 23
Municipal Stadium 6, 13, 37, 73
Munson, Bill 18, 36, 38–39, 43, 48, 60, 71, 76, 84, 90, 110–11
Murchison, Clint 33

Namath, Joe 1, 15, 19, 32–33, 143–44
Neely, Ralph 26, 32, 151
Nelsen, Bill 34, 61, 66–67, 73, 81, 110
Nevers, Ernie 108
New Orleans Saints 53, 146
New York Giants 6–7, 9–11, 27–32, 36–38, 41–42, 45–46, 50–51, 56–58, 61–62, 67, 72–73, 80–81, 85–86, 93–94, 110, 116–17, 145; once-mighty 36; weak 24
New York Jets 19, 32–33, 117, 143, 147
Ninowski, Jim 37, 41, 62, 89, 110
Nitschke, Ray 14, 28, 53, 90, 118, 120, 124, 134, 137
Nixon, Mike 27, 34, 59

Nobis, Tommy 93
Nofziger, Terry 116
Noll, Chuck 9
Nutter, Buzz 128, 130

Oakland Raiders 26, 125, 143, 145, 151
Olsen, Merlin 18, 60, 90, 94, 114
Orr, Jimmy 39, 47, 60, 64–65, 74, 82, 85–86, 99, 103, 106, 141
Orrsville 82
Osborne, Dave 72
Owens, Luke 31

Page, Alan 149
Pappas, Milt 103
Parish, Bernie 79
Parker, Buddy 27, 124
Parker, Jim 7, 9, 31, 104, 123, 126, 140
Parks, Dave 28, 35, 42, 47, 49, 64–65, 68, 70, 77, 100, 107–9, 118–20, 123
Pellington, Bill 8, 10, 32
Perkins, Don 26, 31, 58, 65, 85, 141
Pettibon, Richie 19, 71, 99
Philadelphia Eagles 1, 3, 25–26, 36–38, 41, 46, 49–50, 56, 61–62, 66, 72, 85–86, 89, 94
Pietrosante, Nick 77
Pitts, Elijah 40, 69, 91, 96, 104, 130, 137
Pittsburgh Steelers 6, 27, 38, 56, 61, 94
Plimpton, George 2, 11, 106, 109, 151
Plum, Milt 17, 36, 39, 53, 63, 77, 88, 100
Poage, Ray 36, 82
Povich, Shirley 41
Preas, George 114
Purple Gang 15

Quinlan, Bill 11

Randle, Sonny 37, 49, 67, 76, 142
Rasmussen, Wayne 53
Renfro, Mel 26, 31, 58, 67, 79, 142
Renfro, Mike 45, 142
Renfro, Ray 22
Rentzel, Lance 32, 74, 96
Retzlaff, Pete 66, 85, 123
Rhome, Jerry 46, 50
Rice, Grantland 79
Richardson, Willie 74
Richter, Pat 62
Ringo, Jim 11, 13–14
Robb, Joe 116
Roberts, Walter "Flea" 24, 31, 35, 50, 56, 66
Robinson, Dave 70–71, 76, 85, 96, 104–5, 120, 126, 128–29, 134, 136–37, 146
Robustelli, Andy 27–28, 32
Rooney, Art 112
Rosenbloom, Carroll 33, 75, 131, 144
Rozelle, Pete 10, 12, 20, 29, 33, 44, 102, 123, 143–44, 152

Index

Ryan, Frank 22, 24, 35, 37, 41, 45, 48, 62, 66, 78–80, 116, 134–38, 142

Saban, Lou 18
safeties 28, 39, 69, 71, 91, 99, 104, 124
St. Louis Cardinals 21, 24–5. 27. 30–31, 36–38, 41–42, 44–46, 50–51, 53, 55, 57–59, 61, 66–67, 76–77, 94,110, 115–17
Sample, Johnny 37, 45–46, 57, 67, 117
San Diego Chargers 74
Sanders, Lonnie 92
Sandusky, Alex 7, 114
Sayers, Gale 2–3, 19–20, 36, 38, 43–44, 47–49, 51–53, 60, 62–65, 76–77, 84–85, 89, 98–99, 107–10, 123–24, 142, 147–48, 151–53
Scales, Charley 134
Schafrath, Dick 22–23, 123, 136
Schmidt, Joe 10, 17, 27–28, 68–69, 84
Schramm, Tex 26, 33, 117, 144
Shaw, George 7
Sherman, Allie 28
Shiner, Dick 35, 42, 46
Shinnick, Don 87, 99, 101, 103, 121, 125
Shrake, Edwin 58
Shula, Don 2, 6–9, 32, 35, 40, 99–102, 111–14, 123–24, 126, 131, 140–41, 147
Silas, Sam 31
Skoronski, Bob 14, 90, 95, 121, 134
Smith, Billy Ray 8, 39, 64, 129
Smith, Jackie 25, 116
Smith, Jerry 32, 42, 57, 67, 91–92
Smith, Pat 151, 153
Snead, Norm 25, 46, 50, 82
Snow, Jack 32, 43, 60, 84, 90, 114
Snowden, Jim 35
Snyder, Cameron 111
Spadia, Lou 18
Starr, Bart 13, 43–44, 47–49, 55, 62–63, 68–69, 76, 83, 85, 90–91, 95–96, 102–3, 105–7, 118–19, 125, 132–36, 145–47
Stickles, Monte 119–20
Stonebreaker, Steve 64
Strickler, George 35, 83
Studstill, Pat 68, 77, 86
Stynchula, Andy 38
Sullivan, Billy 144
Sullivan, Dan 2, 8, 106, 129
Summerall, Pat 6, 121
Super Bowl 1, 116–17, 144, 146–47, 149
Svare, Harland 51, 124

Talbert, Diron 93
Tarkenton, Fran 15–16, 34–35, 39, 43, 52, 59, 62, 71, 73, 75, 83, 85, 96–97
Taylor, Charley 25, 37, 46, 62, 72, 81
Taylor, Jim 11, 13, 23, 25–26, 40, 43, 55, 83, 90–92, 103–4, 107, 125, 127–29, 131–36, 138–39
Taylor, Otis 33
Taylor, Roosevelt "Rosey" 19, 38, 63
Thomas, Aaron 61
Thompson, Bobby 47, 55
Thurston, Fred "Fuzzy" 14, 69, 90, 125, 134
Tingelhoff, Mick 123
Triplett, Bill 31, 53, 61, 65, 116
Truax, Billy 90

Unitas, Johnny 6–10, 40–42, 46–49, 56, 60, 64–65, 70, 73–74, 81–82, 85–88, 98–99, 101–3, 105–7, 147, 151

Van Brocklin, Norm 15–16, 39, 59, 75, 97, 148–49
Vander Kelen, Ron 83
Villanueva, Danny 92

Wade, Billy 16, 19, 36, 38, 43, 48
Wade, Tommie 110
Walker, Wayne 17, 39, 47, 54, 60, 68–69, 88, 124, 142
Warfield, Paul 24, 28, 31, 57, 132, 134–36, 138
Washington, Gene 149
Washington Redskins 24–26, 32, 35, 41–42, 45–46, 51, 55, 57–58, 60–61, 67, 72, 81, 91–94, 110, 116–17
Watkins, Tom 69, 84
Watuska, Bob 108
Webster, Alex 32
Welch, Jim 125
Werblin, Sonny 33
White, Jack 18
White, Wilfrid 20
Whitsell, Dave 19, 70
Whittenton, Jesse 15, 25
Wiggin, Paul 135
Wilcox, Dave 77
Willard, Ken 18, 32, 35, 38, 42, 59, 64–65, 67, 100, 109, 119–20
Williams, Clancy 31
Williams, Edward Bennett 57
Williams, Sam 17, 68
Wilson, Butch 56
Wilson, George 27, 124
Wilson, Larry 33, 66, 116
Wilson, Ralph 144
Winner, Charlie 113
Wood, Willie 15, 31, 40, 47, 62, 91, 96, 118–20, 124, 136
Wooten, John 2, 22–23, 31, 111, 136, 138, 153
Wright, Steve 14
Wrigley Field 107

Yary, Ron 149

159

www.ingramcontent.com/pod-product-compliance
Ingram Content Group UK Ltd.
Pitfield, Milton Keynes, MK11 3LW, UK
UKHW042016140426
5217IPUK00015B/1210